The Republican
Virago

The Republican Virago

The Life and Times of Catharine Macaulay, Historian

BRIDGET HILL

CLARENDON PRESS · OXFORD
1992

Oxford University Press, Walton Street, Oxford OX2 6DP
Oxford New York Toronto
Delhi Bombay Calcutta Madras Karachi
Petaling Jaya Singapore Hong Kong Tokyo
Nairobi Dar es Salaam Cape Town
Melbourne Auckland
and associated companies in
Berlin Ibadan

Oxford is a trade mark of Oxford University Press

Published in the United States
by Oxford University Press, New York

British Library Cataloguing in Publication Data
Data available

Library of Congress Cataloging in Publication Data
Hill, Bridget.
The republican virago: the life and times of Catharine Macaulay,
historian/Bridget Hill.
Includes bibliographical references and index.
1. Macaulay, Catharine, 1731–1791.   2. Historians—Great Britain—
Biography.   3. Pamphleteers—Great Britain—Biography.
4. Republicanism—Great Britain—History—18th century.   5. Women in
politics—Great Britain—History—18th century.   I. Title.
DA3.M25H55 1992   941.07'092—dc20   [B]   91–33675
ISBN 0–19–812978–5

Typeset by Best-set Typesetter Ltd., Hong Kong
Printed and bound in Great Britain by
Biddles Ltd, Guildford and King's Lynn

PREFACE

MY interest in Catharine Macaulay dates from many years ago. I had come across several tantalizingly brief references to her and longed to discover more. It proved difficult. Most historians of the eighteenth century omit all mention of her. Yet curiously she is one of the relatively few women included in the *Dictionary of National Biography*. What most intrigued me was that she seemed the exception to all the rules laid down for the behaviour and activities appropriate for women in her period. When I began to read her *History*, and, excited by what I found, started to talk about this remarkable republican historian of the seventeenth century, my husband began to show interest. Through his knowledge of the seventeenth century I grew to appreciate her more. Together we wrote an article on her. The idea of a biography of her had crossed my mind but was given up when I discovered there were no family papers extant and that the available material on her was both fragmentary and anecdotal. Thereafter many things intervened to displace her from my mind until in 1988 a portrait of Catharine Macaulay attracted the attention of two visitors to a Yorkshire country house. This book is the result.

Many people have given generously of their time, their own collected material and their ideas. Among them is the late Dr Richard Hunt of the Bodleian Library, who was responsible for first awakening my interest in Catharine Macaulay. The late Professor David Williams was full of enthusiasm for a study of her life and extremely useful in providing a multitude of references in the early stages. Miss Margaret Sawbridge could not have been more helpful in response to my inquiries about the Sawbridge family and in her offer of illustrative material. Dr Mary Prior, Dr Roger Richardson, and Professor Peter Marshall read sections of the book and provided invaluable criticisms. I am also indebted to Professor Marshall for allowing me to use his notes on the manuscript Hollis diary. Dr John Walsh has been a most generous source of advice and material. In a variety of ways Professor Ian Christie, Dr Roger Lonsdale, Dr Desmond Neill, Peter Brown, Dr Susan Staves, and Marcus Rediker have all contributed to making this book possible. At the Oxford University Press Kim Scott Walwyn and Frances Whistler have been consistently supportive and at the copy-editing stage Dr Leofranc Holford-Strevens made many helpful criticisms. My main debt is to my husband, Christopher, who read every word of it—several times over—and was an unfailing source of stimulus. In particular I acknowledge his help in identifying many of the seventeenth-century tracts in Catharine Macaulay's *Catalogue of Tracts* (1790).

BRIDGET HILL

22 October 1990

ACKNOWLEDGEMENTS

I GRATEFULLY acknowledge the permission of the Manuscript Collection of Rhode Island Historical Society to quote from the letter from Catharine Macaulay to Henry Marchant of October 1774; the Trustees of the Boston Public Library to quote from the letter from Catharine Macaulay to the Committee of Boston of 9 May 1770; the American Philosophical Society to quote from the letter from Catharine Macaulay to Benjamin Franklin of 8 December 1777; and the Beinecke Rare Book and Manuscript Library of Yale University to quote from letters included in the Ezra Stiles Papers.

CONTENTS

ILLUSTRATIONS

PLATES (*between pp. 114 and 115*)

FIGURE (*pp. xii–xiii*)

The plates are reproduced by permission. Pls. 1–6: National Portrait Gallery; pls. 7–8: Bodleian Library; pl. 9: Warrington Public Library; pl. 10: Phillips Fine Arts Auctioneers; pls. 11–13: Department of Prints and Drawings, British Museum.

Pl. 3 has recently been reattributed to Robert Edge Pine, *c*.1774.

FAMILY TREE OF CATHARINE (SAWBRIDGE) MACAULAY

GEORGE SAWBRIDGE = AGNES
of Hill Morton, Warw.
d. 1637

WILLIAM = ALICE
of Hill Morton | living 1652
(1615–73)

JOHN = ANNE
of N. Kilworth, | dau. of Richard
Leics (1617–73) | Turvile of Sheersbury,
Leics.

THOMA
living 16

WARWICKSHIRE LINE

LEICESTERSHIRE AND
NORTHAMPTONSHIRE
LINE

JACOB = ELIZABETH
of London and | dau. of John
'Olantigh', Wye | Fisher of London
in Kent d. 1748

ISAAC
d. 1680

JOHN
d. 168

JOHN = ELIZABETH
of 'Olantigh' | dau. of George
(1699–1762) | Wanley of
Tottenham, Middx
d. 1733

JOHN-ELIAS
of Canterbury
d. unm. 1789

JOSE
d. unn

JOHN of = (1) MARY DIANA
'Olantigh' | dau. of Sir Orlando
(1732–95) | Bridgeman of Castle
Bromwich, Warw.
d. 1763
(2) ANNE dau. of Sir
William Stephenson

REV. WANLEY
d. unm. 1796

3 sons and a daughter

* Opinions differ about the name of Catharine's elder sister. Edward Haste in 1782 called
her Mary and it is as Mary she is usually known. But in this survey of Northamptonshire

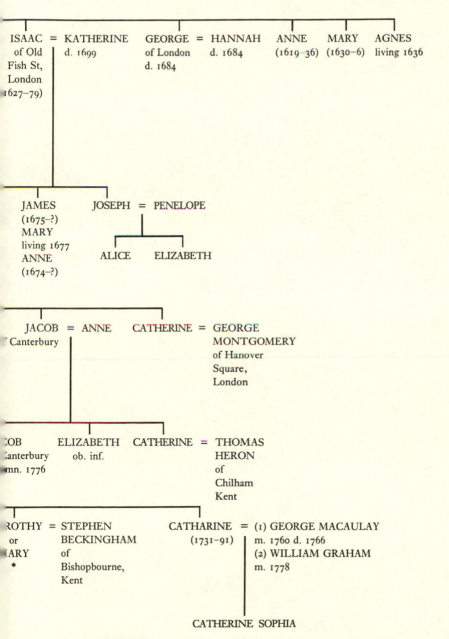

ISAAC = KATHERINE   GEORGE = HANNAH   ANNE   MARY   AGNES
of Old   d. 1699   of London d. 1684   (1619–36) (1630–6) living 1636
Fish St,   d. 1684
London
(1627–79)

JAMES   JOSEPH = PENELOPE
(1675–?)
MARY
living 1677   ALICE   ELIZABETH
ANNE
(1674–?)

JACOB = ANNE   CATHERINE = GEORGE
Canterbury   MONTGOMERY
                              of Hanover
                              Square,
                              London

COB   ELIZABETH   CATHERINE = THOMAS
Canterbury   ob. inf.   HERON
mn. 1776   of
                                     Chilham
                                     Kent

ROTHY = STEPHEN   CATHARINE = (1) GEORGE MACAULAY
or   BECKINGHAM   (1731–91)   m. 1760 d. 1766
ARY   of   (2) WILLIAM GRAHAM
*   Bishopbourne,   m. 1778
         Kent

CATHERINE SOPHIA

(1822–30) George Baker called her Dorothy it is possible she had both names. In his will
her father called her Dorothy'

1. *The Early Years*

I am obliged to you for introducing a Lady to me whose reputation among the literati is high, and whose principles are so justly admired by the friends of liberty and of mankind.

(George Washington to Richard Henry Lee, 22 June 1785, in *Writings of Washington*, ed. John C. Fitzpatrick (39 vols., 1931–44) xxviii, 174.)

Like a Dutch *vrouw*, all shapeless, pale, and fat,
That hugs and slabbers her ungainly brat,
Our Cath'rine sits sublime o'er steaming tea,
And takes her dear Republic on her knee:
Sings it all songs that ever yet were sung,
And licks it fondly with her length of tongue.

(James Boswell, 30 Nov. 1763, from *Boswell in Search of a Wife*, ed. F. Brady and F. A. Pottle (New York, 1956), 171–2 n.)

As a subject for a biography Catharine Macaulay presents certain difficulties. There are no family papers extant. If earlier there were some, as seems likely, almost certainly they were lost in the fire which destroyed the family home in Kent early this century. There are no diaries of Catharine or her brother John, the member of her family to whom she was closest, no journals, and only a few letters, most of them with her friends in America. For information about her life one must depend to a large extent on those outside her family. This means we view her always at a distance through the eyes of observers sometimes sympathetic but often hostile. It makes it difficult to get close to her. There is no such problem with her ideas, whether on history, politics, education, or religion, where her own writings provide ample evidence. Unfortunately, rarely do they contain references to her life. Then there is the problem of the unevenness of material on her. In her lifetime she achieved great fame. It lasted for all of fifteen years, from the appearance of the first volume of her *History* in 1763 to her second marriage in 1778. In that period, from Samuel Johnson, Wilkes, Walpole, and Sylas Neville among many others, from the press, from cartoonists, there came a stream of comment; on her health and appearance, her bons mots and repartee, her travels, her *History*, and her private life. After this date she only emerges from obscurity at infrequent intervals to catch again the public eye.

Whether loved or hated—and reactions to her were inclined to be extreme—Catharine Macaulay was regarded as a quite remarkable phenomenon, and much of the comment on her tends to be a response to the exceptional and unusual, and more particularly to her as a rare—even, as Boswell's scurrilous poem so monstrously depicted her, grotesque—species of the female sex. It is impossible to read such comment without acknowledging the problems faced in the eighteenth century by women whose unique talents made them the focus of attention—intellectual and learned women, women who not only ventured to have opinions but asserted their views with confidence, and, more particularly, women who wrote. The combination of historian and woman was far too unusual to escape comment. As not merely a politician but a republican numerous anecdotes were told of her—most almost certainly mythical.

After the early years when her reputation was made, an increasing amount of such comment was satirical if not downright hostile. One suspects that had she been a man, the nature of such satire, while no less hostile, would have been different. There would not have been the sexual innuendo. Of Samuel Johnson, for example, it was related of one occasion, that 'several persons got into his company the last evening at Trinity, where about twelve, he began to be very great; stripped Mrs Macaulay to the skin, then gave her for his toast, and drank her in two bumpers'. Learning was associated with spinsterhood, and sexual inadequacy, but also, as here, with sexual licence. It is a story that tells us something about Johnson but nothing about Catharine Macaulay except that she was an object of his hatred. Yet hatred alone hardly explains the amount of Johnsoniana focused upon her. She had a fascination for him which he was reluctant to acknowledge. At breakfast one morning, 'unguardedly, [Boswell] said to him "I wish I saw you and Mrs. Macaulay together." He grew very angry; and after a pause, while a cloud gathered on his brow, he burst out, "No, Sir; you would not see us quarrel, to make you sport. Don't you know that it is very uncivil to pit two people against one another?"[1] The trouble with Catharine Macaulay was she was liable to answer back.

At other times the praise and admiration she attracted was so excessively and exaggeratedly adulatory as to be almost equally useless to the biographer. What is in danger of emerging from such sources—if used alone—is a caricature of Catharine Macaulay. Often such caricature is not without some relevance to her life. But usually it throws more light on the author than on the subject. Amongst such anecdotal material there is much that is witty and amusing—and highly readable. There is a great deal that is scurrilous and nasty. As material for a biography it leaves much to be desired. Not only do we learn little of the real-life Catharine Macaulay, but it is near impossible to extract from it a sense of her historical importance, of her claim to be regarded as a serious, republican historian. Nor does it suggest the remarkable, and central, role her writings played in early English radicalism, her friendships and influence with radical dissenters who shared her republican views, and her involvement in practical politics in the period of the Wilkite movement. Her links both with the Sons of Liberty in America and the revolutionaries in France throw light not merely on their revolutions, but on the reshaping of English radicalism in the eighteenth century, its reaction to change, its powerful revival in the final decade of the century, and ultimately, its savage suppression but not demise. Catharine Macaulay's influence, as indeed that of other eighteenth century radicals, can still be traced in the nineteenth century—most notably in the aims and objects of the Chartists.

So although this and other chapters attempt to sketch in all we know of her life, the aims of this book are not just biographical. Nor is its concern primarily a feminist one of recovering from the past a 'remarkable woman', although there is no doubt that Catharine Macaulay was remarkable, and in studying her life and work feminist issues are constantly raised. Its main intention is to justify the claim that she should be seen as an important historical figure whose writings were taken seriously. Her work as a his-

---

[1] *Boswell's Life of Johnson*, ed. G. B. Hill, rev. L. F. Powell, 6 vols. (1934), i. 487; iii. 185.

torian and political polemicist not only influenced English radicalism but American and French revolutionary ideas. She had a
significant and shaping influence on contemporary radical political
debate.

Catharine Macaulay was born on 2 April 1731, the second
daughter of John and Elizabeth Sawbridge of Olantigh, in the
parish of Wye, in Kent. The Sawbridge family had their origins
among Warwickshire yeomanry, and a branch of the family can
be traced at Hill Morton up to the late seventeenth century.
In the first half of that century two other branches of the family
broke away and left Warwickshire—one to become domiciled
at North Kilworth in Leicestershire. It was to split again in
the late seventeenth century, with part moving to Daventry in
Northamptonshire and ultimately settling in East Haddon in the
same county. When in 1773 the open fields of East Haddon were
enclosed, the lordship consisted of about 2,240 acres, of which a
William Sawbridge, the Lord of the Manor, owned more than
half. The other branch on leaving Warwickshire gravitated by way
of London to Kent. It is this last branch with which we are
concerned. Catharine's great-grandfather Isaac Sawbridge had
been in business in London but already roots had been put down
in Kent, for it was in Canterbury that his son Jacob, Catharine's
grandfather, was born.[2]

The family had acquired notoriety long before Catharine came
into the world. In conditions of rapid commercial expansion the
financial structure of the country came under increasing strain.
The absence of adequate and controlled credit facilities invited
financial speculation. Jacob Sawbridge, banker and stockbroker,
and from 1715 MP for Cricklade, was one of a growing group of
businessmen who at the turn of the century set out to exploit the
belief that for the country to prosper an extension of credit
was essential. Those who controlled the newly created Bank of
England enjoyed a highly privileged monopoly, and close financial
ties with the government. Not surprisingly their exclusive privileges were resented. Sawbridge with his two business
associates—the 'three capital sharpers of Britain' as Defoe called
them—set out 'to annex for themselves as large a part as they

---

[2] George Baker, *The History and Antiquities of the County of Northamptonshire*, 2 vols.
(1822–30), i. 160, 161–2.

could of the politico-financial empire' built up by the Bank of England.[3] The South Sea scheme was planned 'to take over a large segment of the national debt at a fixed interest, and to use its credit to finance capital expansion'.[4] With many greedy men anxious to make fortunes as quickly as possible, it was only a matter of time before the crash. When it came in 1720 Sawbridge and his fellow directors of the South Sea Company were deeply involved. An outraged public demanded a scapegoat. The directors of the company who were MPs were found 'guilty of a notorious breach of trust', made responsible for recouping the £250,000 thought to have gone as a bribe to Charles Stanhope and his colleagues at the Treasury, expelled the House, and committed to custody.[5] When called on to reveal his assets, Sawbridge put his as low as £21,000, of which all but £5,000 was expropriated. Hasted valued Jacob's estates and effects on 1 June 1720 at £77,254. More recently his gross assets in 1721 have been estimated at nearer £121,689.[6] Whether guilty or not, Sawbridge still emerged from the crash a rich man. Half a century later Catharine Macaulay, anxious to clear the name of her grandfather, gave her version of events. She argued, with justice, that 'several of the members of both houses of parliament though deeply engaged with the directors... escaped punishment'. She claimed her grandfather 'though carried along with the tide of other men's iniquity', had had no intention of defrauding the public.[7] Whatever the truth of her defence, Sawbridge was no guiltier than many others.

The memory of Jacob's harsh treatment, it was later argued, 'rendered all his successors adverse to everything like arbitrary power'.[8] It was this, it was said, that lay behind her writings and her brother's conduct. But if they were unable to forget their grandfather's disgrace, it was an incident but rarely used against them. Only Horace Walpole, angry at the views she expressed in her *History of England from the Revolution to the Present Time*

[3] John Carswell, *The South Sea Bubble* (1960), 34.

[4] J. H. Plumb, *The First Four Georges* (1966), 62–3.

[5] Carswell, *South Sea Bubble*, 227.

[6] Carswell, *South Sea Bubble*, 257, 283; Edward Hasted, *History and Topographical Survey of the County of Kent*, 4 vols. (1782), i. 576 n. 1.

[7] Catharine Macaulay, *The History of England from the Revolution to the Present Time*, i. (1778), 306–7. Hereafter *History from the Revolution*.

[8] *Memoirs of John Horne Tooke*, ed. Alexander Stephens, 2 vols. (1813), ii. 282.

(1778), in a letter to William Mason, commented spitefully on her grandfather, 'who, *she has been told*, was a mighty worthy man though dipped in the infamous job of the South Sea'.[9] No doubt in ignorance, an article written on Catharine in 1770, described her family as 'through all its descents, highly respectable'.[10]

At the beginning of the eighteenth century Olantigh, where Catharine lived as a child and young woman, was in the hands of a Major Richard Thornhill (see Pl. 7). In 1706 he obtained an act for vesting this and other of his estates in trustees to be sold in order to pay his debts. Jacob Sawbridge, Catharine's grandfather, bought it soon afterwards.[11] It was to remain his home till his death in 1748. He left three sons, John, Jacob, and John Elias. John, Catharine's father, as the eldest, succeeded to the estates, and inherited Olantigh, where he was to live with his family. It was here Catharine Macaulay spent her youth. Unfortunately destroyed in a fire at the beginning of this century, Olantigh was an old house, rebuilt by Sir Thomas Kempe, the founder of Wye College, in the fourteenth century. The ending of the name Olantigh or Olanteigh signifies an island and originally it may well have been situated on one in the River Stour. Pictures of the house as it was after John Sawbridge, Catharine's brother, 'made extensive alterations and improvements, in the interior, as well as exterior; adding the noble entrance-hall, and north front', suggest, above all else, a very large and dignified house. The central section of the frontage—presumably the part added by John Sawbridge some time in the second half of the eighteenth century—was in classical style with four imposing columns. In the eighteenth century Olantigh was said to have been 'the principal' seat in a parish which, at the time of the first Census of Population in 1801, contained about 2,000 inhabitants.[12] It was 'situated on the banks of the Stour, nearly a mile north of the town'.[13] On the opposite side of the river was Godmersham Park, where in 1779 her cousin Catharine was married to Thomas Heron in the Long Room, later so familiar to Jane Austen.[14]

[9] *Horace Walpole's Correspondence*, ed. W. S. Lewis, 48 vols. (1937–83), xxviii. 372.
[10] *The Repository or Treasury of Politics and Literature for the Year 1770*, 2 vols. (1771), ii. 291.
[11] Hasted, *History and Topographical Survey of Kent*, iii. 170.
[12] William S. Morris, *The History and Topography of Wye* (1842), 3, 42–3, 48.
[13] Ibid. 42.
[14] *Archaeologia Cantiana*, 56 (1944), 11.

If the family fortunes had been undermined by Jacob's involvement in the crash of the South Sea Company, they were soon to be retrieved. His son John (1699–1762), who in his youth is said to have been an officer in the Guards, married the daughter and heiress of a London banker, George Wanley of Tottenham. Within a short time of the marriage, she died. Sawbridge was said to have 'retired early to his estate in the country, where he led an inactive life'.[15] According to his daughter, he had been 'a great admirer of Mr. Pulteney', who with Bolingbroke led the opposition against Sir Robert Walpole, until Pulteney accepted a title, when 'the respectful attention of mankind was turned into a studied contempt and neglect'.[16]

During his lifetime Sawbridge significantly increased the size of his estate by purchasing a number of neighbouring properties. John and his second wife Elizabeth had two sons, John and Wanley, and two daughters, Mary and Catharine. John, as eldest son, on the death of his father in 1762, inherited a good fortune as well as an estate that embraced not only Olantigh but 'a very considerable portion of the lands and tenements' in the parish.[17] Under the will Wanley received a legacy of £3,000 but 'in order to secure to him that independence which he himself so highly esteemed', his brother John, in addition, 'made him a present of five thousand pounds'. In contrast the two daughters took a mere £50 each, although we do not know what they received in marriage-portions.[18] Like his father, John 'very early in life captivated a lady with a fortune of £100,000'.[19] She was Mary, daughter of Sir Orlando Bridgeman, who died within two months of the marriage in 1763, but 'such was her gratitude for the pleasure she had tasted, that she rewarded the short services of Mr. Sawbridge with the whole of her fortune'.[20] Two years later he married the daughter of Sir William Stephenson, Alderman of London, one of Sawbridge's future political colleagues and, like him, destined to be a founder member of the Supporters of the Bill of Rights. Of Mary, the eldest daughter, we know little except

---

[15] Mary Hays, *Female Biography*, 6 vols. (1803), v. 288.
[16] Macaulay, *History from the Revolution*, 422.
[17] Morris, *History and Topography of Wye*, 47.
[18] See the will of John Sawbridge, sen., Public Record Office, Prob. ii. 876; *Gentleman's Magazine*, 45 (1775), 216.
[19] *City Biography* (1800), 88.
[20] Morris, *History and Topography of Wye*, 46.

that she married a Stephen Beckingham of Bishopsbourn said to have been 'a gentleman of fortune'.[21] When in 1764 Colonel Edmondstoune wrote to David Hume about Mrs Macaulay's *History*, he mentioned that her sister, 'who seems to be a good sort of woman, a Mrs Buckingham [*sic*]', was staying with him.[22] The youngest of the family, Wanley, who remained unmarried, was destined for holy orders, and became rector of Thundersley in Essex and vicar of Stalesfield not far from the family home in Kent. Evidence suggests he shared the politics of Catharine and John. In 1769, for example, at the time when the House of Commons resolved that Wilkes was 'incapable of being elected' as MP for Middlesex, and recognized Col. Luttrell as having won the seat, the outraged agitation that followed extended as far as Kent, where among the petitioners is the name of the Revd. Wanley Sawbridge, JP.[23] In 1782 Hasted records him as the owner of Otterden Place, south-east of Eyhorne.[24] He died in 1796. It was John and Catharine whose two careers were most closely linked and who were destined for fame.

Elizabeth Sawbridge, 'a beautiful woman, with a delicate and feeble constitution', died in childbirth in 1733. Although she had already borne four children, she was only twenty-two. So from the age of two Catharine was motherless. Her father, 'who severely felt the loss of his wife, almost entirely secluded himself from society, though', it was said, 'possessed of a fortune of £3,000 a year'.[25] We know little of her earliest years. One account of her life in 1770 admitted being 'unable to discover any traces in her infancy of the genius she so *demonstratively possesses*'.[26] Opinions about the nature of her education differ. Two common factors are that, at her father's wish, she was educated privately, and that 'an almost constant residence in the country left her very much to her own inclination in the choice of her studies'.[27] Her father, according to one account, 'paid no attention to the education of his daughters, who were left at the family seat, at Olantigh, to the charge of

[21] Hays, *Female Biography*, 288; and see Horace Walpole, *Memoirs of the Reign of George III*, ed. G. F. Russell Barker, 4 vols. (1894), iii. 191–2.

[22] *Life and Correspondence of David Hume*, ed. J. H. Burton, 2 vols. (1846), ii. 186.

[23] George Rudé, *Wilkes and Liberty* (1962), 143 n., 144.

[24] Hasted, *History and Topographical Survey of Kent*, ii. 506.

[25] Hays, *Female Biography*, v. 288.

[26] *The Repository or Treasury of Politics and Literature for 1770*, ii. 290.

[27] *The European Magazine and London Review*, 4 (1783), 330.

an antiquated, well-recommended, but ignorant, governess, ill-qualified for the task she undertook'.[28]

Unlike her sister, it was said, she found 'the customary avocations of her sex and age' boring. 'Active and curious, she thirsted for knowledge'. She soon became satiated with the 'fairy tales and romances' that 'were put into her hands'. She 'found her way into her father's well-furnished library', where 'she became her own purveyor, and rioted in intellectual luxury'.[29] Here 'her active, elegant, and inquisitive mind, *marked* itself by the food it fed on; history, that noblest of studies, early attached her'.[30] Less elevated was the account that claimed she 'had an early taste for promiscuous reading, which at length terminated in a fondness for history'.[31] According to her own account, she was from a very early age a prolific reader, particularly of 'those histories which exhibit liberty in its most exalted state in the annals of the Roman and Greek Republics'. From childhood 'liberty became the object of a secondary worship' in her imagination.[32] But this was an account directed at her readers and, as her first venture into print, possibly intended to impress them. Rather different is the account which insisted that her education 'was by no means distinguished from that of other young ladies of the same rank', that 'the trifling pursuits of the majority of her sex found sufficient charms to engage her attention, and sufficient employment for every vacant hour'. Her studies 'were of a kind little calculated to lay the foundation of those important works which have since attracted the notice of the public'. It was only 'a year or two before she commenced author' that she began to 'apply herself to the study of politics and moral philosophy'.[33] The truth seems to lie somewhere between the two. Clearly there were two levels to her education; the formal education she and her elder sister, Mary, were intended to receive from their governess which, almost certainly, was indistinguishable from that of the vast majority of their sex; and the informal that relied on her own curiosity and the

---

[28] Hays, *Female Biography*, v. 288.

[29] Ibid. 289.

[30] *The Repository or Treasury of Politics and Literature for 1770*, ii. 290.

[31] Alexander Chalmers, *The General Biographical Dictionary* (32 vols., 1812–17), xxi. (1813) 45.

[32] Macaulay, *The History of England from the Accession of James I to that of the Brunswick Line*, i (1763), p. vii. Hereafter *History of England*.

[33] *The European Magazine and London Review*, 4 (1783), 330–4 at p. 330.

freedom she seems to have had to probe her father's library. On the contents of that library we can only guess. But the Sawbridges appear to have been a bookish family. In 1755 when a Wye Book Club was formed, both John and his father are recorded as members, but no women. But in the custody of the Rector of Crundale, near Godmersham, there was a library of some 2,000 works collected by his predecessor. It was used as a lending library by the local population and a Miss Sawbridge is included in the 'loans book'.[34]

Many years later, when she visited Philadelphia, she told her friend Benjamin Rush 'she was a thoughtless girl till she was twenty, at which time she contracted a taste for books and knowledge by reading an odd volume of some history, which she picked up in a window of her father's house'.[35] This version has an authentic ring to it. Some time in the late 1760s, she told Caleb Fleming she had 'no learning', meaning she knew neither Latin nor Greek.[36] Nevertheless she read Greek and Roman history, claiming they were the inspiration to her turning historian as well as the source of her republicanism. But almost certainly they were in translation. Mary Delany, daughter of Mrs Delany, held that Catharine was virtually ignorant of the principles of English grammar 'until she was thirty years old, and now all her productions go to press uncorrected'.[37]

Was Catharine, as some have said, 'a spoilt child'? One cannot tell, but with little in the way of parental guidance she may well have been a 'wayward, headstrong young woman'.[38] Of her childhood and early adult life we remain almost ignorant. Without a mother and with a father who took little interest in his children, it was almost certainly a lonely life that encouraged her to find her own interests and amusements. It may have been responsible for an independence and intellectual self-sufficiency remarkable in any child in the eighteenth century, but quite extraordinary in a girl. Was it at this stage that she began to discuss her reading with

---

[34] Morris, *History and Topography of Wye*, 164; *A Kentish Parson*, ed. G. M. Ditchfield and Bryan Keith-Lucas (1991), 129.

[35] *The Autobiography of Benjamin Rush*, ed. George W. Corner (1948), 61.

[36] *The Diary of Sylas Neville, 1767–1788*, ed. Basil Cozens-Hardy (1950), 64.

[37] George Paston, *Mrs. Delany: A Memoir, 1700–1788* (1900), 198.

[38] R. E. Peach, *Historic Houses in Bath* (1883), 117 n.

her brother John, and that the first seeds of her republicanism, 'in which she was probably encouraged by her brother', were sown?[39]

We have a rare glimpse of her in 1757 when Elizabeth Carter, a scholar of Latin and Greek who translated the works of Epictetus, visited Canterbury. There, at some annual affair, she met Miss Catharine Sawbridge, then 26 years old. Catharine made a powerful impression on her. In a letter to her friend Catherine Talbot she wrote that Miss Sawbridge figured as a 'very fine lady, who, after curtseying to me for several years past, with more civility than I had any title to, and with much more than fine ladies usually show to such awkward-looking folks as me', finally approached Mrs Carter and took her 'mightily by way of conversation'. Elizabeth Carter was both impressed and a little bewildered by the flow. 'She is a very sensible and agreeable woman, and much more deeply learned than becomes a fine lady; but between the Spartan laws, the Roman politics, the philosophy of Epicurus, and the wit of St. Evremond, she seems to have formed a most extraordinary system.' The account negates any suggestion that Catharine only began to read seriously a year or so before becoming author. During their conversation together they were joined by one of 'the most celebrated beauties in the assembly'—beautiful but dumb—and with humour Elizabeth Carter wrote of how it was 'extremely diverting to see her listen for a considerable time with the most profound attention to a discourse, which must have been for the most part as unintelligible to her as if it had been delivered in Arabic'. Elizabeth Carter was very conscious of how extraordinary—even unseemly—the conversation was at such an assembly, but, as she wrote, was not Catharine Sawbridge 'a fine fashionable well-dressed lady whose train was longer than anybody's train'?[40]

Three years later, just after her marriage, there is an intriguing reference to her in a letter to Lord Lyttelton from Elizabeth Montagu, the 'Queen of the Bluestockings'. 'I would wish Mr. Lyttelton to consider Mrs. Macaulay', it reads, 'as a protégée of the Archbishop of Canterbury'. What request had been made

[39] Chalmers, *Biographical Dictionary*, xxi. 45.
[40] *A Series of Letters between Mrs. Elizabeth Carter and Miss Catherine Talbot*, ed. Montagu Pennington, 2 vols. (1809), ii. 260–1.

of Thomas Secker on her behalf? Whatever it was, Elizabeth Montagu was 'much obliged to his Excellency for his readiness to oblige' her. A little later Lord Lyttelton wrote enclosing a letter from his brother 'about Mrs. Macaulay'.[41]

On 18 June 1760 the marriage was recorded of 'Dr. Macaulay,—to Miss Sawbridge of Olantigh, Kent'.[42] George Macaulay, 'from having an opportunity of becoming Acquainted with her merits, soon became ambitious to be allied to them'.[43] She was 29. The marriage signalled the end of her life in rural Kent; they set up house in London in St James's Place. A Scot, George Macaulay was a physician, who had graduated as a doctor of medicine at Padua in 1739 and was admitted an Extra-Licentiate of the College of Physicians in 1746; when, six years later, he moved to London from Edinburgh, he was elected a Licentiate.[44] At some stage he lived in Poland Street, where he was a neighbour of Dr Burney.[45] He is said to have been a friend of Tobias Smollett and to have helped him in his financial difficulties.[46] Two brothers, John and William Hunter, fellow Scotsmen and both distinguished surgeons, one an anatomist, the other an obstetrician, were among his other friends. When he married Catharine he was physician and treasurer of Brownlow Lying-in Hospital, a post he held until his death in 1766. He was, it seems, dedicated to his work and highly respected by all. 'Never will his name,' it was said in 1770, 'never will his generous attention be forgotten by any of those who obtained admittance in the Brownlow-street lying-in hospital during his period of presidency there.' It was work 'where tenderness, attention, and humanity' were 'particularly essential to soften the two greatest miseries of our nature, sickness and poverty'. He was 'universally beloved'.[47] When about 1756 there was a conference of the leading obstetricians in the country, 'to consider the moral rectitude of and advantages which might be expected from the induction

[41] *Letters of Mrs. Elizabeth Montagu*, ed. Matthew Montagu, 4 vols. (1809–13), iv. 321, 330.

[42] *Gentleman's Magazine*, 30 (1760), 297.

[43] *The Repository or Treasury of Politics and Literature for 1770*, ii. 291.

[44] *Dictionary of National Biography*, under Catharine Macaulay; William Munk, *The Roll of the Royal College of Physicians of London*, 2 vols. (1861), ii. 157.

[45] Peter Cunningham, *Handbook of London* (1850), 403.

[46] *Dictionary of National Biography*, under Catharine Macaulay.

[47] *The Repository or Treasury of Politics and Literature for 1770*, ii. 291–2.

of premature labour in certain cases of contracted pelvis', Dr Macaulay was one of those who took part. When it was agreed to adopt the procedure in future it fell to Dr Macaulay to undertake the first case, which he performed with success.[48] Apart from two fascinating medical case-histories contributed to the Medical Observations of the Society of London Physicians, he left no trace of literary activity.[49] His marriage to Catharine Sawbridge was his second marriage. His first in 1744 was to an heiress, Leonora Maria, daughter of Peter Bathurst, brother of Allen, first Earl Bathurst. It was an old Northamptonshire family and Leonora seems to have inherited the manor and much of the estate at Gretworth. In 1751 she and George Macaulay, jointly with Thomas Cooper, are recorded as selling the estate.[50] It was probably soon after this time they moved to London for his appointment at the Lying-in Hospital dated from the following year. Leonora died in 1760. Within a few months he had remarried. He was fifteen years older than Catharine.

Of George Macaulay all too little is known. He was described as 'a gentleman of great worth and integrity' and as 'the twin-brother of Benevolence'.[51] His marriage to Catharine seems to have been happy. One of the few insights we have of it comes from Richard Baron, the republican dissenter and friend of Thomas Hollis. He must have known George Macaulay well—indeed, rather better than he knew his second wife. After Macaulay's death Baron confided to Sylas Neville that he could not 'prevail on himself to go to the house', although Catharine had 'inquired of Timothy Hollis and others the reason of his not calling on her'. Baron described George Macaulay as 'a most worthy and benevolent man'. At that time, Baron was rather in awe of Catharine. He thought her 'quite a phenomenon—a woman without passions'. 'Her face' he described as 'abstract as the print of Mr. Locke'. But he admitted George Macaulay was devoted to her. As he told Baron: 'You may think that Catherine from her application to study is not an attentive wife, but there

---

[48] Munk, *The Roll of the Royal College of Physicians*, ii. 181.
[49] *Gentleman's Magazine*, 27 (1757), 224, 362.
[50] Baker, *History and Antiquities of Northamptonshire*, i. 509.
[51] *European Magazine*, 4 (1783), 330; *The Repository or Treasury of Politics and Literature for 1770*, ii. 291.

never was a more affectionate wife, or more tender mother.'[52] Baron remained fascinated by her. After George Macaulay's death, an entry in Thomas Hollis's diary reads: 'With Baron . . . much conversation with him, relating to . . . the Times, Popery, Archdeacon Blackburne, Mrs. Macaulay etc.' A week later they converse 'on the same subjects'.[53] The Macaulays at this period enjoyed an active social life. 'Their table was open to every man of worth in the circle of their acquaintance, which was pretty extensive.'[54]

During her first marriage, a glimpse of Catharine was caught by Alicia Lefanu, the daughter of Mrs Frances Sheridan (1724–66), novelist and playwright. Mrs Sheridan left Dublin for London in 1754, where she and her husband moved in a small circle that included Samuel Johnson, Mrs Cholmondeley, younger sister of Peg Woffington and Horace Walpole's niece, Samuel Richardson, and Catharine Macaulay—'one more London acquaintance of Mrs. Sheridan' as her daughter put it. Although only nine or ten years old, Alicia Lefanu later wrote an account of the first meeting between the two. It must have been soon after the first volume of Catharine Macaulay's *History* appeared. She wrote how both were quick to compliment the other on their writing but that by the manner in which they did so, she got the impression 'neither of them had read the works of the other'. Alicia Lefanu was a little disappointed in Mrs Macaulay's appearance. She lacked 'those charms so profusely ascribed to her by a female biographer' (Mary Hays). On the other hand she found in her 'none of that levity or extravagance of dress imputed to her by one of the other sex' (Dr Johnson). It was a comment later endorsed by a gentleman friend, who thought she dressed well. 'Her cloaths are fashionable', he wrote, 'but well fancied . . . though neat, she is far from being finical.' With Richard Baron, Alicia Lefanu found Catharine 'cold'. She thought her, a 'plain woman,—pale, tall . . . and formal, with nothing reprehensible in her manners, nor any thing peculiarly fascinating in her address'.[55] As the verdict of a 10-

[52] *The Diary of Sylas Neville*, 20.

[53] MS of diary of Thomas Hollis, Houghton Library, Harvard University, entries for 6 and 13 Dec. 1766.

[54] *Town and Country Magazine*, 1 (1769), 92.

[55] Alicia Lefanu, *Memoirs of the Life and Writings of Mrs. Frances Sheridan* (1824), 232–3.

year-old, it is in strong contrast to that of a gentleman friend who thought she had 'a very handsome face and person' and 'uncommon ease and affability of behaviour', and to the most detailed description of her given by her sister-in-law and friend Mrs Arnold, who found her 'elegant in her manners, delicate in her person, and with features, if not perfectly beautiful, so fascinating in their expression, as deservedly to rank her face among the higher order of human countenances'. Yet Mrs Arnold had observed her closely. She was 'above the middling size, inclining to tall; her shape slender and elegant; the contour of her face, neck, and shoulders, graceful. The form of her face was oval, her complexion delicate, and her skin fine; her hair of a mild brown, long and profuse; her nose between the Roman and the Grecian; her mouth small, her chin round'. But it was on her eyes that Mrs Arnold dwelt most. They were 'beautiful as imagination can conceive, full of penetration and fire, but their fire softened by the mildest beams of benevolence; their colour was a fine dark hazel, and their expression the indication of a superior soul'.[56] (See Pl. 2 for an artist's impression of her in 1764.)

In the six years of marriage to George Macaulay, Catharine became seriously interested in writing history and set herself the momentous task of completing an eight-volume history of England. Her husband must have been unusually enlightened to have encouraged her to pursue a career viewed by many as unladylike if not worse. When at David Hume's own request, a copy of Catharine Macaulay's first volume was sent to him and, after nearly five months no response had been forthcoming, it was George Macaulay who wrote to remind him—but most courteously—that although the volume had been sent, no acknowledgement had been received. He must have felt immense pride in Catharine's achievement as a historian. His friendship with Richard Baron and Timothy Hollis suggests he may have shared her republican and radical ideas. In 1766, aged 50, he died 'sincerely lamented by his friends, and equally so by his widow'. Catharine wrote a long epitaph for him that expressed both admiration and real affection:

The Virtues of his Life were too numerous to be contained in an Epitaph;

---

[56] *Town and Country Magazine*, 1 (1769), 92.

Let it suffice to observe,
That in his character were comprehended,
Pure Morality, untainted by Superstition;
An ineffable Sweetness of Temper,
which Sickness and Death could not discompose;
The Excellencies which flowed from a good Heart,
and a sound Understanding;
With the peculiar Graces of Genius and Learning,
And every social Virtue,
in the highest Degree of Perfection.
He lived an Ornament to his Family;
an Honour to his Country:
And departed this Life,
when he had attained the age of Fifty Years,
On the sixteenth of September, 1766,
To the inexpressible Sorrow of his Family,
his Friends,
and a numerous Train of Mourners,
The Objects of his Charity, Benevolence and Generosity.[57]

Besides his widow George Macaulay left one daughter, Catherine Sophia.

At the time of her first marriage Catharine Sawbridge was almost completely unknown outside her circle of friends and acquaintances, except for a few who, meeting her by chance, were never to forget her. Three years later the first volume of her history appeared. Overnight she became 'the Celebrated Mrs. Macaulay'. In the next ten years Catharine Macaulay remained in London, enjoying the success and fame it had brought her. She produced four more volumes by 1773. She also wrote two pamphlets, which were published anonymously; *Loose Remarks on certain Positions to be found in Mr. Hobbes's 'Philosophical Rudiments of Government and Society'*, which appeared in 1767, and her *Observations on a Pamphlet entitled 'Thoughts on the Cause of the Present Discontents'*, of 1770. She moved in at least two, almost distinct, social circles; the first a group involved in practical politics, in which her brother John Sawbridge played a leading role as a Wilkite and a founder-member of the Society of the Supporters of the Bill of Rights. The second was that of the Real Whigs, mainly, but not exclusively, dissenters with republican tendencies,

---

[57] *European Magazine*, 4 (1783), 332; Hays, *Female Biography*, v. 293.

to which Thomas Hollis, Richard Baron, and Sylas Neville all belonged. In the 1760s and early 1770s they were more interested in spreading ideas than in practical politics. Nevertheless, if they did not overlap much with the Wilkite group, the two had ideas in common. Both were focused on London, although both had members and sympathizers outside the metropolis.

Thomas Hollis knew both the Macaulays, and was a frequent visitor to their home. In February 1764 he recorded in his diary one such visit when he 'stayed with her till dinner time, conversing agreeably about her History, Politics & Virtu'.[58] The little knowledge we have of Catharine Macaulay's social life in this period we owe in large part to Sylas Neville's diary and to Wilkes's correspondence with his daughter Polly. Neville's diary covers the 1760s and 1770s. From it we learn how Timothy Hollis, first cousin once removed to Thomas, had been introduced to Mrs Macaulay in Bath by William Harris, the dissenting historian. She was, Hollis thought, 'a most agreeable Lady'. He found 'her conversation is of the same kind with her writings, and though she plays at cards and talks of different subjects, she always returns to that, being absorbed in such speculations'. It was, he thought, 'an odd character for a Lady, but not unbecoming because uncommon'. He thought her history was sometimes written 'with too much asperity' but as Neville told him 'the characters & measures of these times deserved to be treated with asperity'. One day in July 1767, while Sylas Neville and Timothy Hollis were taking tea together, 'a card' was 'brought from Mrs. Macaulay offering a visit' in the coming week. Neville was delighted to be included in the invitation from Timothy Hollis to join the gathering, to which it was proposed asking 'some of the mutual friends of Liberty'. From Neville we also learn of Mrs Macaulay's belief that 'all stomach complaints proceed from relaxation and that ice-cream strengthens and braces the stomach'. It is an indication of how early her health became a constant preoccupation. Neville immediately tried the recipe and recorded: 'I actually did not feel dinner heavy as I often do.' In January 1768 he attends a Twelfth Night Rout at Mrs Macaulay's house. Clearly it had been a good party. Games were played but Neville had no time for them: 'How unworthy of reasonable beings are

---

[58] Diary of Thomas Hollis, entry for 4 Feb. 1764.

modern fashionable amusements!' He left at half-past midnight but the party only broke up at three in the morning. Although he had now met her several times, there had been no chance of talking at length with her. Caleb Fleming, Independent minister and preacher at Pinners Hall, a friend of both Neville and Catharine Macaulay, finally wrote to her of Neville's desire 'to exchange a few ideas with her'.[59] The result was an invitation for the morning of 30 April 1768. Neville recorded the visit in some detail in his diary. Accompanied by Fleming he had reached her house in St James's Place about eleven o'clock. 'She received us with great civility in her study', Neville recorded, 'where we drank chocolate'. Neville was entranced by her, and found her 'a charming creature'. In an age of such corruption, he was amazed to find 'her penetration, her judgment, her knowledge, her virtue, her love of Liberty, her greatness of soul which shines with the greatest of lustre in her truly free and benevolent principles'. She had talked at length with them and Neville recorded her every word.[60]

St James's Place remained her home in London until some time in 1769, when she moved to Berners Street, Oxford Road. There both Wilkes and Hollis were among her visitors. Wilkes very nearly became her neighbour. On 11 May 1770, in a letter to his daughter, he mentioned that the day before he had visited Mrs Macaulay and that he was toying with the idea of moving into a neighbouring house in Berners Street. His daughter Polly had particularly liked the house, but there were problems about the lease and the idea was abandoned. At the end of May he planned to take Polly to spend a week in Dover, 'and then to Mr. Sawbridge's for a few days'. Two years later he wrote that Mrs Macaulay had just left Bath. In the summer of the same year Polly sent her father an account of her stay with a Mr and Mrs 'Molyneux' (Molineux) in Ilford, adding 'Mrs. Macaulay was there at the time, which contributed to make the visit extremely agreeable'. Crisp Molineux, MP for King's Lynn, was one of the twelve MPs who belonged to Wilkes's party, the 'twelve apostles', as Wilkes called them. Ten days later both the Molineux and Mrs Macaulay visited Polly Wilkes. Mrs Macaulay, she wrote to

[59] *The Diary of Sylas Neville*, 13, 14, 18, 20, 29, 32.
[60] G. M. Ditchfield, 'Some Literary and Political Views of Catherine Macaulay', *American Notes and Queries*, 12 (1974), 70–6, at pp. 72–3.

Wilkes, was to spend the rest of the summer in Norfolk with the Molineux family. She had planned to go to the Isle of Wight and, Polly wrote to her father, 'would have been very glad if she could have gone while you were there'. September found them all at Garboldisham in Norfolk, the Molineux's country home.[61]

Some time early in 1770 shortly after her return from Bath, Thomas Hollis visited her at Berners Street. The house was apparently 'a new one' and he described it as 'furnished handsomely'. Despite Hollis's own rejection of luxury or display of any kind, he was clearly impressed by the grandeur of her way of living. He thought 'she had the air of a princess', and 'out-Cornelised the Cornelisians'. Her visit to Bath had restored her to health, for as Hollis commented she 'had the frank Bath air upon her countenance'. 'It seems she keeps two servants in laced liveries,' he wrote to Theophilus Lindsey, 'treats cleverly and elegantly, and, in short, author or fine lady, surpasses all her sex'. And lest Lindsey should interpret his remarks as in any way critical of her, he added: 'all this in *confidence* for I respect her exceedingly, and she is to be maintained in much just commendation for her many extraordinary qualities and the cause sake'.[62] 'In her person', went an account of her in the same year, 'Mrs Macaulay is above the common size, in her connections genteel, and in her manner of living, unites elegance with hospitality'.[63]

The publicity her fame attracted took many forms. Under the unlikely name of Jacobina Henriques, in 1766 there appeared in the *Annual Register* a 'Humorous Proposal for a Female Administration' in which was included a list of women to occupy each office. As to their abilities for holding such office, readers were asked only to compare them 'with the *males* who at present enjoy those places'. 'It is naturally to be presumed', wrote the author, 'that a *female ministry* may restore our decayed constitution and enable it to exert its pristine vigour.' Ironically, given her hatred of the monarchy, Catharine Macaulay was given the role of

---

[61] *Correspondence of the Late John Wilkes with his friends*, ed. John Almon, 5 vols. (1805), iv. 31, 34–5, 44, 118.

[62] *Memoirs of the Late Revd. Theophilus Lindsey. M. A.*, ed. Thomas Belsham (1812), 508–9. 'out-Cornelised the Cornelisians': Cornelia, a virtuous and accomplished woman, came of a distinguished family. The daughter of Scipio Africanus, she married Ti. Sempronius Gracchus, gave birth to two tribunes, Tiberius and Gaius, and was idolized by the people.

[63] *The Repository or Treasury of Politics and Literature for 1770*, ii. 292.

Royal Historiographer.[64] Few historians can have had the distinction of having so many poems written to them as Catharine
Macaulay. The *London Chronicle* in November 1770 carried two
by a John de Brent, said to have been a pseudonym used by
Thomas Hollis. Dedicated to Mrs Macaulay, one included the
lines:

> Proceed, great Writer! brave the school
> Of Barbarism, and misrule.
> Nor cease t'explore the hideous cell,
> Where Tyranny and Popery dwell.[65]

Although the playwright, religious reformer, and bluestocking
Hannah More was later to criticize Catharine Macaulay savagely,
earlier she was her admirer, and included her with other distinguished women writers in a poem published in 1774, where she
argued that attitudes to women writers had changed.

> But in our chaster time 'tis no offence,
> When female virtue joins with female sense;
> When moral Carter breathes the strain divine,
> And Aikin's life flows faultless as her line;
> Where all-accomplish'd Montagu can spread
> Fresh-gathered laurels round her Shakespeare's head;
> When wit and worth in polished Brooke unite,
> And fair Macaulay claims a Livy's right.[66]

An interesting poem was that ascribed to Dr William Robertson
(1705–83), a pupil of Francis Hutcheson, who, ordained priest in
1727, became a curate in Co. Carlow. Later he had doubts about
his faith, and resigned all benefices because he felt he could
not hold them consistently with the principles of liberty. Subsequently, under the influence of Joseph Priestley and Theophilus
Lindsey, he adopted Unitarian ideas. Lindsey described him as
'the father of unitarian non-conformity'.[67] After leaving Ireland he
became a master at Wolverhampton Grammar School. He was

---

[64] *Annual Register*, 9 (1766), 209–12. I owe this reference to John Walsh.

[65] *London Chronicle*, 28 (1770), 4.

[66] From 'Epilogue to the Search after Happiness: A Pastoral Drama', as quoted in
Eighteenth-Century Women Poets: An Oxford Anthology, ed. Roger Lonsdale (Oxford,
1989), 325.

[67] *The Monthly Repository of Theology and General Literature*, 1 (1806), 169, 225–8,
282.

described as a man of 'great learning and good judgement'. Whether or not he was responsible for the poem *Eleutheria* inscribed to Catharine Macaulay, and published in 1768, John Disney had 'good reason to believe' him its author.[68] Sylas Neville entertained no doubts. The entry to his diary for 8 June 1768 reads: 'Ended reading Eleutheria, a poem inscribed to Mrs. Macaulay by the truly honest and disinterested Dr. Robertson'.[69] In the poem, Jove, concerned at the

> Corruption, Luxury, Venality,
> Division, Vanity and fell Oppression,

he sees in Britain, sends Eleutheria accompanied by

> the shades
> Of patriotic heroes

to restore liberty. In her search for a mortal in whom to dwell she finds

> A breast replete with virtues all divine.
> Joyful, she enter'd into this bright FORM
> And said, her ORACLES she now would give
> From the well-guided pen of fair MACAULAY.[70]

The same year a play, *The Devil upon Two Sticks* by Samuel Foote, was staged in London. In it Mrs Macaulay is represented as Margaret, sister of a Sir Thomas Maxwell whose daughter Harriet wished to elope with 'a paltry clerk'. As 'a Lady of great political knowledge, and a zealous supporter of the rights and privileges of her sex' her advice is sought.[71] Certainly the character of Margaret was inspired by Mrs Macaulay, and no one who saw the play could have remained ignorant of Foote's intentions. The reviewers were in no doubt. 'This character', wrote one, 'is said to be drawn for a celebrated Female Historian, who has greatly distinguished herself in the cause of Liberty'.[72] The play opens with Sir Thomas arguing with his sister over what was the proper treatment of his daughter. In an impatient aside to the

---

[68] *Gentleman's Magazine*, 53 (1783), 745.
[69] *The Diary of Sylas Neville*, 34.
[70] *Eleutheria: A Poem Inscribed to Mrs. Macaulay* (1768), 2, 7.
[71] Samuel Foote, *The Devil upon Two Sticks* (1778), 1.
[72] *London Chronicle*, 23 (1768), 525.

audience he exclaims: 'Why the woman is mad! these curs'd newspaper patriots have shatter'd her brains, nothing less than a senator of seven years standing can conceive what she means.' Then turning to Margaret he asks 'why the devil can't you converse like the rest of the world? . . . because I lock up my daughter to prevent her eloping with the paltry clerk of a pitiful trader, it is forsooth an invasion of the Bill of Rights, and a mortal stab to the great Charter of Liberty.' Margaret accuses him of being incapable of managing his daughter. 'Had you, with me,' she cries, 'traced things to their original source; had you discovered all social subordination to arise from original compact; had you read Machiavel, Montesquieu, Locke, Bacon, Hobbes, Harrington, Hume; had you studied the political testaments of Alberoni and Cardinal Richelieu . . . had you analiz'd the Pragmatic Sanction, and the family compact; had you toil'd through the laborious page of the Vinerian professors or estimated the prevailing manner with the vicar of Newcastle; in a word, had you read Amicus upon taxation, and Inimicus upon Representation, you would have known . . . that in spite of the frippery French salic laws, woman is a free agent, a noun substantive entity.' When Sir Thomas claims a parent's 'Natural Rights', she responds angrily. 'Natural rights! Can a right to tyrannise be founded in nature?' Fearful that his daughter might hear more of these 'romantic republican notions', Sir Thomas asks Margaret to leave. She was intending to, she replies, 'and without taking leave; nor will I reside on a spot where the great charter of my sex is hourly invaded'. As a parting thrust she warns Sir Thomas that once she has returned to the 'land of liberty', he can expect to have his 'despotic dealings properly and publicly handled'. Foote's intention was to make learned women objects of ridicule. But if a caricature of Catharine, it has more than a grain of truth. It gives us an idea of the impression she made upon people. She was seen as too learned by half, and an active politician in the cause of liberty. Margaret's conversation echoes Elizabeth Carter's account of the meeting at a Canterbury Assembly. What is interesting is the feminist stance Margaret adopts in the face of her brother's assumptions of the rights of parents towards daughters. As she tells her brother there is no need for her 'to turn author' for 'liberty has already a champion in one' of her sex: 'The same pen that has dar'd to scourge the arbitrary actions of some of our monarchs' would 'do equal justice to the oppressive power of parents.' It was to prove a prophetic remark, although whether Catharine Macaulay was in fact an active champion of her sex is questionable.[73]

The play was a great success. Horace Walpole was one of those who set off to see it but was unable to get in. The following week he was successful and shared his 'niece Cholmondeley's box' with Catharine Macaulay, 'who', he wrote, 'goes to see herself represented, and I suppose figures herself very like Socrates'. Early in 1769 Walpole recorded dining with 'the famous Mrs. Macaulay' and the Duke de La Rochefoucault, one of the leading aristocratic patriots in the early years of the French Revolution. 'She is one of the sights', he wrote, 'that all foreigners are carried to see.'[74]

The completion of the fourth volume of her *History* seems to have left her exhausted. She had produced a volume a year since 1766. In January 1769 she returned to London from Bath, where she had gone seeking a cure. The following summer, along with Elizabeth Carter and 'several other Literary Ladies', she was invited to attend the Shakespeare Jubilee celebrations at Stratford-upon-Avon, but ill-health prevented her. Instead she went to Tunbridge for a few days and then on to her brother at Olantigh in Kent. A month later, 'much recovered from her late indisposition', she arrived back in London.[75] It was in this period that Lord Lyttelton wrote of Mrs Macaulay as 'a very prodigy'. Portraits of her were 'on every print-seller's counter'.[76] There was even a Derby figure of her made in porcelain.[77] In 1772 Mrs Patience Wright arrived in London from America 'to make figures in wax of Lord Chatham, Lord Lyttelton, and Mrs. Macaulay'.[78] Patience Wright had already acquired something of a reputation in America for life-sized coloured wax figures. That of Catharine Macaulay was one of the first completed. The *New York Gazette*

---

[73] Foote, *The Devil upon Two Sticks*, 1–6.

[74] *Horace Walpole's Correspondence*, xxiii. 92.

[75] *London Chronicle*, 26 (1769), 208, 288.

[76] Sir George Otto Trevelyan, *The American Revolution*, 2 vols. (1903), ii. 275.

[77] N. B. Penny, 'The Whig Cult of Fox in Early Nineteenth-Century Sculpture', *Past and Present*, 70 (1976), 94–105, at p. 103. There is such a figure in the Fitzwilliam Museum, Cambridge; see also Claire Gilbride Fox, 'Catherine Macaulay, an Eighteenth Century Clio', *Winterthur Portfolio*, 4 (1968), 129–42.

[78] *Horace Walpole's Correspondence*, xxxii. 98.

reported it 'the most striking Likeness ... of Mrs. Catharine
M'Cauley, so much admired for her great Learning, Writing and
amiable Character'.[79] Two years later the *London Magazine* noted
that, of all the figures completed, hers was the 'most familiar'. She
would 'live by the fingers of Mrs. Wright as long as in her
republican history, wherein she has given us a picture of her
mind; but Mrs. Wright has preserved to us the person of this
celebrated and patriot female'.[80] She was still unwell and in
search of a healthier environment when in 1774 she moved to
Bath.

   In Bath she was to share the house of the Revd Thomas
Wilson, an ardent Wilkite and a founder-member of the Society
of Supporters of the Bill of Rights. The adulation continued, but
tempered with the extravagant praise poured out on her there
were beginning to be signs that many rejected precisely those
aspects of her that earlier they had admired. Times had changed.
Her fame was to come to an abrupt halt when in 1778 she
provided the excuse many had long been seeking for dropping
her. She remarried. Her second husband, also a Scot, was more
than twenty years her junior—and a ship's steward. The marriage
marked her abandonment by many of her former friends and
admirers. From constantly being in the public eye she disappears
into obscurity only to emerge briefly from time to time. Yet her
writing continued—both the completion of her *History* and her
political polemic—right up to her death in 1791.

   [79] Charles Coleman Sellers, *Patience Wright* (1976), 52.
   [80] *London Magazine*, 44 (1775), 556.

2. *The* History

There was a Macaulay's History of England long before Lord Macaulay's was heard of; and in its day a famous history it was.

(R. Chambers, *The Book of Days* 2 vols. (1863–4), i. 810)

But there is another characteristic of Mrs. Macaulay's History still more respectable than her love of liberty, and that is, *her love of truth.*

(Edit. footnote, *Gentleman's Magazine*, 64 (1794), ii. 805)

CATHARINE MACAULAY was a political polemicist, the author of works on philosophy, ethics, and education, but above all she was a historian. It was on her history that her main claim to fame rested. It represents by far the largest part of her writings and within it lie perhaps the most important clues to her character, and to her values. So it is with her as a historian we must begin. What strikes one immediately is her uniqueness. It is not just that no other English woman had written history before her, that among her contemporaries there were no other women historians, but that little history was read, let alone written, by women. As Catherine Morland asked, why should women read history with 'the quarrels of popes and Kings, with wars and pestilences, in every page; the men all so good for nothing, and hardly any women at all'?[1] In the course of the eighteenth century a number of men expressed growing concern with the state of women's education and recommended a study of history as admirably suited to their needs. David Hume, who as a historian was one of Catharine Macaulay's chief rivals, thought there was nothing he 'would recommend more earnestly to his female readers than the study of *History*'.[2] He seems not to have contemplated women as the writers of history until confronted by Catharine Macaulay. For him as for other historians, it was an unexpected invasion of a field hitherto monopolized by men.

---

[1] Jane Austen, *Northanger Abbey*, ch. 14.
[2] David Hume, *Essays Moral, Political, and Literary* (1903), 558.

The History of England from the Accession of James I to that of the Brunswick Line was to run to eight volumes and 3,483 quarto pages.[3] The first four volumes were completed within five years. It took her twenty years to complete the eight, but there was a ten-year gap between Volumes V and VI, when she interrupted the work to write, among other things, a *History of England from the Revolution to the Present Time*.[4] Only the first volume, which carried the story up to 1733, was completed. It may have been written when she recognized that her original intention of ending her *History* in 1714 was not to be realized. After finishing the fifth volume, she still thought that within three more she could reach 'the elevation of the house of Hanover'. Subsequently she acknowledged the impossibility of achieving her aim and when she went back to completing the last three volumes she changed the title to *The History of England from the Accession of James I to the Revolution*.[5] Earlier she had announced her intention of following her survey of the seventeenth century by a study of the Tudors and a broad-sweep introduction which would 'begin with the earliest account of Britain, and stride down to her History of the Tudors'.[6] Neither plan was to be realized. Yet by any standard what she achieved was quite remarkable.

Her eight-volume *History* is a political history of the seventeenth century. The first two volumes cover the period from 1603 to 1641. The pace thereafter slows, and the next two volumes are closely focused on the 1640s—an indication of just how important she considered these years. Her fifth volume begins in 1648 and ends with the Restoration. At this point the ten-year pause occurred. When, finally, the *History* was resumed, two volumes cover the period from the Restoration down to 1683. In the last volume she again concentrates closely on just five years, 1683–9. Her reason for choosing the seventeenth century, she wrote, was 'to do justice . . . to the memory of our illustrious ancestors'. People in her own time, she argued, had forgotten that the privileges they enjoyed had had to be fought for by 'men that, with the

[3] Catharine Macaulay, *History of England* 8 vols. (1763–83).

[4] *History from the Revolution*, i (1778).

[5] This was in fact her third title, for after vol. ii she changed it to *The History of England from the Accession of James I to the Elevation of the House of Hanover* for the next three volumes.

[6] *Memoirs of the Late Revd. Theophilus Lindsey, M. A.*, ed. Thomas Belsham (1812), 508.

hazard and even the loss of their lives, attacked the formidable pretensions of the Stewart family, and set up the banners of liberty against a tyranny which had been established for a series of more than one hundred and fifty years'. The *History* was written, wrote James Burgh in 1774, 'for the purpose of inculcating on the people of Britain the love of liberty and their country'.[7]

She was not the first historian in the eighteenth century to concentrate on an analysis of the years 1603–89. Others had written of the period long before either she or David Hume came on the scene. Clarendon's *History of the Rebellion*, although written much earlier, was not published until 1702–4, when his son, the Earl of Rochester, calculated it would provide a useful reinforcement of the Tory version of seventeenth-century events.[8] Certainly the Whigs regarded it as a 'partisan, Tory history'.[9] It was widely read and proved immensely influential. Catharine Macaulay found it 'as faithful an account of facts as any to be found in those times'. 'The characters', she wrote, 'are described in strong if not just colours, but the style is disagreeably pompous', and all too often 'the author's conclusions are so much at war with his facts that he is apt to disgust a candid reader with his prejudices and partiality'.[10] The debate that followed the publication of Clarendon's *History* 'showed . . . how controversial a subject the English Revolution still remained . . . Whig and Tory interpretations . . . became an essential ingredient in the subject matter of eighteenth-century politics'.[11]

In the course of that debate numerous Whig and Tory versions of events in the seventeenth century appeared by historians with varying claims to scholarship; those of White Kennett, Laurence Echard, John Oldmixon, Paul de Rapin-Thoyras, James Ralph, William Guthrie, and many more.[12] Acknowledged to be by far

---

[7] Macaulay, *History of England* i (1763), pp. viii–ix; James Burgh, *Political Disquisitions* 3 vols. (1774–5), i, p. vii.

[8] Edward Hyde, Earl of Clarendon, *History of the Rebellion and Civil Wars in England*, 3 vols. (1702–4).

[9] R. C. Richardson, *The Debate on the English Revolution Revisited*, 2nd edn. (1988), 37.

[10] Macaulay, *History of England*, vi. 262–3.

[11] Richardson, *Debate on the English Revolution*, 37, 38.

[12] See White Kennett, *A Compassionate Enquiry into the Causes of the Civil War* (1708); id., *Complete History of England* (1706); Laurence Echard, *History of England from Julius Caesar to 1689*, 3 vols. (1707–18); John Oldmixon, *Critical History of England*, 2 vols. (1724–6); id., *History of England during the Reigns of the Royal House of*

the best history that appeared in the first half of the century was
Paul de Rapin-Thoyras's *Histoire d'Angleterre*. It was published
at the Hague from 1724 to 1727 in ten volumes and almost
immediately translated into English by Nicholas Tindal, and
published in fifteen volumes between 1723 and 1732. Catharine
Macaulay made frequent use of the work. 'England', she recognized, 'was obliged to a foreigner for . . . the most faithful narrative of the civil and military achievement of her gallant sons.' She
acknowledged its popularity 'but it was more from the circumstance of his having no competitor', she wrote, 'than from the
intrinsic merit of his work'. She admitted 'he was infinitely less
partial in his account of the civil wars . . . than almost any other
writer of that period', but he was 'very prolix', and his writing was
'destitute of all those animating graces and justifications which are
necessary to form an agreeable and instructive history'.[13] But
together with 'that honest historian', James Ralph (1705?–1762),
and the Scot William Guthrie (1708–70), he was 'classed among
the few faithful historians' whose works 'abound with very just
remarks and pertinent reflections'. Guthrie's style could on occasion 'rise even to the sublime', but both these historians were
found 'too careless writers' and like Rapin 'very prolix to a degree
of tediousness'.[14] It was a criticism later levelled at her own
history.

The historian perhaps closest to her in objectives was William
Harris (1720–1810), a Dissenting minister who wrote a series of
historical biographies of, among others, Charles I, Charles II, and
Cromwell. He did not pretend to be impartial. 'His reasonings',
we are told, 'are strongly tinged with his early prejudices', but 'his
notes are full of information from sources not easily accessible'
and 'the evidence on both sides is given without mutilation'.[15]
One other earlier history must be mentioned here. Daniel Neal's
The History of the Puritans (1732–8) in four volumes, was re-

Stuart (1730); Paul de Rapin-Thoyras, *Histoire d'Angleterre*, 10 vols. (1724–7); James
Ralph, *The History of England during the Reigns of King William, Queen Anne, and King
George I*, with an Introductory Review of the Reigns of the Royal Brothers Charles and
James (1744); William Guthrie, *History of England from the Invasion of Julius Caesar to
1688*, 4 vols. (1744–51).

[13] Macaulay, *History of England*, vi, p. vi.

[14] Ibid. vii. 484; vi, p. vi.

[15] *Dictionary of National Biography*; Alexander Chalmers, *The General Biographical
Dictionary*, xvii (1812), 182–4.

printed and edited by Joshua Toulmin in 1793–7. Neal was a Protestant Dissenter, pastor to an Independent congregation in London. His was essentially a religious history written from 'an utter aversion to imposition upon conscience in any shape'.[16] It was a work much used by both Harris and Mrs Macaulay. What made it something of a milestone in historical writing was its scholarship. In the 1793 edition Toulmin, also a dissenting historian, frequently quoted with approval Mrs Macaulay's *History*.

Although not all seventeenth-century history written in the eighteenth century was clearly Tory or Whig in sympathy, it tended to be claimed by one side or the other and became actively used in the battle of party politics. This was particularly true of David Hume (1711–76). Although Rapin's history was not uncritically Whig, it was as a Whig historian that he came to be attacked by Hume. When the first volume of his *History of England* (1754–62) appeared, Hume had been an admirer of Rapin but later admiration turned to scorn. Rapin became one of the 'most despicable' historians.[17] Subsequent volumes of Hume's *History* were directed against Rapin's Whig interpretation. Yet, ironically, when he commenced historian Hume was far from being straightforwardly Tory. 'I have the impudence to pretend that I am of no party', he wrote, 'and have no bias.' He was genuinely surprised to find he was 'commonly numbered among the Tories'. His history from the date of the first volume was detested by the Whigs. Pitt viewed it with hostility and later, as Lord Chatham, was to attack it in the House of Lords. It came to be seen as the classic exposition of the Tory view of history, particularly constitutional history. Later Hume was to write how when he came to revise his *History*, the alterations he made, were 'invariably to the Tory side'.[18] Little wonder if he was labelled as a Tory historian. But bitterness against the Whigs led him to exaggerate. Most of his revisions were made in the period immediately following publication, when he was peculiarly sensitive to its hostile reception and to the severe criticism it received at the hands of the Whigs.[19]

[16] Daniel Neal, *The History of the Puritans*, ed. Joshua Toulmin, 3 vols. (1837), from 'Memoir of the Life of Mr. Daniel Neal', p. li.

[17] From David Hume, *History of England* (1793), viii. 323 as quoted Richardson, *Debate on the English Revolution*, 52.

[18] E. C. Mossner, *The Life of David Hume* (1980), 311.

[19] E. C. Mossner, 'Was Hume a Tory Historian?', *Journal of the History of Ideas*, 2 (1941), 225–36, esp. 231–3.

Hume's *History* remained the dominant interpretation for the next sixty years. Despite its initial failure—more particularly in England—after ten years it became a best-seller. Widely read, it had great influence on all subsequent eighteenth-century historians. Thomas Babington Macaulay called Hume 'the ablest and most popular of modern historians', while at the same time losing no opportunity of criticizing him in his desire to supersede him in the public eye.[20] The *History*, wrote Gavin Hamilton, Hume's publisher, was 'the prittyest thing ever attempted in the English History'.[21] It was in similar terms, if not with the same intention, that Catharine Macaulay described his *History* as serving as 'an elegant pastime for the hours of leisure or idleness, leaving the reader perfectly ignorant as to character, motives, and other facts'.[22] The reasons for his popularity were clear to Mrs Macaulay. As his prejudices 'have fallen in with the prejudice of the prevailing faction in this country', she wrote, 'and as his admirable genius is fully equal to the inspiring every unlearned, incurious and negligent reader with the prejudice of the author, he has for a long time maintained an unrivalled popularity in the walk of English history'.[23] No wonder Whigs were concerned at his influence and sought an alternative interpretation. Catharine Macaulay's *History* (at least the early volumes) was welcomed as providing just that—a Whig counterpart to Hume—and her explanation of Hume's continued popularity is not without relevance to the decline of her own. To the work of Hume, and almost all these eighteenth-century historians who wrote about the seventeenth century, Catharine Macaulay made reference in her *History*.

What distinguished her *History* from that of contemporaries was not just that it was seen as a Whig answer to Hume, but that it was the first republican history of the seventeenth century based on an extensive knowledge of hitherto unused tracts of the 1640s and 1650s. Two of the main sources for her knowledge of such tracts were Thomas Hollis and Richard Baron. The influence

[20] T. P. Peardon, *The Transition in English Historical Writing* (New York, 1933), 19 n. 23, quoting from *The Edinburgh Review*, May 1828, 359; and see Richardson, *The Debate on the English Revolution*, 69.

[21] Mossner, *Life of David Hume*, 303.

[22] Macaulay, *History of England* vi, p. vi.

[23] Ibid.

they had on her republican ideas is dealt with in a later chapter. The historian William Harris, a friend of Catharine Macaulay, also benefited from the generosity of Hollis in making available material that had been lost or mislaid, especially tracts of the Civil War period. Unlike many historians of the time, both Harris and Mrs Macaulay reveal in their work extensive reading and a wide knowledge of sources.

Like many eighteenth-century radicals Catharine Macaulay looked back to Anglo-Saxon England and the time before popular liberties had been crushed by the Norman yoke. Common law was grounded on 'the Saxon institutions'. In the period before the Norman Conquest lay the origins of our true constitution, when the English enjoyed freedom and equality under representative institutions. The constant struggle to win back those lost rights had led to some recovery, but it had been thwarted by the Reformation and the uniting in the same person of political and ecclesiastical power. From Henry VIII's time England 'had preserved a steady course towards slavery and public ruin', only briefly interrupted in the seventeenth century by the Commonwealth, when 'the English after the expense of a ten-years civil war, had totally subdued the despotic family of the Stewarts, and overturned the tyranny settled by the Norman invader'. But 'instead of returning to the more wholesome principles of the Saxon constitution', Parliament had 're-established in its full extent a government from which the people had never received other than bitter fruit, and . . . let loose upon the public an enraged faction, supported by the unprincipled son of a father'. Nor was 1688 a step towards liberty, but inaugurated a system with the vices of 'all the monarchical, oligarchical, and aristocratical tyrannies in the world'.[24] 'The plan of settlement' was not 'agreeable to the regularity of the Saxon constitution which effectually secured every privilege it bestowed'.[25] For Catharine Macaulay, history was the story of struggle to recover those ancient rights. Later radicals were to make extensive use of the Norman Yoke theory, but Catharine Macaulay's *History* was 'an important landmark'.[26] If not central to her work the theory

---

[24] Ibid. i. 387; vii. 332; vi. 71–2; viii. 330.
[25] Macaulay, *History from the Revolution*, i. 5.
[26] Christopher Hill, *Puritanism and Revolution* (1986), 99.

occurs frequently throughout her eight volumes. She was far from
alone. It was, according to Albert Goodwin, a 'bogus but strongly
held historical myth'. He sees it as a 'harking back, often consciously, to the behaviour and political attitudes of the "real
Whigs" or "eighteenth-century Commonwealthmen"' of nearly a
century earlier.[27]

Alfred, 'a prince of the most exalted merit that ever graced the
English throne', had a central role in the theory of the Norman
Yoke.[28] To him was owed much that was good in our ancient
law—not least, trial by jury. When wishing on a rare occasion to
praise Charles II for his speech to parliament in 1662, the best
thing Catharine Macaulay could find to say of it was that 'it would
have done honour to the character of an Alfred'.[29] In the 1770s
she lived at Alfred House, Bath, where a bust of Alfred stood over
the door. Of the six odes written for her birthday in 1777, three
make reference to Alfred.[30]

Her *History* reveals her as a shrewd judge of character and a
witty and lively writer. Of Elizabeth she wrote that 'her good
fortune is in nothing more conspicuous, than in the unmerited
fame it has to this day preserved to her'. 'This contemptible
time-server', as she called Bacon, 'was the greatest preferment-
seeker of the age, to the abuse of his excellent talents.' Raleigh's
'apprehension was quick, his parts subtle; he had an indefatigable
industry, and a great command of temper; but his judgement was
clouded with partial views of self-interest, and the servile prejudices of the times; though guiltless of any attrocious [*sic*] crimes,
yet his morals had taken a deep tint from the vices of the court'.
'The virtues' possessed by James I 'were so loaded with a greater
proportion of their neighbouring vices, that they exhibit no lights
to set off the dark shades.' 'He snuffed up continually the incense
of his own praise.' The Duke of Buckingham exhibited 'a mixture

---

[27] Albert Goodwin, *The Friends of Liberty* (1979), 33.
[28] Obadiah Hulme, *Historical Essay on the Constitution* (1771), 23–4; examples of the
same attitude to Alfred in the 18th c. are not difficult to find; see e.g. Toplady's praise
of him as 'an individual and as a chief magistrate', who 'came the nearest to moral and
political perfection, of any regal character which adorns the page of secular history',
and, at the time of George III's accession, Thomas Hollis's hopes that 'his pattern be
that of Alfred': *The Works of Augustus Toplady* (1853), 845; *Memoirs of Thomas Hollis*,
ed. Francis Blackburne, 2 vols. (1780), i. 98.
[29] Macaulay, *History of England* vi. 109.
[30] *Six Odes Presented to the Justly-Celebrated Historian, Mrs Catharine Macaulay, on her
Birthday* (1777), 17, 35, 42–3.

of Gallic licentiousness and British roughness'. On Charles II she commented that 'when he was forced, or inclined to do obliging things, he did them in the most obliging manner'. Of his consistent failure to act according to his promises she concluded either that 'he was one of those unfortunate lunatics, who preserve a sufficient appearance of soundness of understanding to give the colour of guilt to their enormities; or that he was a downright hypocrite, and to serve a present purpose, spoke a language not only opposite to his intentions, but to his judgement and convictions'.[31]

Her *History* also reveals her familiarity with the literature of the period. Andrew Marvell she considered 'the greatest wit and one of the honester men in the age'. She commented that there were again in her own day a few who recognized 'the illustrious champions of the public cause'. The poet Cowley was 'no longer preferred to the sublimer Genius of Milton, in whose comprehensive powers were united the highest excellencies of poetry, the acuteness of rational logic, and the deep sagacity of politic science'. She noted how the diligence of the licenser of the press in 1667 had led to 'Milton's Paradise Lost, a poem which has reflected the highest honours on the English nation for its unparalleled merit' being 'very nearly lost to the public'.[32]

It was her fourth volume of 1768 that provoked the greatest discussion. 'Till its author shall descend to times and characters which wear complections very different from those she has hitherto discussed,' as one review of her third volume put it, nothing 'decisive' could be said 'as to the general scope and tendency of this work'.[33] Advertised as extending to 'that important period of the English annals, the Execution of Charles I', it met with criticism from both sides.[34] Timothy Hollis, cousin of Thomas, admitted that while he liked the volume, he was 'surprised with other friends of liberty at the favourable character' she gave to Charles.[35] She wrote how while 'the partizans of Liberty applaud his fate; the liberal and humane condemn and pity him', and both views shaped her verdict.[36] By other critics she was accused of 'attempting to throw the whole blame of the

[31] Macaulay, *History of England* i. 2, 102 n. 99, 137, 265, 8, 218; vi. 420.
[32] Ibid. v. 379, 382; vi. 106.
[33] *Critical Review*, 23 (1767), 168.
[34] *London Chronicle*, 24 (1768), 479.
[35] *The Diary of Sylas Neville*, ed. Basil Cozens-Hardy (1950), 58.
[36] Macaulay, *History of England* iv. 417.

civil war on the unfortunate victim of it'.[37] In the character of
Charles, she wrote, were found 'the qualities of temperance,
chastity, regularity, piety, equity, humanity, dignity, condescension, and equanimity'. Some had 'gone so far as to allow him
integrity'. But she warned of the danger that in dwelling so much
'on the suffering prince, we are apt to overlook the designing
tyrant, to dwell on his hardships and forget his crimes'—his
'passion for power' and 'idolatry to his royal prerogatives'.[38] She
'seems to think it possible,' wrote one reviewer tentatively, 'that a
great monarch may be a low, shuffling, disingenuous slave to
bigotry and love of power'.[39]

Claiming that like the court Charles was dissipated and his
conversation indecent, she quoted Milton against the assertions of
Clarendon to the contrary. She concluded that were Charles'
chastity allowed, 'it was tainted by an excess of uxoriousness
which gave it the properties and the consequences of vice'.[40] Her
critics were quick to reply. 'Amongst all the hardships and cruelties
inflicted upon Charles the First', wrote 'An Old Bachelor' in the
London Chronicle, 'I think it was by no means the least that ladies
should rise up in this generation, who after having stripped him of
all other virtues, will not allow him even the cold comfort of
chastity, or suffer him even to kiss his own wife with impunity.'[41]
Significantly it was not so much her criticism that was attacked
but the fact that it came from a 'lady'. Many were convinced by
her portrait. 'See Charles's face drawn by Clarendon', wrote
William Cowper, 'and it is an handsome Pourtrait; see it more
justly exhibited by Mrs. McAulay, and it is deformed to a degree
that shocks us. Every feature expresses Cunning . . . .'[42]

Opposition to Charles I was, she thought, 'grounded more on
religious prejudices, on personal dissatisfaction, on the prevalency
of a faction about him, on the natural principle of resisting an
high degree of oppression, than on any enlarged notions of government'. The terms on which Parliament offered peace to
the king were 'more the cautions than the principles of the

---

[37] *London Chronicle*, 25 (1769), 228.
[38] Macaulay, *History of England* iv. 418–19.
[39] *Critical Review*, 27 (1769), 81.
[40] Macaulay, *History of England* iv. 422.
[41] *London Chronicle*, 25 (1769), 45.
[42] *The Letters and Prose Writings of William Cowper*, ed. James King and Charles
Ryskamp, 5 vols. (1981), ii. 17.

Presbyterians', who, she wrote, 'had no dislike to royal authority, nor to tyranny itself, provided it was directed according to their own fantastic ideas and notions'. It was not only enmity from 'the formidable factions of Cavalier and Presbyterian' that Parliament had to face. In their own party there were those 'disgusted with the oligarchical form into which they had modelled the government, and the undivided authority they had assumed to themselves'. Among the opposition there were 'some few . . . who, from the first, looked forward to the reformation of the principles, as well as the executive part, of the government'.[43] She called them republicans.

The period of the Commonwealth was 'the brightest age that ever adorned the page of history'. She rejected those who represented it 'in a pitiful light, despised and disregarded by the people, which gave Cromwell the boldness to act as he did'. The reverse was true. 'Never did the annals of Humanity furnish the example of a government, so newly established, so formidable to foreign states as was at this period the English Commonwealth'. It was Parliament's proposals for reform of the system of law, 'the rendering its execution less tedious and burdensome to the subject, the correcting the abuses of the courts of justice, and reducing the clergy to a more evangelical constitution' which had so alarmed 'the greater part of the lawyers and clergy' as to provide the conservatives with an argument for a protectorate.[44]

When she described the Long Parliament as 'the most patriotic government that ever blessed the hopes and military exertions of a brave people',[45] a critic wrote that while he revered 'the memory of those real patriots who have spent their blood and treasures to preserve our constitution, yet I cannot allow that the majority of the members who composed the long parliament, deserved that glorious appellation.'[46] Her description of the parliamentary army whose fighting 'was not a trade of blood, but an exertion of principle, and obedience to the call of conscience, and their conduct was not only void of insolence but benevolent and humane' produced an angry reaction.[47] How could she so flatter 'men

[43] Macaulay, *History of England*, iv. 159, 160; v. 6; iv. 160.
[44] Ibid. v. 382, 108–9, 79, 120.
[45] Catharine Macaulay, *A Modest Plea for the Property of Copyright* (1774), 23.
[46] *Gentleman's Magazine*, 44 (1774), 218.
[47] Macaulay, *History of England*, iv. 181–2.

whose horrid cruelties disgraced their country, their religion, and
even human nature itself?'[48]

In justifying regicide, she used the arguments of Goodwin,
Locke, Sydney, and Milton, among others, to make her case.
She wrote that 'Kings, the servants of the State, when they
degenerated into tyrants, forfeited their right to government'.[49]
But was Charles I a tyrant? James Burgh was quick to defend her,
calling on the reader to study Mrs Macaulay's 'history of his
horrid reign . . . and determine whether exempting him from the
guilt of tyranny, it is possible to fix it on any prince that ever disgraced a throne, or filled a kingdom with confusion and blood-
shed.'[50] Summarizing Milton's arguments in *Defence of the People
of England against Salmasius*, she concluded that 'the oaths of
allegiance were to be understood as conditionally binding, according to the observance of the oaths kings made to their people. And
neither the laws of God nor nature were against the peoples
laying aside Kings and Kingly government, and the adopting more
convenient forms.'[51] While regretting that she had not dealt more
directly with the legality of the execution of the King before
espousing 'the proceedings of the regicides', the *Critical Review*
nevertheless declared itself 'in favour of Mrs. Macaulay's narrative' which was 'concise, clear, and candid' and 'worthy a warm
friend to liberty'.[52]

For Cromwell, 'the vain-glorious usurper', she reserved her
greatest condemnation. He was an 'individual, no ways exalted
above his brethren in any of those private endowments which
constitute the true greatness of character, or excelling in any
quality, but in the measure of a vain and wicked ambition'. With
approval she quoted William Harris's *Life of Cromwell*. The cause
of more evil than any other character in history, Cromwell was
'more diabolically wicked than it was possible for the generality of
the honest part of mankind to conceive'. He was motivated by 'the
most sordid principles of self-interest, with their concomit-
ant vices, envy, hatred, and malice'. It was Cromwell she held
responsible for ending a 'period of national glory . . . when

---

[48] *Gentleman's Magazine*, 44 (1774), 303.
[49] Macaulay, *History of England*, iv. 28.
[50] Burgh, *Political Disquisitions*, i. 185.
[51] Macaulay, *History of England* iv. 428–9.
[52] *Critical Review*, 27 (1769), 95.

England after so long a subjection to monarchical tyranny bad fair
to out-do in the constitution of its government ... every circumstance of glory, wisdom and happiness related of ancient or
modern empires'. Fearful of the increase of power of the republican party, and conscious of the decline of his own, he set out
to undermine and destroy it.[53]

It was her earlier admiration for the parliamentary army that
provoked Horace Walpole, in an almost hysterical outburst, to ask
'is some Cromwell to trample on us because Mrs. Macaulay
approved the Army that turned out the House of Commons?' And
again 'when did an army bestow freedom? Did that army which
raised Cromwell to the throne—those republican heroes of Mrs.
Macaulay? The Parliament was the true barrier against the King's
usurpations, and had done its duties nobly. Reformation, not
destruction of the constitution, was its aim; and therefore, in her
eyes, it was not less guilty than the King.' But some of her critics
ignore the fact that Catharine Macaulay's attitude towards the
army changed after Cromwell was elevated to sole power in 1653.
When he defended his assuming the Protectorate, 'for as they
were entrusted in some things, so was he in others', she noted it
was the same argument 'which, on occasions something similar,
had been used by the late king'.[54]

Familiar as she was with all the Leveller manifestos, it was that
of 1 May 1649, *An Agreement of the Free People of England*, the
product of the imprisonment in the Tower of Lilburne, Walwyn,
and Overton, she favoured as 'a better model than any which had
yet been offered to the public'. It was, she noted the 'high tone of
authority' with which any who ventured to show discontent were
treated, 'conduct ... ill suited to the independent spirit of the
Levellers', that 'provoked them to assemble at Burford' in an
army mutiny.[55] Disastrous, in her opinion, had been parliament's
entrusting the command of the army to Cromwell on Fairfax's
resignation in 1650. She believed that had parliament countered
the power of Cromwell with 'an equal military command in the
hands of the brave and honest Ludlow ... till time and opportu-

---

[53] Macaulay, *History of England*, v. 95, 101, 124, 129, 172.
[54] *Horace Walpole's Correspondence*, ed. W. S. Lewis, 48 vols. (1937–83), xv. 129;
Memoirs of the Reign of George III, ed. G. F. Russell Barker, 4 vols. (1894), iii. 121–3;
Macaulay, *History of England*, v. 146.
[55] Macaulay, *History of England*, v. 129, 124, 101, 95, 146.

nity had enabled them totally to destroy an influence which from the first establishment of the Commonwealth had threatened its existence', the Restoration would never have happened. She wrote of the growing despair of 'the Republicans', many of whom had left the government 'unable to hold office compatible with their principles'. 'Many sensible and spirited pamphlets' were written in an attempt 'to awaken men to a sense of ... the danger of those evils which awaited them', to reveal how 'the passions of hope, despair, fear, and revenge affected the tranquillity of the public and rendered the desire of a settlement on any terms general'. The tragedy was the sacrifice of 'all those principles of Liberty and Justice which had been established by the successful contests of the people with the crown ... all the advantages which had been gained by a long and bloody war'. Scornfully she described the growth of 'the abject vice of servility' at the Restoration, of 'the transport with which the giddy multitude, and all ranks of men, received this new pageant of royalty, to which they had been so long unaccustomed'. To the Royalist stories of 'men who died with the pleasure they received on this joyful event', she reacted with characteristic scepticism: 'This premature ... mortality was in all probability incurred by inebriety'.[56]

Her opinion of Cromwell was not one shared by many of her contemporaries. She noted the extravagant praise he had received, and scorned 'that party among us who call themselves Whigs' for their adoption of so false a representation. 'Historians, either from prejudice or want of attention' had 'in general given into those ill-founded encomiums so prodigally bestowed on the usurper'.[57] Her friend Augustus Toplady was not convinced that Cromwell had been 'so utterly destitute of conscience and principle', and entered into 'an amicable controversy' with her. He could perceive 'in various features of his [Cromwell's] mental character', he wrote, 'some striking symptoms of magnanimity and virtue'. While agreeing that many of his principles and much of his conduct were indefensible, he thought she was judging him by 'too exalted a standard'. 'Much allowance', he argued, 'must be made for the times in which he lived' and 'the situation in which he was gradually placed; much for that teeming train of events which

---

[56] Ibid. 378, 380, 323, 381–2 (*recte* 391–2), 363, 378.
[57] Ibid. 202–3.

appear to have drawn him in step by step.' Exactly how she countered Toplady's argument we do not know. She would have had little sympathy with it. But three months later Toplady proposed a compromise formulation from Lord Lyttelton which ended: 'he trampled on the laws of the nation, but he raised the glory of it; and it is hard to say, which he most deserved, a halter or a crown'.[58] Catharine Macaulay may have accepted the compromise for she firmly believed good could come out of evil. Toplady's view of Cromwell was shared by others. 'However unjustifiable we admit the conduct of Cromwell to have been, in the measures which he pursued for obtaining the protectorship', wrote *The Critical Review*, 'it is certain that neither the glory nor strength of the empire suffered any abatement from the elevation of that celebrated usurper.'[59]

Her choice of Cromwell for the most damning criticism that any individual received in her *History*, is in line with the importance she attached to individual morality. The worst fault of any king, statesman or politician in her eyes was self-interest, 'their apparent devotion to politics for personal gain rather than for the advancement of liberty', for in their hands lay the shaping of history. Her approach was essentially a moral one, and it is notable that when in her *History* she wished to consider all sides of a question, she nearly always resorted to an analysis of the moral character of the individuals concerned. It went with her conviction that only a virtuous people could achieve a real republic. As Lynne Withey has suggested, 'individual morality lay at the heart of Macaulay's writing of history'. Without it there could be no progress.[60]

The response to the first volume of Catharine Macaulay's *History* was enthusiastic. It 'was received with great applause, and the public, ever in extremes, gave it a reception not less flattering to the ambition than satisfactory to the interest of a writer'.[61] It was widely reviewed. One of the first comments on it came from Thomas Hollis, who recorded in his diary on 30 November 1763,

---

[58] *Works of Augustus Toplady*, 844–5, 851.
[59] *Critical Review*, 31 (1771), 176.
[60] Lynne E. Withey, 'Catharine Macaulay and the Uses of History: Ancient Rights, Perfectionism, and Propaganda', *The Journal of British Studies*, 16 (1976), 59–83, 72; this article also demonstrates how her religious beliefs informed her view of history.
[61] *The European Magazine and London Review*, 4 (1783), 330–4, at pp. 330–1.

'finished the reading of the first volume of Mrs. Macaulay's *History* . . ., the history is honestly written, and with considerable ability and spirit; and is full of the freest, noblest, sentiments of Liberty'.[62] A month later Horace Walpole, in a letter to the Revd William Mason, asks: 'Have you read Mrs. Macaulay? I am glad again to have Mr Gray's opinion to corroborate mine that it is the "most sensible, unaffected and best history of England that we have had yet".'[63] Later in a letter to the Revd James Brown, Gray was to write 'you have doubtless heard of the honour done to your friend Mrs. Macaulay. Mr. Pitt has made a panegyric of her *History* in the House.'[64] This cannot have pleased Hume, but what caused him 'the greatest vexation he ever experienced' was that Pitt went on to make 'strictures on the Tory bias of his work'.[65] Mrs Macaulay also won approval from rational Dissenters like Joseph Priestley, who for 'a good antidote to what is unfavourable to liberty in Mr. Hume' recommended 'the very masterly history of Mrs. Macaulay'.[66] Among her many other admirers in the 1760s and 1770s, John Wilkes referred to 'that noble English historian who does so great an honour to her own sex, and ought to cover ours with blushes'.[67] Nor was it only in this country that her *History* won acclaim. Benjamin Franklin, in a letter to a newspaper in 1765, talked of that 'honest set of writers . . . who always show their regard to truth . . . to . . . the infinite advantage of all future Livies, Rapins, Robertsons, Humes, and McAulays who may be sincerely inclin'd to furnish the world with that *rara avis* a true history'.[68] In France, Madame Roland was inspired by Catharine Macaulay's history, which she regarded as hardly inferior to that of Tacitus, to become 'la Macaulay de son pays'.[69]

Much later, in 1782, when her popularity had waned, William Cowper, the poet, read her *History* and was moved to write of it to his friend Joseph Hill that 'the men whose integrity, courage, and

[62] *Memoirs of Thomas Hollis*, ed. Francis Blackburne, 2 vols. (1780), i. 210.
[63] *Horace Walpole's Correspondence*, xxviii. 3.
[64] *Letters of Thomas Gray*, ed. D. C. Tovey, 3 vols. (1900–12), iii. 106.
[65] As quoted Mossner, *Life of David Hume*, 310.
[66] Joseph Priestley, *Lectures on History and General Policy*, 2 vols. (1803), i. 340.
[67] *The Correspondence of the Late John Wilkes with His Friends*, ed. John Almon, 5 vols. (1805), iv. 139.
[68] *The Writings of Benjamin Franklin*, ed. A. H. Smyth, 10 vols. (1905–7), iv. 370.
[69] *The Private Memoirs of Madame Roland*, ed. E. G. Johnson (1901), 366.

Wisdom broke the bonds of tyranny, established our constitution upon its true basis, and gave a people overwhelmed with the Scorn of all countries an opportunity to emerge into a state of the highest respect and Estimation, make a better figure in History than any of the present day are likely to do'.[70] But Mrs Macaulay's 'emphatic Whiggism', which predisposed Horace Walpole in her favour, had the opposite effect on others. 'I am glad to find you hear Mrs. Macaulay's book so much commended,' wrote Elizabeth Carter in 1764, 'the few extracts which I have seen of it have given me a high idea of her talents. From the accounts of others I apprehend there is too violent a party spirit runs through it, at which I am exceedingly vexed.'[71]

At the end of October 1763, Dr Macaulay, apparently acting on Hume's instructions, sent him a copy of the first volume of his wife's *History*. No acknowledgement was received. Hume, however, was constantly reminded of its existence by his correspondents. Allan Ramsay, the painter, shortly after its publication, wrote to him of 'somebody under the name of Mrs Catharine Macaulay' who 'has written a romance, called "James the First", the secret design of which is to abuse you and me, and all the other people of consequence, whom she calls the creatures of a court and the tools of tyranny'. Later Colonel Edmonstoune, a cousin of Lord Bute's, wrote asking him: 'What is this McCaulay history? I saw in the newspapers an extract of a preface that seemed to me to be the rhapsody of a crazy head. I hear it is in opposition to your History.'[72]

When still receiving no word of acknowledgement, Dr Macaulay on the 22 March 1764, wrote again to Hume to tell him that the first volume had been sent to him the previous October adding how he 'now thought proper to send you this intelligence, lest you should imagine that we were chargeable with any want of punctuality'.[73] Hume, full of apologies, wrote back from France, where he was basking in the sort of praise England had denied him, thanking Catharine for the 'agreeable present' and for 'the

---

[70] *The Letters and Prose Writings of William Cowper*, ii. 13.

[71] *Memoirs of the Life of Mrs. Elizabeth Carter*, ed. Revd Montagu Pennington (1807), 481–2.

[72] *Letters of Eminent Persons to David Hume*, ed. J. H. Burton (1849), 29–30; id., *Life and Correspondence of David Hume*, 2 vols. (1846), ii. 186.

[73] *The Letters of Eminent Persons to David Hume*, 112.

pleasure your performance has given me; and for the obliging manner in which you mention me even when opposing my sentiments'. She did him the honour, he added, 'to keep me in your eye, during the course of your narration; and I flatter myself that we differ less in facts, than our interpretation and construction of them.' But honesty forced him to admit a difference in 'some original principles, which it will not be easy to adjust between us'. For example, he wrote, 'I look upon all kinds of subdivision of power . . . to be equally legal if established by custom and authority; I cannot but think that the mixed monarchy of England, such as it was left by Queen Elizabeth, was a lawful form of government, and carried the obligations to obedience and allegiance.' 'Every kind of government may be legal,' she responded, 'but sure all are not equally expedient; and an individual, who rigorously maintains and enlarges his power, in opposition to the inclination and welfare of a people is, in my opinion, highly criminal.' She claimed that Hume's views on the obligations to obedience and allegiance to all lawful forms of government involved 'all reformers in unavoidable guilt, since opposition to established error must needs be opposition to authority'. Hume was stung to retort: 'I grant that the cause of liberty which you Madam, with the Pyms and Hampdens have adopted, is noble and generous, but most of the partizans of that cause, in the last century, disgraced it, by their violence, and also by their cant, hypocrisy and bigotry, which, more than the principles of civil liberty, seem to have been the motive of all their actions.'[74]

After this outburst Hume the gentleman reappears, and with tongue firmly in cheek, he claimed that 'had these principles always appeared in the same amiable light which they receive from both your person and writings, it would have been impossible to resist them; and however much inclined to indulgence towards the first James and Charles, I should have been the first to condemn these monarchs for not yielding to them.' Finally he expressed again, 'lest you should think that the air of this place has infected me with the style of gallantry', his 'great esteem' for her work and his 'great personal respect' for her person. Catharine rose to the occasion, rejecting the suggestion that 'his high strain of gallantry' had anything to do with the French air, 'since those who have had

[74] *European Magazine*, 4 (1783), at p. 331.

the pleasure of conversing with Mr. Hume know, that he unites with the utmost candour, all that engaging politeness which marks the gentleman, as well as the philosopher.' Conscious how such gallantry was occasioned by her sex rather than her *History*, she wrote jokingly of the arbitrary princes of the Stuarts who had a very effective way of protecting themselves against 'female opposers, since cropping of ears close to the head, slitting of noses, and branding of foreheads, must needs be as formidable to women, as Caesar's attack on the face was to the Roman petit-maitres.'[75] The *European Magazine* had no doubt who had won in this debate. 'It is unnecessary to observe, that the celebrated Scotch historian, in the present correspondence, is manifestly inferior to the lady, at least in argument.'[76] In Joseph Towers's review of Hume's *History of England* it was recommended to readers 'that after they have perused Mr. Hume's *History*, they will qualify it with a quant. suf. of Mrs. Macaulay's; and the real state of truth and things may probably be found in the mean between them'.[77]

Hume was surprised and disappointed by the initial English reception of his first volume in 1754, which was in marked contrast to the praise later occasioned by the appearance of Mrs Macaulay's. 'I was assailed by one cry of reproach, disapprobation, and even detestation,' he wrote, 'and what was still more mortifying, the book seemed to sink into oblivion.' Apparently only forty-five copies were sold in the first year. He blamed the Whigs, who had treated his history with contempt, and designed 'to ruin him as an author'. It may have contributed to his going out of his way to discredit them in subsequent volumes. On the cause of its initial failure, he was almost certainly nearer the truth when he confessed to harbouring 'some vague misgivings concerning the influence of the London booksellers in retarding sales'. When his publisher moved to London, took a shop, and tried to sell his work to booksellers, 'none of them would deal with an interloper'. Hume must have resented the success with which, initially, Mrs Macaulay's *History* was met.[78] 'The Strictures made upon his History ... were ... carried to an extraordinary length', wrote

[75] Ibid.
[76] Ibid. 332.
[77] *Westminster Magazine*, 6 (1778), 230.
[78] Mossner, *The Life of David Hume*, 312.

Lord Charlemont, the Irish statesman, Hume's friend and
admirer, 'when Mrs. Mc Cauly, as an Historian, was preferred to
him, and her constitutional Writings were declared to be the only
Antidote to his Poison.'[79] How did he react to the many inquiries
directed at him about her work? What reply did he give, for instance, to the letter from Mademoiselle de l'Espinasse in October
1767, asking, 'Est-il vrai qu'il y ait une histoire d'Angleterre faite
par une Écossaise qu'on dit être très républicaine?', and adding, 'il ne peut y avoir qu'une femme qui soit assez hardie pour
oser courir carrière après vous'.[80] Hearing of the 'extraordinary
ovations from enthusiastic admirers' she received in Bath, how did
he feel when his own visit to that town passed unnoticed?[81] In
December 1770 the *London Chronicle* carried a story of 'a certain
Lady, well-known in the republic of letters', who 'a few days since
was favoured by a visit from an author, who had been very severe
on some striking passages delineated by that Lady, relative to the
Stuart family; as soon as he entered the anti-chamber, or levee-
room, our heroine, with the spirit of an amazon, instantly laid hold
of his nose, in that posture conducted the trembling author to the
door, then suddenly turned herself about, absolutely kicked him
fairly into the street.'[82] It is, no doubt, an apocryphal story but the
identity of the characters is clear.

The attitude of Horace Walpole to her *History* deserves some
explanation. Nineteenth-century editors of Walpole's memoirs
and letters were clearly at a loss to account for his devoting so
much space and critical energy to Mrs Macaulay's *History*. That
Walpole should mention it in the same breath as Dr Robertson's
Charles the Fifth seemed an inexplicable 'perversion of judgement'.[83] Yet there is no doubt Walpole thought very highly of her
earlier volumes, even if this admiration rapidly became mixed with
feelings of envy if not downright jealousy. Probably such feelings
were not unconnected with Walpole's own venture into publication as a historian. His *Historical Doubts on the Life and Reign of
Richard III* appeared in 1768—the year in which Catharine

[79] As quoted ibid. 310.

[80] *Letters of Eminent Persons to David Hume* (1849), 211.

[81] A. Birabeau, *Life and Letters at Bath in the Eighteenth Century* (1904), 171.

[82] *London Chronicle*, 27 (1770), 3.

[83] Horace Walpole, *Memoirs of the Reign of George III*, 4 vols. (1894), iii. 321–3
editorial n. *b*.

Macaulay's fourth volume was published. One of Walpole's biographers wrote that his work was 'an original and spirited piece of special pleading but its theories were based on inadequate material, and were often supported by decidedly flimsy reasoning.'[84] In fact the work was an immediate success, but although he was loyally defended by his friends, the weakness of his argument was an open invitation to serious criticism. He was convincingly attacked by Gibbon and Hume as well as by other historians whose opinion Walpole could not easily dismiss. Such criticisms were bitterly resented by Walpole not least because, as his biographer has said, his brand of snobbishness led him to feel that 'his books, the productions of a gentleman of leisure, ought to be exempt from the searching criticisms of professionals.'[85]

Walpole did not venture into print again as historian, and the controversy into which this one venture led him continued for the rest of his life. Against this background it must have been galling for him to see the steady flow of Catharine Macaulay's *History*. The barely concealed anger of his outbursts against her were surely, in part, expressions of this jealousy. 'The female historian', he wrote, 'as partial to the cause of liberty as bigots to the Church and royalists to tyranny, exerted manly strength with the gravity of a philosopher. Too prejudiced to dive into causes,' he went on, 'she imputes everything to tyrannic views, nothing to passions, weakness, error, prejudice, and still less to what operates oftenest and her ignorance of which qualified her less for a historian—to accident and little motives.'[86]

When Catharine Macaulay published her *History of England from the Revolution to the Present Time in a Series of Letters to a Friend* (1778), Walpole called it a 'foolish and absurd "Summary"' and claimed it was nothing but 'a wretched compilation from magazines, full of gross mistakes'.[87] Not all agreed with him. The *Critical Review* thought 'her observations' were 'frequently judicious and liberal' and that she displayed 'the same spirit and elevation as in her *History*'.[88] In this first volume she covered the period from the Revolution up to 1733. A second would have

---

[84] R. W. Ketton-Cramer, *Horace Walpole* (1940), 247.
[85] Ibid. 172.
[86] Walpole, *Memoirs of the Reign of George III*, iii. 121–3.
[87] *Horace Walpole's Correspondence*, xxviii. 371.
[88] *Critical Review*, 45 (1778), 134.

brought the story down to her own time, but it was never completed. In the form of letters to Thomas Wilson, it adopts a conversational tone, and, unlike previous volumes, it is without footnotes. It was written in Bath, where she no longer had access to the British Museum, but besides her own books Wilson had put his library at her disposal, so that she was not deprived of all material. The more likely explanation of her omitting all footnotes lies in the preface to Volume VI of her *History* published three years later. 'Having heard that long notes were tedious and disagreeable to the reader', she had decided to change her method of presentation and had 'woven into the text every part of the composition which could be done without breaking into the thread of history'.[89] She was trying to cover a far broader sweep of years in the 1778 volume and, as she intended it to be a popular history, footnotes were less appropriate.

Her views of the 'Glorious Revolution' were here laid out in detail. She agreed that the Revolution marked a change in the constitution. The power of the Crown was no longer recognized as depending on 'hereditary indefeasible right' but derived from 'a contract with the people', who 'were now looked up to as the only legal source of sovereign authority'. 'Allegiance and protection were declared reciprocal terms.' But given the great opportunities offered them, so anxious were they 'to establish the personal interest of their leader', that patriots neglected 'this fair opportunity to cut off all the prerogatives of the crown' to which they had 'justly imputed the calamities and injuries sustained by the nation'. The settlement, she claimed, failed to 'admit of any of those refinements and improvements, which the experience of mankind had enabled them to make in the science of political security'.[90]

In 1781 she wrote of her efforts to make her *History* 'useful to men of all conditions'. Later, in her *Letters on Education* (1790), she was to emphasize the importance of a study of history in the education of the young. She was all too aware of how little regard was had for it in universities. If she was clear of what the task of

---

[89] Macaulay, *History of England* 6, advertisement before text.

[90] Ead., *Observations on a Pamphlet Entitled 'Thoughts on the Cause of the Present Discontents'* (1770); ead., *History from the Revolution*, i. (1778), 4–5, 72; and see Barbara B. Schnorrenberg, 'An Opportunity Missed: Catharine Macaulay on the Revolution of 1688', *Studies in Eighteenth-Century Culture*, 20 (1990), 231–40.

the historian consisted: 'Labour, to attain truth, integrity to set it in its full light', she admitted it was not always easy. In 1768 she told Sylas Neville that her fourth volume was proving 'a very troublesome one' to complete.[91] When it came to periods of the past, the execution of Charles I or the Revolution of 1688/9 for example, on which passions remained high, a historian 'to contradict the opinion of his countrymen' needed the 'enthusiasm of a martyr'. 'The most invidious and the most distressful part of historic composition' was, she found, 'the drawing the character of those unfortunate individuals whose conduct is the proper object of satire rather than of panegyric.' When she resumed her *History*, she wrote bitterly of how 'the public advantages which must attend a disinterested principle in historians' were acknowledged by all parties, and by all parties were 'equally hated and equally persecuted'.[92]

There are those who, attacking her work as a 'masterly example of how not to write history', have argued that she was no scholar.[93] While admitting she may occasionally have consulted some British Museum manuscripts, they have accused her of carelessness in consulting original authorities and of unfairness in the way in which she used them. Yet the footnotes to her *History* show she frequently referred to manuscripts in the British Museum. A list of the authorities consulted for each volume of her history is impressive. The fact that she made use of such original source-material was in sharp contrast to Hume, who apparently never consulted manuscripts. In fairness he never claimed to have written a 'scholarly' history. 'I have inserted no original Papers', he wrote, 'and enter'd into no Detail of minute, uninteresting Facts.' Research, he once claimed, was the 'dark industry'.[94] Catharine Macaulay read and was closely acquainted with many seventeenth-century tracts. If the whole study of that century has been profoundly affected by the use of such material, she was certainly one of the first to draw on it extensively. If there remains any doubt of

[91] Macaulay, *History of England* vi, p. xiii; i, p. x; G. M. Ditchfield, 'Some Literary and Political Views of Catherine Macaulay', *American Notes and Queries*, 12 (1974), 70–6, at p. 74.

[92] Macaulay, *History of England* viii. 59, 329; vi, p. v.

[93] T. P. Peardon, *The Transition in English Historical Writing*, 60.

[94] Mossner, *Life of David Hume*, 316; Arthur Marwick, *The Nature of History* (1970), 31.

her scholarship, there is the evidence provided by *A Catalogue of Tracts* [belonging to Mrs Macaulay] printed in 1790, a year before her death. Whether it was a record of her working library or of those works that she had decided to sell we do not know. But the list is a fascinating one. It consists of nearly 5,000 tracts and sermons mainly covering the seventeenth and eighteenth centuries. Of just over 4,100 tracts rather more than half are from the seventeenth century, and there are over 500 where the date is omitted. Of course the fact that such works were in her library does not necessarily mean they were read. But against every work there is a number and it is clear the whole collection was carefully catalogued according to subject. The system that emerges suggests a much-used collection. There are references to many of the tracts in her *History*. The collection is remarkable for its range of seventeenth-century source material, much of it from the period 1640–50. It includes twenty manuscript sources, and several tracts unknown to modern seventeenth-century specialists.

Today we tend to forget that to be a scholarly historian in the eighteenth century was not just a matter of dedication and method. It was also necessary to have access to primary source-material. This was often difficult for the period of the Civil War, for many of the tracts had not been reprinted, had been destroyed or mislaid, or were difficult of access. For a historian sympathetic to republican ideas, like Catharine Macaulay, there were real problems. To be a historian at all required free access to libraries. London at this time possessed no public libraries and only in 1759 was the British Museum opened. Thomas Hollis was in large part responsible for introducing Catharine Macaulay—and others—to many Civil War tracts and pamphlets. Her *History* shows not merely that she used such material but that she also consulted recently published debates and state papers. We shall look more closely at Hollis's role as a rescuer of rare and inaccessible tracts, and at his influence on Catharine Macaulay in Ch. 8. She was not only on the receiving end of this collecting. The *Memoirs of the Life of Colonel Hutchinson*, perhaps one of the most interesting biographies of a Parliamentarian leader in the Civil War, was finally published in 1810. In the preface it was said that the memoirs had been in the hands of the late Thomas Hutchinson, who 'had been frequently solicited to permit them to be published, particularly by the late Mrs. Catharine Macaulay, but had uniformly refused'.[95]

For all the criticism subsequently levelled at her *History*, there is little doubt that in the 1760s and 1770s it met with considerable success, was widely read and as widely praised. 'We by no means profess ourselves Mrs. Macaulay's panegyrists,' said the *Critical Review* of her third volume, 'and it is with no small degree of surprize we have perceived it hitherto not only unanswered, but unattacked.'[96] There had always been critics, but most of the abuse directed at it came later—even after her death—when her initial reputation was almost forgotten. It was natural that as the first English female historian she should have received particular attention. But this hardly accounts for the warmth of praise coming from, among others, intelligent critics whose views cannot easily be discounted. Unable to explain the phenomenon one account shrewdly sidestepped the issue, stating that 'the adventitious events which produced this perversion of judgement in a large portion of the public have long ceased to operate.'[97] It had a point. In a future chapter we shall look more closely at these 'adventitious events', how they changed, and what were the consequences for her reputation. We can learn much of the woman from the history. Besides great industry and scholarly research it reveals humour, a dry wit, a shrewd judgement, a strong moral approach, and considerable humanity. Her *History* does not focus on women but, as we shall see in Ch. 6, there is a sympathetic awareness of them.

Her *History* brought her not only fame but a quite considerable income. If Mr Cadell, printer and bookseller, reaped the biggest profits from the serial publication of her *History*, which began in 1768, as an undoubted best-seller it must have brought comfortable returns to her. An advertisement in the press of July 1768 read: 'Mrs. Macaulay having been informed, that the present Mode of publishing her History renders the Purchase of it inconvenient to many who wish to peruse it, has directed that Work shall be divided into Weekly Numbers, for their Accommodation';[98]

[95] *Memoirs of the Life of Colonel Hutchinson*, ed. C. H. Firth, 2 vols. (1885), i, p. x.
[96] *Critical Review*, 23 (1767), 82.
[97] Walpole, *Memoirs of the Reign of George III*, iii. 121–3 n. *b*.
[98] *London Chronicle*, 24 (1768), 13.

each volume of her *History* was divided into fifteen numbers, one of which was published each week, price 1s. With no. 31, which began the third volume, a print of the author in the character of the *Libertas* on the medals of Brutus and Cassius was given to the reader (see Pl. 1). The serialization of her work is indicative of its popularity and also of the nature of the reading public interested in history. Those who read her were not restricted to any narrow circle, and the weekly serialization was surely aimed at readers of only moderate income who were not prepared to pay 30s. or thereabouts for a thick folio volume. In fact each bound volume of her *History* sold at £4. 10s. per copy.

Some time shortly before her fifth volume appeared she changed her publisher and sold to Messrs Dilly in the Poultry for £900 'the power of making an octavo edition of her works, she reserving the right afterwards in those works . . . Also the right of every future volume which she shall write for one thousand pounds each volume.' Thomas Hollis thought this a very good financial arrangement, perhaps even too favourable. 'It would be a sad case', he wrote, 'to write of liberty and magnanimity, at a price, and against a season, at any price!' Apparently she had negotiated with Cadell, her previous publisher, when she had finished the first three volumes of her *History*, with the intention of persuading him to buy the copyright of them. But 'he chose not to meddle with her history in so imperfect, uncertain a state'. Later he may well have regretted his decision. He certainly regretted the fact that he was not consulted about the octavo edition, in which he would have liked to have shared, but he confessed that *he* could not have agreed to the financial arrangements for, as he put it, 'the future unbegotten volumes'.[99]

In a study of an eighteenth-century historian, it may seem idiosyncratic to focus so much on the history of the seventeenth century. It was, it is true, the subject of her *History*, and she herself made clear the importance she attached to the period and what she saw as its relevance for contemporary politics. But quite apart from her own views, any study of eighteenth-century radical politics cannot ignore the history of the seventeenth century and the conflicting interpretations of events in that era on which so much of the political debate centred. It was not only English

---

[99] *Memoirs of the Late Rev. Theophilus Lindsey*, 508.

radicals that drew analogies—whether or not mistakenly—
between present politics and those of the pre-Civil War period. As
the crisis in relations with the American colonies worsened many
Sons of Liberty were interpreting government policy towards the
colonists in terms of seventeenth-century English experience. In
her interpretation of the early stages of the French Revolution in
seventeenth-century English terms, Catharine Macaulay was far
from alone. Many revolutionaries in the 1790s concerned with the
legitimacy of removing, and possibly executing, a king looked
back to seventeenth-century England. Burke's condemnation of
the French revolutionaries, as indeed the many answers, including
Catharine Macaulay's, that condemnation provoked, hinged on
different interpretations of the achievements of the 'Glorious
Revolution' of 1688. For those contemplating revolutionary
change what more natural than to examine and draw lessons from
an earlier revolution—and one sufficiently distant to allow for
a relatively dispassionate analysis? For the French as for the
American revolutionaries there were parallels to be drawn and
lessons to be learnt from the events of the previous century in
England. Knowledge of those events relied on an understanding
of seventeenth-century English history. Catharine Macaulay's
History played no small part in providing the basis of such
understanding.

3. *Politics in the 1760s and 1770s*
Catharine Macaulay, John Sawbridge, and the Revival of English Radicalism

> Of vice the secret friend, the foe professed;
> Of every talent to deceive possessed;
> As mean in household savings, as profuse
> In vile corruption's scandalous abuse;
> Mentally blind; on whom no ray of truth
> E'er glanced auspicious e'en in bloom of youth.
> What though inimitable Churchill's hearse
> Saved thee from all the vengeance of his verse,
> Macaulay shall in nervous prose relate
> Whence flows the venom that distracts the State.
>
> (Written of George III in 1770; quoted Sir George Otto
> Trevelyan, *The Early History of Charles James Fox* (1901),
> 129 n. 1)

THE two groups in which Catharine Macaulay moved in the 1760s and 1770s were the Real Whigs and the Wilkites. In ideas and outlook they had much in common. Their political sympathies largely coincided and they came to share the demand for a radical reform of parliament. That such groups should have roughly defined Catharine Macaulay's social milieu is in itself extraordinary. It would be more easily comprehensible if it was merely as a wife or sister that she related to them. But George Macaulay was dead by the time Wilkes's Middlesex campaign was fought and her involvement with the Wilkites was certainly not merely that of a sister to John Sawbridge. Indeed, at least for a time, it seems there was some disagreement between them over Wilkes and his policies.

The Real Whigs—never more than a very loosely defined group—saw themselves as descendants of Commonwealthmen of both the seventeenth and eighteenth century, whose ideas, they argued, formed the foundation of true Whiggery. Not all shared Catharine Macaulay's passionate admiration for their seventeenth-century forebears, but their enemies did not distinguish between them. They tended still to be identified as 'sectaries and King-Killers'.[1] Mainly an urban, and more particularly, a London phenomenon, they drew support from the prosperous middle classes—small merchants, tradesmen, and artisans—much the same group as were to form the hard core of the Wilkites. If the majority were dissenters, there were also those like Theophilus Lindsey, who in 1774 left the Church of England to set up the first Unitarian chapel at Essex Street in London, and his brother-in-law John Disney, who eight years later followed to become his assistant. Others like Catharine Macaulay, her brother John Sawbridge, and Archdeacon Francis Blackburne, biographer of Thomas Hollis, remained within the Established Church. What they all shared was a passionate belief in freedom of conscience and an equal conviction that such toleration should never be extended to Catholics.[2]

Anti-Catholicism has been seen as one of the 'less attractive' aspects of eighteenth-century radicalism.[3] It 'represents a stain on the *whole* Commonwealth tradition'.[4] Such views perhaps underestimate not only how keen the memory remained of persecution in the seventeenth century, but how real at times in the eighteenth century the threat seemed of a re-enactment of those events. If such views were particularly held by Dissenters they were not confined to them. The belief in an international Catholic plot against English independence persisted. Unattractive, 'un-Christian', and mistaken, as it may seem to the eyes of the twentieth century, the anti-Catholic and anti-episcopal attitudes of many Real Whigs—and others—represented a view that not only had deep roots in the seventeenth century, to which so many radicals looked back for guidance, but remained very much alive

---

[1] Anthony Lincoln, *English Dissent, 1763–1800* (1971), 4–5, 6–7.

[2] On the Real Whigs see Verner W. Crane, 'The Club of Honest Whigs', *William and Mary Quarterly*, 3rd ser., 23 (1966), 210–33; Martin Hugh Fitzpatrick, 'Rational Dissent in the Late 18th Century with Particular Reference to the Growth of Toleration', D.Phil. thesis (University of Wales, 1952); Lincoln, *English Dissent, 1763–1800*; P. D. Marshall, 'Thomas Hollis (1720–74): The Bibliophile as Libertarian', *Bulletin of the John Rylands University Library of Manchester*, 66(2) (1984), 246–63; Caroline Robbins, *The Eighteenth-Century Commonwealthman* (1959); John Sainsbury, *Disaffected Patriots* (1987).

[3] Linda Colley, 'Radical Patriotism in Eighteenth-Century England', in Raphael Samuel (ed.), *Patriotism: The Making and Unmaking of British National Identity*, 1: *History and Politics* (1989), 170.

[4] Fitzpatrick, 'Rational Dissent in the Late Eighteenth Century', 294.

in the eighteenth. Her *History* leaves us in no doubt that Catharine Macaulay shared this attitude. Musing on the Irish rebellion she wrote of the Papists' 'never-ceasing attempts by every kind of means, to bring all things again to subjection to the Church of Rome; their avowed maxim that faith is not to be kept with heretics; their religious principles calculated for the support of despotic power, and inconsistent with the genius of a free constitution'.[5] Such a view was not peculiar to her. It was shared by Wilkes and many of his followers, as well as by other Real Whigs, and, coupled with anti-episcopacy, persistently occupied the minds of American dissenters in the years before the Revolution. She had no time for those urging toleration of Catholics. In conversation in 1768 with Caleb Fleming, the Independent pastor at Pinners Hall, and Sylas Neville, she criticized those 'who pretend to be friends of Liberty and (from an affectation of a liberal way of thinking) would tolerate Papists'. Even in 'the best constituted Democracy' it was to tolerate 'a sect which proposes to do all it can against the state'. She was to add that in a monarchy the danger was that much greater for 'the Court would soon become proselytes to their faith'.[6]

Soon after the accession of George III the high expectations Real Whigs had of the new reign were quickly thwarted. The failure to repeal the Test Acts, contrary to their hopes, threatened what they had believed secured by the Revolution of 1688–9. Earlier they had expressed admiration for the British constitution as it emerged after the 'Glorious Revolution', but increasingly they adopted Catharine Macaulay's attitude in stressing its inadequacies. Earlier, in so far as they had adhered to any political group, they had seen the Whigs as most closely representing the values dear to them and many of them had been, and were to remain, devoted followers of Pitt. But in their opinion contemporary Whigs had turned their backs on all the Old Whigs had valued. When they renewed their demand for toleration it was on

---

[5] *Memoirs of Thomas Hollis*, ed. Francis Blackburne, 2 vols. (1780), i. 225; Catharine Macaulay, *History of England*, iv. 73.

[6] G. M. Ditchfield, 'Some Literary and Political Views of Catherine Macaulay', *American Notes and Queries*, 12 (1974), 70–6, at p. 73; for a reassessment of the importance of the Catholic factor in the outbreak of the Civil War see Caroline Hibbard, *Charles I and the Popish Plot* (North Carolina Press, 1983); for an account of how far the anti-Catholic, anti-episcopal ideas of many Real Whigs were shared by American dissenters, see Carl Bridenbaugh, *Mitre and Sceptre* (1962).

the basis of natural rights. The focus of their argument had shifted from theology to politics. Increasingly they saw their hopes for toleration as depending on a radical reform of parliament.

After the accession of George III the peace concluded with France was unpopular with both Pitt and the City. Discontent in the City grew and it moved into opposition. Pitt had already resigned. The post-war economic depression and consequent social unrest combined to consolidate this opposition. The Wilkes case was to provide it with a focus for its grievances. To win support for its policies the government launched a new journal, *The Briton*. John Wilkes, MP for Aylesbury since 1757, and Charles Churchill, the poet, responded in June 1762 by publishing *The North Briton*—a vehicle for ridiculing the government and its handling of affairs. A few months before the first volume of Mrs Macaulay's *History* was published in 1763, the notorious No. 45 appeared attacking the King's speech, and by implication the King himself. It was the opportunity the government had been waiting for, a chance both of silencing Wilkes and of suppressing opposition to the peace proposals. Wilkes was accused of seditious libel and a 'general' warrant issued against the authors, printers, and publishers. After his arrest Wilkes was committed to the Tower, but not before he had arranged for an application to be made for a writ of *habeas corpus* to secure his release. It was granted and Wilkes was released. Overnight Wilkes became a popular hero. Later general warrants were declared illegal, and Wilkes and the printers of No. 45 received extensive damages. Unfortunately, just after his release from prison and while Wilkes was absent, a copy of an obscene poem, a parody of Pope's *Essay on Man*, which Wilkes intended printing for private circulation, was discovered among his papers, and read aloud in Parliament. Wilkes, still convalescing from a wound he had received in a duel, was summoned by Parliament to answer further charges. Wisely he decided to withdraw temporarily from politics and before the end of the year he left England for France. In January 1764, failing to appear before the court, he was expelled from the House of Commons and outlawed.[7] Four years later despite his outlawry he returned to England.

One of the first acts of Wilkes was to become a freeman of the

[7] George Rudé, *Wilkes and Liberty* (1962), 20–4, 26, 28, 34–5.

Company of Joiners, which gave him access to City politics. Like the Real Whigs the Wilkite movement, although not confined to the metropolis, was to be centred in London within the City Corporation. After standing unsuccessfully as candidate for the City, Wilkes announced his intention of contesting a Middlesex seat. In March 1768, much to the delight of his supporters, he was duly elected. A month later he was arrested and imprisoned, pending trial for the charges brought against him in 1764. In June his sentence of outlawry was lifted, he was fined £1,000 and sentenced to 22 months' imprisonment. The following February he was expelled from the House of Commons. In the same month, in March, and again in April he was three times re-elected for Middlesex and three times expelled the House of Commons. After his election for the fourth time the House of Commons decided that the ministerial candidate Col. Luttrell, who had polled a mere 296 votes, 'ought to have been returned a member for Middlesex', and duly declared him elected.[8]

In the 1760s and early 1770s, when the Wilkes campaign was at its height, the vast majority of the Real Whigs, while sympathetic, and sharing Wilkes's political ideas and objectives, remained apart from involvement in Wilkite politics. They were vigorous pamphleteers, concerned with the theory of politics, but they were not on the whole active Wilkites. So Catharine Macaulay, and her brother John Sawbridge, were almost unique in having a foot in both camps, closely associated with Real Whigs and, at the same time, participants in the Wilkes campaign. The reason for the distancing of Real Whigs from the Wilkites lay in a certain ambivalence in attitudes to Wilkes. That it should have been he who succeeded in rousing popular feeling to such an extent that it seriously embarrassed the government was viewed with 'mixed feelings amongst the Hollis circle'. Indicative is Catharine Macaulay's comment to Caleb Fleming and Sylas Neville in April 1768, that 'the attachment to Wilkes' was 'a strong instance of the peculiar spirit' of the nation, 'as a man guilty of so many excesses and inconsistencies would have been deserted in any other'.[9] She must have been aware of the reservations about Wilkes of many of

---

[8] Ibid. 70.
[9] Ditchfield, 'Some Literary and Political Views of Catherine Macaulay', 71, 74.

her friends. To some extent she shared them, but this did not prevent her from actively supporting his campaign.

In his diary in 1768 Sylas Neville noted that Caleb Fleming agreed with him in thinking that Wilkes 'being an enemy of every obligation of religion and morality cannot be a true friend of liberty'. Fleming was pessimistic about 'success if he is to be Capt. General on the side of Liberty'. Later they were reassured to hear that Thomas Hollis was 'a friend of Wilkes' and vouched for him not accepting 'a place or a bribe, tho' not a man of virtue'.[10] 'I am sorry for the irregularities of W—kes', Hollis wrote, 'they are, however,' he went on to add, 'but as spots on the sun.' He was 'worthy of every respect'.[11] When later Richard Price confessed to finding 'an immoral patriot' a contradiction in terms, he may well have been thinking of Wilkes.[12] Certainly both he and Joseph Priestley, while sympathetic to Wilkes, were not uncritical. Nevertheless Hollis seems to have been partially successful in reassuring others of his circle that however despicable his morals, Wilkes was to be trusted. But a coolness between them persisted. In February 1769, at Fleming's suggestion, Sylas Neville called on Wilkes to warn him of the Court's intention of disqualifying him the day before the Middlesex election, and putting up a candidate of its own. Neville had suggested that Wilkes distribute handbills recommending 'any gentleman he knows to be honest' to the Middlesex freeholders as an alternative candidate. Although Wilkes rejected the plan, he apparently thanked Neville 'for his interest', but, as Neville noted in his diary, 'did not ask me to sit'.[13]

The role Catharine Macaulay played in practical politics in these years is difficult to assess. She was more interested in political polemic than everyday strategy. But one thing is clear. Close though her relations were with the Real Whig circle, she 'did not entirely share their aloofness from politics'.[14] If female historians were rare in the eighteenth century, female politicians were even rarer. It was virtually impossible for women to partic-

[10] *The Diary of Sylas Neville, 1767–1788*, ed. Basil Cozens-Hardy (1950), 30–1.
[11] *Memoirs of Thomas Hollis*, i. 289–90.
[12] Richard Price, *Observations on the Nature of Civil Liberty* (1776), 43.
[13] *The Diary of Sylas Neville*, 30, 31, 61–2.
[14] Ian Christie, *Wilkes, Wyvill and Reform* (1962), 17–18.

ipate actively in politics when they were debarred from membership of any political association or society, and had no voice in the election of representatives. In December 1769, when an aldermanic seat became vacant Horace Walpole could write to the Countess of Ossory, 'I hope they will elect Mrs. Macaulay'—but it was intended as a joke.[15] It is a measure of the remarkable influence Catharine Macaulay exerted that she was regarded as in any way a participant in the politics of the time.

One of Wilkes's earliest supporters was John Sawbridge, Catharine Macaulay's brother. Of his political career it was said that if John Wilkes 'introduced this Gentleman into the *practice* of politics in the *theory* he had early made a rapid progress, under the auspices of *Mrs. Macaulay*'.[16] Walpole thought it was 'independence and his sister's republicanism' which 'had thrown him into [an] enthusiastic attachment to liberty'.[17] Always close, they must frequently have discussed politics together. Sadly nothing remains of such exchanges. By the time John Sawbridge succeeded to the extensive family estate at Olantigh and to 'a very princely fortune', Catharine was already married and living in London.[18] In 1763 he too married but within two months was a widower. He acquired, on the death of his wife, an addition to his fortune of £100,000. Two years later he married Anne, daughter of 'the opulent Alderman Sir William Stephenson', a hop-merchant and distiller, his business partner, and later a fellow-Wilkite.[19] He rented a London house in New Burlington Street, St James's, which was 'assessed for the Watch Rate' at £90 per annum, and had landed property in Edmonton and Tottenham as well as extensive estates in Kent.[20] Like his father-in-law, John Sawbridge was a hop-grower and distiller. By any standards he was a very rich man, 'a Kentish Gentleman of Fortune' as Lord Holdernesse was to describe him.[21] As with Catharine we know

[15] *Horace Walpole's Correspondence*, ed. W. S. Lewis, 48 vols. (1937–83), xxxii. 40.
[16] *City Biography* (1800), 87.
[17] Horace Walpole, *Memoirs of the Reign of George III*, ed. G. F. Russell Barker, 4 vols. (1894), iii. 192.
[18] *Gentleman's Magazine*, 65 (1795), 216.
[19] Ibid.; see also Christie, *Wilkes, Wyvill and Reform*, 33–4.
[20] Edward Hasted, *History and Topographical Survey of Kent*, 4 vols. (1782), iii, 171; Rudé, *Wilkes and Liberty*, 87.
[21] George Wilks, *The Barons of the Cinque Ports and the Parliamentary Representation of Hythe* (Folkestone, 1892), 113.

very little of his upbringing except for the fact that part of his education was spent at the Academy at Caen in Normandy, to which he was later to send his son.[22]

'A school friendship', we are told, 'introduced him to the notice of Lord Chatham, through whom he was brought into Parliament'. According to the *City Biography*, 'their mutual friendship reflected honour on each other. The peer aided one who wanted patronage, and the party obliged, repaid it by proper but independent exertions of gratitude and genius'.[23] That friendship lasted throughout Pitt's life; like Pitt's friendship with Thomas Hollis, it was based on great admiration and deep affection. In 1764, at the time Wilkes was going into exile, John Sawbridge is listed as a member of the Club in Albemarle Street, where the opposition had 'the pleasure of meeting and conversing with each other'.[24] He became MP for Hythe in Kent in 1768, and put himself under the leadership of William Beckford, 'Chatham's mouthpiece in City politics'.[25] Sawbridge's arrival in the House of Commons coincided with Wilkes's decision, despite his outlawry, to return from four years of exile.

Sawbridge, after his election to parliament, planned to become a City alderman—and in consequence, eligible as a candidate for a City constituency. In May 1769 he too purchased the freedom of the City. He became a freeman of the Company of Framework Knitters in anticipation of 'offering himself for one of the next vacancies in the Court of Aldermen'.[26] In June, Sawbridge together with James Townshend were 'unanimously chosen' as Sheriffs 'for their spirited conduct in support of the rights of the people'.[27] In July 1769 at a 'numerous meeting' Sawbridge, by a decisive vote given 'with joyful acclamation', was elected Alderman of the Langborne ward.[28] The fight by Wilkes and his supporters against the decision over the Middlesex election occupied the next five years. In this fight Sawbridge played a leading role. 'In defiance of the Bill of Pains and Penalties held

---

[22] *Memoirs of John Horne Tooke*, ed. Alexander Stephens, 2 vols. (1813), ii. 282.
[23] *City Biography*, 87.
[24] John Almon, *History of the Late Minority* (1766), 297, 299.
[25] Rudé, *Wilkes and Liberty*, 151.
[26] *London Chronicle*, 25 (1769), 426.
[27] *Gentleman's Magazine*, 39 (1769), 317; *Annual Register*, 17 April 1769, 91.
[28] *Gentleman's Magazine*, 39 (1769), 361; *London Chronicle*, 26 (1769), 6.

out by the Government, he persevered in his duty [as Sheriff], and returned Mr Wilkes to parliament five successive times'.[29] There was even a rumour after the third Middlesex election that he and Townshend were also to be expelled for their 'temerity in proposing Wilkes after he had been thrice rejected'.[30] But 'though their conduct as members was most indecent and disrespectful to the House,' wrote Walpole, 'the Ministers did not dare to call them to account'.[31]

The main characters in the Wilkite movement were well known to each other. 'So great is the spirit of Patriotism', wrote a newspaper correspondent in March 1769, 'that the newborn daughter of a certain baronet in Great G—— Street, is to be baptised by the name of Libertina, the Rev. Mr. Horne of Brentford is to perform the ceremony, and the sponsors are Mr. Alderman Wilkes, Mr. Sergeant Glynn, a celebrated Female Historian and Miss Wilkes—Mr. Humphrey Cotes is to stand proxy for Mr. Wilkes on this occasion'.[32] The baronet was Sir Edward Astley, who was to become an active member of the Society of the Supporters of the Bill of Rights, as were Horne, Wilkes, and Glynn—all founder members of the Society. When William Beckford was installed as Lord Mayor on 9 November 1769, we are told that a 'magnificent entertainment' was afterwards provided at the Guildhall. With the two Sheriffs, Sawbridge and Townshend, Beckford's election provided the opposition with a strong axis, and as the government clearly thought, a cover for Wilkes. The government set out to boycott the party at the Guildhall in order to discredit the mayoralty. Nevertheless the occasion we are told was graced by a 'numerous and splendid company'. Sheriff Sawbridge had invited his sister 'the celebrated Mrs. Macaulay . . . at the particular request of the new Lord Mayor'.[33] When suddenly the following year, and before his term had ended, Beckford died, Lord Lyttelton wrote to Mrs Montagu that he 'was sorry for his death' but would 'leave his funeral oration to Mrs. Macaulay'.[34]

[29] *City Biography*, 87.
[30] Horace Bleackley, *Life of John Wilkes* (1917), 223.
[31] Walpole, *Memoirs of George III*, iii. 230–1.
[32] *London Chronicle*, 25 (1769), 240.
[33] *London Chronicle*, 26 (1769), 456.
[34] *Mrs. Montagu 'Queen of the Blues': Her letters and Friendships from 1762 to 1800*, ed. Reginald Blunt, 2 vols. (1923), i. 234.

The same month as Sawbridge was elected Alderman, the Society of Supporters of the Bill of Rights was founded. Wilkes had spent not only his own fortune but that of his wife. By the time of his imprisonment he was deeply in debt—probably by rather more than £6,000. Already some of his friends had clubbed together to help him. Sawbridge was reputed to have sold an estate in order to subscribe to Wilkes's support.[35] But in comparison with what he owed, such private subscriptions proved totally inadequate. Meanwhile his debts grew. Under the leadership of the Revd John Horne—later Horne Tooke—on 20 February 1769, Wilkes's friends met together in the London Tavern in Bishopsgate Street and formed the Society with the intention of giving Wilkes financial support. John Sawbridge was one of its founder-members along with the two City MPs, Aldermen Richard Oliver and James Townshend, and the two Middlesex members, Sergeant Glynn and John Wilkes. Also a founder-member was the Revd Dr Wilson, rector of St Stephen's, Walbrook, later to share his Bath house with Catharine Macaulay. 'The members were few at first', wrote Horne Tooke, 'but respectable both for wealth and talents.'[36]

Evidence suggests Catharine Macaulay was deeply involved in Wilkite politics. Behind all references to her in these years there is the assumption that she was a 'patriot', a supporter of Wilkes. If the Society of Supporters of the Bill of Rights had enlisted women members, she must have been the first admitted. Most of its original members were as well known to her as to her brother. She moved freely in Wilkite circles. We have already seen how in the late sixties and most of the seventies, she was on friendly terms with Wilkes and his daughter Polly. With Polly she visited the home of Crisp Molineux, an ardent Wilkite of Garboldisham in Norfolk. Wilkes and Catharine Macaulay continued to visit each other, to dine together, to express mutual admiration, and Wilkes certainly regarded her as one of his supporters. Their close acquaintance continued right up to the time of her leaving Bath in 1778 but perhaps more through Wilkes's relations with his loyal supporter Thomas Wilson than through his friendship with Catharine Macaulay. In fact, as we shall see, that friendship

[35] *Memoirs of John Horne Tooke*, ii. 283.
[36] Ibid., i. 164.

noticeably cooled. In 1774, at his fifth election for Middlesex, Wilkes took his place in Parliament. On the occasion of his first speech Dr Thomas Wilson wrote to congratulate him, adding that Mrs Macaulay thought it 'a manly, plain, intrepid exertion of true English spirit'. She had compared it favourably with 'some of her favourite speeches of 1639 etc.'[37]

The Society of the Supporters of the Bill of Rights led the campaign over Wilkes and the Middlesex election. It took the initiative in petitioning Parliament and the King. In May 1769 a committee consisting of Sawbridge, Townshend, Bellas, and Horne had been appointed to act as a pressure-group in the petitioning campaign. It was they who prepared the petition of the county of Middlesex to the King of 24 May 1769. The dominant role played by the Society was reflected in the list of grievances the petition listed. Apart from the violation of the rights of electors and the outlawry and imprisonment of Wilkes, it also listed attacks on the freedom of the press, arrests by general warrants, neglect of *habeas corpus* and trial by jury, and the mismanagement of the American colonies. According to an account by Richard Rigby, among those presenting the petition to the King were 'Sergeant Glynn; an old parson, Dr. Wilson, prebend of Westminster; Messrs. Townshend, Sawbridge, Bellas, and one other ill-looking fellow [Horne Tooke?], whose name I could not learn'. Apparently the King received it 'with proper contempt, not speaking to any of them; but an impropriety seems to have been committed, by their being permitted to kiss the King's hand, all of them except the old parson [Dr Wilson] and Sawbridge'.[38]

Before any division appeared in the ranks of Wilkes's supporters, an event was temporarily to unite the opposition. General Pasquale Paoli had been overpowered in his defence of Corsica against the French. In 1769 he fled from the island and sought refuge in England. He reached London on 20 September, when he received an enthusiastic welcome and was established in 'magnificent lodgings . . . arranged for him in Old Bond Street'.[39] Long before he arrived a group of his supporters and sympathizers had formed under the leadership of James Boswell, whose

[37] *The Correspondence of the Late John Wilkes with His Friends*, ed. John Almon, 5 vols. (1805), iv. 174.

[38] Sir George Otto Trevelyan, *The Early History of Charles James Fox* (1901), 200 n. 1.

[39] Peter Adam Thrasher, *Pasquale Paoli: An Enlightened Hero, 1725–1807* (1970), 158.

An Account of Corsica. The Journal of a Tour to that Island; and Memoirs of Pascal Paoli, had been published early in the previous year. Highly successful, within a year it had run to three editions. Others of the same group of sympathizers were Lord Lyttelton, Edward Dilly, the bookseller and publisher of Boswell's *Account*, and Catharine Macaulay. Boswell had visited Corsica in 1764, had met Paoli, and was completely won over to the Corsican cause.[40] Catharine Macaulay had few illusions about Boswell. As she told Sylas Neville, 'he sets out a Tory, and has no idea of True Liberty'. She was critical of his first *Account of Corsica* but thought the *Journal* was 'better and written with a good deal of spirit'. Of the books Boswell had sent to Paoli, she approved of Sydney and Locke but was appalled that Milton—'much more proper for such a man and more calculated to enlighten a people under Popish Superstition'—had been omitted.[41]

On the occasion of Paoli's birthday in 1768, 'many companies of the true Friends of Liberty' had met to drink the health of 'that illustrious Hero, and success to the brave islanders'.[42] In a meeting in the Queen's Arms in St Paul's Churchyard 'a very respectable company' presided over by James Boswell, having drunk Paoli's health, followed it by drinking, 'amongst others', that of Catharine Macaulay.[43] On the Corsican cause all groups within the radical opposition were united. A 'Corsican Subscription' fund was started in 1769, and sympathizers were called on to 'show their generosity upon this trying occasion'. A sum of £2,400 was donated by the Society of Supporters of the Bill of Rights. In all, over £20,000 was contributed to the Corsican cause.[44] Catharine Macaulay's support of Paoli was not merely financial. Earlier in her *Short Sketch of a Democratical Form of Government in a Letter to Signor Paoli* (1767), she had outlined the essential ingredients of a democratic republic. It was her first open confession of republican sympathies, and no doubt served to confirm her critics' worst suspicions. She wrote that she favoured a two-chamber state, the Senate and the People. 'The second order is necessary', she wrote, 'because ... without the people have auth-

[40] Ibid. 163.
[41] Ditchfield, 'Some Literary and Political Views of Catharine Macaulay', 74.
[42] *London Chronicle*, 23 (1768), 328.
[43] Ibid. 334.
[44] *London Chronicle*, 25 (1769), 31.

ority enough to be thus classed, there can be no liberty.' There must be a power of appeal from every court of justice both to the Senate and to the representatives of the people. To guard such a state against corruption there should be rotation of all places of trust, the whole Senate to be changed once in three years by a third retiring annually. As an admirer of Harrington, she went on to explain how an Agrarian law, by limiting the amount of land individuals could inherit, would prevent the growth of a landed aristocracy.[45] She ended her *Letter* by promising Paoli further details on the militia, the police, the education of youth, and 'other points necessary to good government, and the further security of liberty', if he should so desire it. Finally, recognizing the necessity of having 'an unrestrained power lodged in some person, capable of the arduous task of settling such a government', she concluded that there was 'no person so capable of this high employment' as Paoli himself. Together with her letter to Paoli she sent a copy of her *History*.[46]

It is not surprising that Paoli and his cause were so closely identified not only with the opposition to the administration but specifically with Wilkes. Paoli and Liberty were synonymous in men's minds, and as his biographer argues, he could 'have become a focus for this opposition'. But clearly he chose not to. He had made up his mind in advance that he would 'not be caught up in any faction', and despite the difficulties this involved, and 'misinterpretations' that were put on his actions, 'he carefully avoided any utterance or activity at this time which would have identified him in any way with either the Government or the Opposition'.[47] Such apparent detachment laid him open to criticism.[48] Of his reception, Horace Walpole was to write in 1769 that 'the opposition was ready to receive and incorporate him in the list of popular tribunes. The Court artfully intercepted the project, and', added Walpole cynically, 'deeming patriots of nations equally corruptible, bestowed a pension of £1,000 a year

---

[45] Catharine Macaulay, *Loose Remarks on Certain Positions to be Found in Mr. Hobbes's 'Philosophical Rudiments'... with a Short Sketch of a Democratical Form of Government in a Letter to Signor Paoli* (1767), 30, 31, 33, 36, 37. For her proposals for limiting the inheritance of land and a discussion of how her agrarian balance would work see Ch. 8.

[46] Ibid. 38.

[47] Thrasher, *Pasquale Paoli*, 163.

[48] Ibid. 164.

on the un-heroic fugitive'.[49] The pension Paoli received was, in fact, £1,200, but on this sum he had to support the considerable body of dependants he had brought with him from Corsica. In accepting the pension he was careful to make clear he regarded it as 'from the King as the representative of the English people, and certainly not from any political party'.[50]

'The court have artfully adopted him', wrote Walpole, 'and at least crushed one egg on which faction, and her broodhen, Mrs. Macaulay would have been very glad to have sat.' Later, he wrote that 'the King and Queen both took great notice of him' and he was 'everywhere received with much distinction; so Mrs. Macaulay, it seems, has not laid him under an interdict'.[51] Later still, under the title 'Picture of a complete Gentleman', an article appeared in the *Monthly Miscellany*, in which it was concluded that a man 'who could win the petty opinion of the vain and ignorant James Boswell to *tataow* his character, and . . . refuse to visit that amiable and glorious daughter of Liberty, Mrs. Macaulay, for fear of offending the narrow mind of a British King' could be 'no gentleman'.[52] It had a point. Admittedly Paoli trod a difficult path. On the one hand he had been influenced in his decision to come to England by the knowledge of the existence, in the City and in the country at large, of an active sympathy with the cause of the Corsican people. But as he put it, 'I am not English but Corsican; my sole and only political interest is the interest of Corsica.'[53] His only aim in England, he explained, was to keep enthusiasm for the Corsican cause alive until such time as an open conflict between France and England developed. With this object in view, he avoided being too closely associated with the government, and while he certainly had some relations with the opposition he 'avoided the political embraces of the more furious opponents of the King, such as Mrs. Macaulay'.[54] The comment is revealing on how Mrs Macaulay was already regarded: a 'furious opponent of the King'.

[49] Walpole, *Memoirs of the Reign of George III*, iii. 258.
[50] Thrasher, *Pasquale Paoli*, 165; Robert Chambers, *The Book of Days*, 2 vols. (1863–4), i. 810.
[51] *Horace Walpole's Correspondence*, xxiii. 145.
[52] *Monthly Miscellany*, 1 (1774), 118.
[53] Thrasher, *Pasquale Paoli*, 163.
[54] Ibid. 166.

A letter in the *London Chronicle* in 1769 signed by 'A Republican' suggested Paoli had been advised it would be impolitic to see Catharine Macaulay. According to this account about two weeks after Paoli's arrival in England, she received from him a 'verbal message ... in which he excused himself for having been in the Kingdom so long without waiting on her'. But now, he added, he would take the first opportunity of doing so. Mrs Macaulay had replied expressing her pleasure at a visit from him 'when it was agreeable'. The General agreed to call on her the following Saturday between six and seven, but on the day a messenger arrived at seven o'clock to say the General had been 'taken suddenly ill with a giddiness in the head' but would wait on her directly he was better. 'Mrs. Macaulay has neither seen or heard of him since', the account continued, 'although he has been out every day.' The letter ended with a question: 'Can it be imagined that the General's sudden illness was other than political?' It was proof, the writer concluded, that Paoli was 'an abject slave in the freest country in Europe'.[55] His frequent visits to the Duke of Grafton and his apparent wooing of the Court was noted as further confirmation that Paoli was corruptible.

Whatever the truth of his relations with Mrs Macaulay, both before and after his arrival, their names continued to be linked. In the popular imagination Mrs Macaulay was inseparably coupled with the Corsican patriot. Early in 1770 an advertisement for the *Ladies Annual Journal* promised 'Approved Likenesses of Mrs. Macaulay, the Patriotic Historian, and Pascal Paoli; the celebrated Corsican General'.[56] There were rumours and counter-rumours in 1769. 'It is imagined the report of Pascal Paoli's arrival at Mrs. Macaulay's', went one account in July of that year, 'is either premature or that it is to be kept a profound secret.' Significantly it went on to comment that Paoli's visit 'at this very critical time, has given some umbrage to a certain personage, who seems to be frightened even at the shadow of a Liberty Man'.[57] According to Horace Walpole, when Mrs Macaulay offered to visit the General he had asked her to excuse him as 'he had no woman to receive her', and as Walpole claimed 'she resents it and they do not meet'.

[55] *London Chronicle*, 26 (1769), 336.
[56] *London Chronicle*, 27 (1770), 48.
[57] *London Chronicle*, 26 (1769), 106.

Nevertheless she was said to have put her house at his disposal, and there were even rumours of an impending marriage between 'the unfortunate defender of Corsican Freedom ... and the lady who employed her pen with equal zeal in the cause of British freedom'.[58] The *London Chronicle* reported 'an elegant entertainment' given by Paoli 'to several of the Nobility at his house in Dover Street, at which Mrs. Macaulay was present'. Yet a few months later it carried a denial: 'we are assured General Paoli has not yet seen Mrs. Macaulay'.[59] Lord Lyttelton wrote to Mrs Montagu in October 1769, of how proud he was 'that Paoli has made England the place of his retreat'. Had he been Lord Mayor, Paoli would have received 'as fine an entertainment as the King of Denmark' for 'exiled heroes are more illustrious guests than travelling Kings'. But, he continued 'as he has not paid his homage to Mr. Wilkes in the Fleet or Mrs. Macaulay in her closet, so he will not be acknowledged for a hero in the City, or for a patriot in the country'.[60]

William Beckford died in April 1770, two months after Wilkes's release from prison. During Wilkes's imprisonment it had been Beckford who led the City opposition. Under him the dominance of the Court faction in City politics began to be challenged in both the Common Council and among the aldermen. It had been on his instructions that Sawbridge took up the freedom of the City and thus became eligible for the Shrievalty and Aldermanic Council. When Wilkes was first released from prison relations between him and the City were close. In August 1770 when he went to Dover to meet his daughter Polly on her return from France he paid 'a short visit to Alderman Sawbridge at Olantighe' where 'the most reputable of Wilkites were summoned to meet him'.[61]

There soon began to appear signs of increasing tension in the relations of the new City leadership—Sawbridge, Townshend, and Oliver—with Wilkes. On his release from prison, it has been suggested, he 'made the tactical error' of invading 'their own

[58] *Horace Walpole's Correspondence*, xxiii. 145–6 n. 29.
[59] *London Chronicle*, 26 (1769), 319, 438.
[60] *Mrs. Montagu—Queen of the Blues*, i. 230.
[61] Horace Bleackley, *Life of John Wilkes*, 255; see also *Correspondence of Wilkes*, iv. 34–5.

special domain'.[62] From September 1770 the Society of the
Supporters of the Bill of Rights was torn by dissension. It was not
helped by Wilkes's 'rudeness to his city colleagues' and his failure
'to disguise his contempt for his fellow citizens'.[63] From the start
relations between Horne Tooke, who had been mainly responsible
for founding the Society, and Wilkes were bad. They rapidly
deteriorated. A stream of angry letters passed between them and
the quarrel was given maximum publicity in the press. Sawbridge,
Townshend, and Horne Tooke were having serious doubts about
Wilkes. In November of 1770, the three leaders of the City
opposition, together with Horne Tooke and others, broke with
Wilkes and seceded from the Society of the Supporters of the Bill
of Rights to form a separate Constitutional Society.

Whatever the causes of the secession, John Sawbridge was at
the centre of the disagreement with Wilkes. He and others in the
Society thought that Wilkes was attempting to confine its objects
and to manipulate it to his own financial advantage. But it was
also a disagreement on policy. Horace Walpole wrote that while
'Wilkes and his friends' were 'inclined to riots and tumult,
Sawbridge, and the more real patriots . . . were for proceeding
more legally and temperately'.[64] At a meeting of the Westminster
electors in October 1770, Sawbridge and Wilkes disagreed over
the best way to carry on the policy of protest against the government. Wilkes favoured the passing of a motion instructing the
Westminster MPs 'after the manner of our great ancestors' to
impeach Lord North 'the chief instrument of the tyranny we
groan under, at home and in the colonies'. Sawbridge thought
such instructions 'nugatory, ridiculous and ineffectual', and
although, at first, the meeting refused to listen to him, he finally
won them over.[65] With the feeling of the meeting behind him he
proposed a further remonstrance to the King. If former petitions
to the throne had failed to succeed, they must not 'be dis-
couraged; for that the people, had never persevered in vain'.[66] If
Wilkes was more than a little annoyed at failing to get his way, he
hastened to correct the account of the meeting which appeared in

---

[62] Bleackley, *Life of John Wilkes*, 253.
[63] Ibid. 255.
[64] Walpole, *Memoirs of the Reign of George III*, iv. 121.
[65] *London Chronicle*, 28 (1770), 426.
[66] Ibid.

the *London Chronicle*. He sent them a letter in which the debate between himself and Sawbridge was described as of 'the greatest temper and candour, to the satisfaction of every Gentleman present'. He insisted that 'no man, Sir, can honour Mr. Sawbridge more than I do for every publick and private virtue which constitutes a great and amiable character'.[67] Sawbridge, Walpole argued, 'was by no means attached to Wilkes, nor led by him. The strictness of Sawbridge's principles... had made him look with aversion on the profligacy of Wilkes.'[68]

By the end of 1770 some £17,000 of Wilkes's accumulated debts had been paid or compounded and, according to Almon, there were others in the Society besides Sawbridge who felt their obligation to Wilkes had been more than met.[69] Horne Tooke thought the time had come to emphasize that the Society had pledged itself to support Wilkes's cause only 'so far as it was a public cause'.[70] There were other causes of equal importance that had a claim on the Society. Earlier a printer, Bingley, had been imprisoned for printing a letter from Wilkes said to have reflected on the administration and the courts of justice. When the printer was in his third year in prison, after behaving with great courage during his trial, Tooke wanted the Society to make some contribution to the losses he had sustained. He moved a resolution at a meeting of the Supporters of the Bill of Rights to open a subscription of £500. But even though, as it was argued, 'it was extremely politic at that moment, in order to encourage the printers to resist the menaces of the house of commons', Wilkes and his friends opposed it.[71]

After the split between John Sawbridge and Wilkes had caused the former to secede from the Society, a correspondence was carried on by Junius, the unknown author of a series of letters to the *Public Advertiser*, with Wilkes and Horne Tooke, over Sawbridge's candidacy for the mayoralty in 1771. The object of Junius was to restore unity, and he saw Horne Tooke's public quarrel with Wilkes as destructive and doing the cause nothing

---

[67] Ibid. 455.

[68] Walpole, *Memoirs of the Reign of George III*, iv. 121.

[69] G. S. Veitch, *The Genesis of Parliamentary Reform* (1965), 30; see also *Correspondence of Wilkes*, iv. 13–14.

[70] Veitch, *The Genesis of Parliamentary Reform*, 31.

[71] *Memoirs of John Horne Tooke*, i. 168–9.

but harm. Angrily he told Horne Tooke how astonished he was that Sawbridge 'whose character I really respect', failed to see through his 'duplicity'.[72] He urged Wilkes to make his peace with Sawbridge for, as he wrote, 'the appearance of your acting together . . . would . . . contribute to give you a more secure, a more permanent, and, without offence to any man, a more honourable hold upon the city'. Sawbridge's 'reputed firmness and integrity' could be 'a capital resource' to Wilkes. Sawbridge 'ought to be Lord Mayor' and he ought to become Lord Mayor as a result of Wilkes's support. It was a futile appeal. Wilkes responded that Junius had 'too favourable sentiments of Sawbridge. I allow him honest', he continued, 'but think he has more mulishness than understanding, more understanding than candour. He has become the absolute dupe of Malagrida's [Shelburne's] gang'. Sawbridge, Junius was told, had 'openly acted against us. Our troops will not be brought at present to fight his battles.' Finally, he was to add, and it is significant of the importance he attached to her support, 'Mrs. Macaulay has warmly espoused the common cause, and severely condemns her brother.'[73]

Whether or not Wilkes's claim was true Catharine Macaulay may have found herself with divided loyalties. She was, after all, both a friend of Wilkes, and of his loyal supporter, the Revd Thomas Wilson. She may have been rather more of a Wilkite than her brother, and remained in sympathy with the Society of the Supporters of the Bill of Rights after her brother's secession. The fact that in April 1769 Sir Edward Walpole had written to his brother suggesting that she was Junius—a notion Horace immediately dismissed—might indicate she was against the split, and more sympathetic to Wilkes than to Horne.[74] But earlier she had 'actively' supported her brother, 'who shared her republican principles', and the two were more often in agreement than in opposition.[75] There is evidence that she too entertained doubts about Wilkes. Her friendship with Dr Wilson may have prevented her voicing them. Some time in 1770, while she was still seeing a great deal of Wilkes's daughter Polly, his friends the Molineux, as well as Wilkes himself, she wrote him a letter. It seems she had

[72] *The Letters of Junius*, ed. John Cannon (1978), 258.
[73] Ibid., 399, 400, 415.
[74] *Horace Walpole's Correspondence*, xxxvi. 52.
[75] Ibid. xxxii. 40 n. 24.

subscribed generously to his support—in part in the form of a loan. She reminded him of 'an higher principle on which I act than the relative ties of common life and that it is the duty of a good Citizen to assist as far as circumstances will allow every individual under sufferance for exertion in the cause of liberty'. But, she continued, she now needed some repayment as the sum she had sacrificed was required by her own necessities, her expenses included furnishing an entire house and paying a fine on her estate. Finally she declared: 'the sum which was legally due to me from you would have made me easier'.[76] Whether this letter prompted a response from Wilkes we do not know. It may well have contributed to the cooling in her relations with Wilkes. It suggests that with her brother she was critical of Wilkes's use of the Society of Supporters of the Bill of Rights for his own financial ends.

The quarrel between Wilkes and his friends, and Horne Tooke and his supporters, was disastrous for the City opposition and 'finally proved of but little service to either of the belligerents'.[77] In his address to the Livery after being elected one of two candidates for the choice of mayor in 1771, John Sawbridge made his own views of the split clear. 'I cannot but regret the unhappy differences which have arisen amongst men professing the same principles, and who honestly can have but one common cause.'[78] Yet on certain issues the opposition was temporarily reunited. In the case of the printers, for instance, Wilkites, and the leaders of the Shelburne and Rockingham parties, again worked together.

It had long been illegal to publish parliamentary debates in newspapers. From time to time there had been cases of breaching the ban but in the late 1760s, encouraged by certain editors like John Almon, there was an increase in the practice. By early 1771 'over a dozen daily and weekly papers were regularly reporting debates'.[79] Attempts to enforce the ban had met with open defiance. The House of Commons set out to tighten the ban and apprehend all transgressors. In February 1771 the printers of the *Middlesex Journal* and the *Gazette* were ordered to attend the

---

[76] British Library, Add. MS. 30870. fo. 242.

[77] *Memoirs of John Horne Tooke*, i. 175.

[78] *London Chronicle*, 30 (1771), 366.

[79] Peter D. G. Thomas, 'The Beginning of Parliamentary Reporting in Newspapers', *English Historical Review*, 74 (1959), 623–36, at p. 632.

Commons. When they went into hiding and failed to appear the King issued a proclamation offering £50 reward for their arrest.[80] Sawbridge called the proclamation 'waste paper' and claimed it could not be acted upon without offending the law of the land.[81] In March six more printers were ordered to attend the House of Commons. Four did so, but on 15 March 1771, according to the terms of the proclamation, John Wheble of *The Middlesex Journal*, who had refused to attend the summons, was apprehended by one of his servants and brought before Wilkes, who happened to be the sitting Alderman at the Guildhall at the time. Wilkes ordered his release on the grounds that the proclamation did not authorize arrest. His servant was prosecuted on charges of assault and false imprisonment. The same day a House of Commons messenger tried to arrest another publisher of parliamentary debates, who, on being ordered to attend at the House of Commons, refused. John Miller, a freeman of London, and publisher of the *London Evening Post*, questioned the validity of the warrant, charged the messenger with assault and false imprisonment, and helped by a constable, escorted the messenger to the Mansion House. A court consisting of the Lord Mayor Brass Crosby, Alderman Oliver MP, and Wilkes, confirmed the warrant was illegal. The messenger was ordered to appear at the next quarter sessions to answer the charge.

John Sawbridge went out of his way to congratulate the Lord Mayor on his action as 'worthy of the thanks of every Englishman'.[82] The three magistrates were summoned to the House to answer for their conduct. Wilkes, using the occasion to reopen the Middlesex election issue, refused to attend, as he had not been summoned as a Member of Parliament. Crosby and Oliver were sent to the Tower. Mrs Macaulay, when 'informed of the proceedings of the Lord Mayor and Aldermen, respecting the printers and messengers of the House of Commons, applauded their conduct, and declared that they had proved themselves real guardians of the Citizens, and justifiable Defenders of the Liberty of the Subject'.[83] Her brother, together with Townshend, had taken part in the debate in the Commons censuring the Lord

---

[80] Rudé, *Wilkes and Liberty*, 155–6.
[81] Ibid. 157.
[82] Ibid. 159.
[83] *The Public Advertiser*, 25 Mar. 1771.

Mayor and Oliver, declaring that 'had their situation been the same with that of the Mayor, they would have acted in the same manner'.[84]

If the opposition was temporarily united over the issues of Wilkes's expulsion from the Commons, Paoli, and the case of the printers, the unity was short-lived. The Wilkite movement had pinpointed what was wrong with political life and the constitution. It had brought Middlesex freeholders into head-on confrontation with the House of Commons. Parliament had been shown to be unrepresentative, based on privilege and corruption. The growth of political frustration in the City and country had reached an explosive state. But the opposition was anything but in agreement as to the solution to the problem, or indeed on the analysis of the nature of the malaise. Fundamental differences of opinion between the City radicals and the moderate Whigs had already been revealed in the conduct and content of the petitioning campaign to the King in 1769. Vain attempts had been made to co-ordinate the action of the opposition groups. The moderate Whigs had wanted to confine their campaign to the Middlesex issue, whereas the City, and more particularly, the Supporters of the Bill of Rights, had tried to make Wilkes's disqualification the occasion for a general attack on government policies and the ventilation of grievances. While all groups were prepared to consider reform, not all were agreed on what reform involved.

The moderate Whigs were critical of the new methods being used to win over public opinion and were anxious to resume leadership of the opposition. To do so they needed publicity for their limited aims and a reasoned argument against the City radicals. They found their spokesman in Edmund Burke, who in 1770 produced his *Thoughts on the Cause of the Present Discontents*. Walpole, despite being allied with the moderate Whigs under Rockingham's leadership, asserted that the pamphlet was 'designed for the manifesto of the Rockingham party'.[85] A more recent judgement has seen the pamphlet as the first clear expression of the need for party government by which the whole administration would be under a single party.[86] Burke made clear that the

---

[84] Ibid. 27 Mar.

[85] *Horace Walpole's Correspondence*, xxiii. 209 n. 6.

[86] Carl B. Cone, *Burke and the Nature of Politics*, 2 vols. (University of Kentucky Press, 1957), i. 195, 198.

Rockingham Whigs not only were unconcerned with parliamentary reform but thought any tampering with the constitution
undesirable. Their sole object was to attack the Court faction, and
to separate the ministries from it. They attacked what they saw as
the system of a 'double cabinet': the outer cabinet of the Ministry,
and the inner of favourites close to the Crown who actually
possessed the power and controlled the administration. It was 'this
unnatural infusion of a *system of favouritism* into a government'
which was the cause of 'the present ferment in the nation'.[87]
Burke was pleased by the reception given the pamphlet. Nevertheless there were critical voices. Walpole talked of 'a long
and laborious pamphlet' which 'tired the informed, and was
unintelligible to the ignorant'. It was 'in point of judgement...
totally defective ... calculated for no one end but to deify Lord
Rockingham'. It had 'disgusted the popular party'.[88]

In the spring of 1770 a young American was dining with the
Dillys in the company of Mrs Macaulay. She had given him a
preview of her answer to Burke, which was about to be published. He had found it 'very well written—very nervous—
very spirited'.[89] It was short but succinct. Burke's pamphlet was
written with 'great eloquence, acuteness and art', but it contained
'a poison sufficient to destroy all the little virtue and understanding of sound policy which is left in the nation'. Behind the
pamphlet's apparent concern with 'the dangerous designs of a
profligate junto of courtiers' lay 'the corrupt principle of self-
interest' of 'Aristocratic faction and party' only anxious for their
own return to power.[90] James Burgh was later to make a similar
comment. Burke had 'held the grievances were only remedied by I
know not what public men, who were to be responsible. But most
people thought this a very gross confession, that he did not mean
the public advantage; but that he wanted to be one of the public
responsible men'.[91] In concentrating their attention on present misuse of kingly power they seemed to forget, Catharine

[87] Edmund Burke, *Thoughts on the Present Discontents* (1770), 29.
[88] Walpole, *Memoirs of the Reign of George III*, iv. 86.
[89] L. H. Butterfield, 'The American Interests of the Firm of E. and C. Dilly, with
their Letters to Benjamin Rush, 1770–1795', *Papers of the Bibliographical Society of
America*, 45 (1951), 283–332, at pp. 287–8.
[90] Catharine Macaulay, *Observations on a Pamphlet entitled 'Thoughts on the Cause of
the Present Discontents'* (1770), 6.
[91] James Burgh, *Political Disquisitions*, 3 vols. (1774–5), i. 173.

Macaulay argued, 'the more atrocious crimes of his tyrannic predecessors' and failed to see the origin of the present evils. The fault lay in the 'system of corruption' which 'began at the very period of the Revolution'. Parliament, from having 'a controuling power over the executive parts of government, became a mere instrument of regal administration'. It preserved the form of the constitution but 'annihilated its spirit'. Among the evils in the system of government produced by the Revolution were a standing army 'contrary to the very existence of real liberty', the 'army of placemen and pensioners', septennial rather than annual parliaments, and 'heavy taxes imposed for the single advantage and emolument of individuals'.[92]

She attacked those responsible for the Revolution 'who called themselves Whigs, but who in reality were as much the destructive, though concealed, enemies of public liberty' as the Tories. If now they resented their loss of power it was their own doing in allowing the power of the Crown to grow. Yet while deploring a House of Commons at odds with the people, Burke could claim that 'frequent elections' led to 'horrible disorders among the people'. He would be 'fearful of committing, every three years, the independent gentlemen of the country into contest with the Treasury'. If the motive of those who stood for Parliament lay in the 'lucrative prospect', then Mrs Macaulay thought the best cure, as Harrington had earlier suggested, was a system of rotation. By changing a half or the whole of parliament yearly, and by debarring every member from re-election for a term of years, corruption would be reduced. She recommended a Place Bill, which Burke had argued would 'set the executive power at variance with the legislative, and hazard the forms of our excellent constitution'; she wanted 'a more extended and equal power of election', something Burke had totally ignored; and finally she warned that unless the people's representatives were held to 'some political promises of real public service', they would continue planning 'schemes of private emolument and private ambition'.[93] Her pamphlet underlined the essential difference between the radicalism of the 1760s

[92] Macaulay, *Observations on a Pamphlet Entitled 'Thoughts on the Cause of the Present Discontents'*, 6–7, 10–11.

[93] Ibid. 12, 15–16, 17, 18, 19, 20; see also Muriel C. Beckwith, 'Catharine Macaulay: Eighteenth-Century Rebel', *Proceedings of the South Carolina Historical Association*, 1958, 12–29, at pp. 20–3.

and 1770s and that of the Country Opposition earlier. It was not that it did not share concern over increased court influence in parliament, and fully endorse the demand for Place and Pension Bills, but that it went much further in demanding a fundamental reform of parliament with an extension of the franchise and a redistribution of seats. Behind this new emphasis lay a new evaluation of the 'Glorious Revolution', in which Catharine Macaulay had given the lead.

Walpole thought well of the pamphlet and that her censure of Burke was just. Her 'principles were more sound and more fixed than Burke's', he wrote, and her 'reasoning was more simple and more exact'.[94] James Burgh was to talk of her 'shrewd answer'.[95] Recently an American historian has described Catharine Macaulay in 1770 as the leader of 'the vocal radicals'. The reply to Burke of 'this remarkable woman', he writes 'would be repeated many times in the future when the struggle between the forces of conservatism and of radical reform became fully engaged... Mrs Macaulay led the advance guard of the reform movement.'[96] It is not an excessive claim. We need to pause fully to appreciate just how remarkable Catharine Macaulay was. She did not hesitate to take on the most powerful political propagandist of the age. In the context of women's total lack of any political identity it is extraordinary that not only did she enter the political debate but that she was taken seriously. In the opinion of contemporaries and, more recently, experts on Burke's political thought, hers was a powerful and telling retort. The pamphlet was an important contribution to the reshaping of English radical ideology in this period. In her rejection of the traditional Whig interpretation of the 'Glorious Revolution' she underlined the distinction between moderate and radical reformers. In her outline of a policy of parliamentary reform she anticipated not only the programme put forward a little later by the Supporters of the Bill of Rights, and the breakaway group, the Constitutional Society, but that of Major John Cartwright and, much further ahead, the Chartists. Catharine Macaulay and her brother, John Sawbridge, shared a passionate and consistent commitment to radical politics and the

---

[94] Walpole, *Memoirs of the Reign of George III*, iv. 86–7.
[95] *Political Disquisitions*, i. 173.
[96] Cone, *Burke and the Nature of Politics*, i. 206–7.

cause of parliamentary reform. Whether she was regarded as the 'broodhen' of 'faction' or 'that amiable and glorious daughter of Liberty', no one after the 1760s could remain in any doubts where her political sympathies lay.[97] But more important, her contribution to the political debate must be recognized as significantly shaping radical ideas in England, and also, as we shall see later, in America and France.

[97] *London Chronicle*, 25 (1769), 26; *Monthly Miscellany*, 1 (1774), 18.

4. *The Bath Period, 1774–1778*

> Here, my poetic Patriot efforts end,
> Unskill'd alike, to *praise*, as to *defend*;
> Happy my F A I R! for works like thine indeed,
> Which neither *one*, nor *other*, of them need;
> To *neither*, therefore, daring, I aspire,
> My great ambition, Lady!—to *admire*!

(From a poem by J. D. B. dedicated to Mrs Macaulay in *The London Chronicle for 1770*, 495)

ILL health finally forced Catharine Macaulay to leave London. She moved to Bath and took a house in St James's Parade. It is unclear whether at this time she intended to stay permanently. Probably she did not know. Her move to Bath was in search of better health. In a letter written early in 1774 to her friend Augustus Toplady, she said only that her stay would be 'of considerable duration'.[1] She had been a widow for eight years; her daughter Catherine Sophia was still a child. In London, surrounded by friends and acquaintances, and in frequent contact with her brother, she had led an active social and political life. She had just experienced a most exciting period in the development of radical politics. She was no stranger to Bath. It was there that some time in the 1760s she had been introduced to Timothy Hollis by the historian William Harris.[2] In January 1772, Wilkes had written to his daughter that 'Mrs Macaulay has just left Bath'.[3] But if Catharine Macaulay knew Bath already and had friends there, they were almost certainly far fewer than those in London. As a single woman in a town that hitherto she had known only from brief visits, she may have been lonely at first. She was certainly unwell.

Eighteenth-century Bath was a spa and one of the great playgrounds of the pleasure-seeker. It was also a cultural centre, but far from being the focus of radical politics that London rep-

---

[1] *The Works of Augustus Toplady* (1853), 855, letter dated 18 Feb. 1774.
[2] *The Diary of Sylas Neville, 1767–1788*, ed. Basil Cozens-Hardy (1950), 13.
[3] *The Correspondence of the Late John Wilkes with his Friends*, ed. John Almon, 5 vols. (1805), iv. 97.

resented. She had completed five volumes of her *History* in eight years. To move from a hard-working, politically active life in the metropolis to Bath must have presented problems. For the first time in years she may have had time on her hands—and found it near-unbearable. The Revd Thomas Wilson was known to her already as a founder member of the Society of the Supporters of the Bill of Rights, a close friend of Wilkes and of her brother John. In 1775 he had written a letter to Wilkes from Gay Street in Bath, in which he referred to 'our dear friend, Mrs. Macaulay'. He had pressed Wilkes to bring his daughter Polly to visit Bath, where he would find a group of 'choice friends', and he added, 'amongst these give Mrs Macaulay and myself leave to say, that you have not many sincerer'. Catherine Sophia, Mrs Macaulay's daughter, Wilson described as a 'pretty miss' who returned 'the kiss you sent her by me'. The letter suggests the friendship between Wilson and Catharine Macaulay was already an established one, close but not intimate. In October of the following year Wilkes writes to tell his friend Mr Pettie (*sic*: probably Sam Petrie) that Dr Wilson had dined with him and was now 'returned to Bath for the remainder of his life, after having sent there all his furniture from the Cloister of Westminster'.[4]

Within a few months of his arrival in Bath, the Doctor invited Catharine Macaulay and her daughter to come and share his house. He promised to put his entire library at her disposal. In his letter to Sam Petrie, Wilkes had mentioned, and apparently he did not find it unusual, that Wilson was 'to live in the same house at Bath as Mrs. Macaulay, who had paid me a most friendly visit'.[5] Once the invitation was given she appears not to have hesitated. Very soon she was firmly installed at Alfred House, No. 2, Alfred Street. She was then 45; Thomas Wilson was 73. Given her veneration of the Anglo-Saxon monarch it was appropriate that the bust of King Alfred was placed above the porch of the house.

Born in 1703, Thomas Wilson was the son of the Bishop of Sodor and Man. In 1737 he was made one of the king's chaplains and, the same year, presented to the rectory of St Stephen's, Walbrook, which he held until his death in 1784, although he does not appear to have ever resided there. In 1743 he was made

[4] Ibid. iv. 174–5; v. 29.
[5] Ibid. v. 29.

prebendary of Westminster and held the rectory of St Margaret's from 1753. He had married his cousin in 1734, but she died a few years before Catharine Macaulay's move to Bath, not long after Wilkes had written to his daughter in January 1772 that Dr and Mrs Wilson were 'very poorly'.[6] Earlier he and his wife had regularly dined with Wilkes, and appear to have been on very friendly terms with Wilkes's daughter Polly. The 1760s found Wilson an ardent Wilkite who engaged 'with great eagerness in the political feuds of the day'.[7] He was to remain a loyal friend of Wilkes until his death in 1784. A kindly man, he gave considerable sums to charity, but, it is suggested, 'his rich preferments, his private estate which accumulated over the years, and his wife's inheritance' made him well able to afford them. He was also a cultured man, the owner of an extensive library, and a considerable book collector—factors that must have played their part in persuading Catharine Macaulay to share his house.[8]

Both Catharine Macaulay and Dr Wilson may have felt the need for company. After the death of his wife in 1772, we are told, Wilson found his house in Westminster School 'very lonely and forlorn'. He rarely resided there 'making his permanent home at Alfred House'.[9] As this was before Mrs Macaulay was invited to share the house it suggests Wilson had purchased it well before the invitation was issued. An account of how Wilson came to invite Mrs Macaulay to share Alfred House, on the other hand, claimed he 'purchased, and presented her with a mansion, which he called by the name of Alfred House, a library, servants, and every article of luxury and splendour'.[10] In a letter to Hugh Blair, Hume mentioned that Mrs Macaulay had now settled in Bath, and added that she was 'if not a more illustrious, yet a more fortunate Historian, than either of us. There is one Dr. Wilson, a man zealous for Liberty, who has made her a free and full Present of a house of £2,000 Value, has adopted her Daughter by all the Rites of Roman Jurisprudence, and intends to leave her all his Fortune, which is considerable.'[11]

[6] Ibid. iv. 99.
[7] *The European Magazine and London Review*, 4 (1783), 332.
[8] *The Diaries of Thomas Wilson D.D.*, ed. C. L. S. Linnell (1964), 6.
[9] Ibid. 17.
[10] *European Magazine*, 4 (1783), 332–3.
[11] *The Letters of Hume*, ed. J. Y. T. Greig, 2 vols. (1932), ii. 321.

There are some puzzling aspects to Wilson's relationship with Catharine Macaulay. The *Town and Country Magazine*, admittedly fond of gossip and any hint of scandal, regularly carried a column entitled 'Histories of the Tête-à-Tête annexed'. In 1771 one was devoted to 'Memoirs of the Reverend Joiner, and Mrs. L——n'. There can be no doubt of the identity of 'the Reverend Joiner'. Wilson, after Wilkes had acquired the freedom of the company of Joiners, in order to further his hero's ambitions within the City of London, became master of that company. Prefacing the article were two prints, one of them captioned 'The Reverend Joiner', the other, 'The Female Politician'. The latter shows a remarkable likeness to other prints of Catharine Macaulay. The article traces the career of 'this extraordinary character . . . Dr. W—' who was 'at once a priest, a patriot, and a politician' from his time at university, to taking orders, after which 'he constantly attended the late Duke of Newcastle's levee, in order to obtain preferment; but after a series of years spent in fruitless pursuit, the duke dying, and all hopes of lawn-sleeves vanishing, from an obsequious courtier he changed his opinion with his circumstances, being now in possession of an affluent fortune, and is at present as vociferous a patriot as he was before a ministerial advocate'.[12] Other accounts confirm this picture of an 'obsequious courtier'. His biographer suggests that 'he was careful to keep on the right side of "the great men"'. He 'embarked upon a pursuit of preferment which must appear to modern readers as quite shameless. He had only to hear that the holder of some rich city living was ill, or even only indisposed, or likely to be preferred elsewhere, and he was off doing the best he could to secure it for himself.'[13] In the early years after George III's accession, Wilson was asked to preach 'before the new King, whose favour was not conciliated by the means which were taken to obtain it'. The sermon, the report continued, 'was couched in terms of flattery so gross, as to be noticed with some degree of censure'.[14] On one occasion the king, 'upon hearing a flattering sermon from Dr. Wilson', asked that he be told 'that he came to church to hear God praised, not himself'.[15] One can see why

---

[12] *Town and Country Magazine*, 3 (1771), 681.
[13] *The Diaries of Thomas Wilson D.D.*, 10–11.
[14] *European Magazine*, 5 (1784), 250.
[15] *The Letters of Mrs. Elizabeth Montagu*, ed. Matthew Montagu, 4 vols. (1813), iv. 356, in a letter to Elizabeth Carter.

Walpole called him 'that dirty disappointed hunter of a mitre'.[16]
Of this part of Wilson's life Catharine Macaulay almost certainly
remained ignorant. The Wilson she knew was the 'patriot and
politician'.

There is more in the *Town and Country Magazine* about
Wilson's loyalty and generosity to Wilkes, and of the leading
role he played in the Wilkes campaign. It noted his failure to
reform that 'libertine . . . who still pursues his course of dissipated
pleasures', with a suggestion that 'even the reverend liveryman,
though now approaching his grand climacteric', was 'not without
his tender alliances'. The names of three were hinted at. But once
a patriot, the account continues, 'he sought everywhere for a
female patriot . . . but . . . was informed there was but one in
England, and she was Mrs. Macaulay'. We are told that 'thus
frustrated, he was upon the point of giving up all intercourse
with the fair-sex when he fortunately fell in company with Mrs
L——n'. She was described as 'a woman entirely after his own
heart, and, to complete her character, a *public writer*'. It seems
curious that after mention of Mrs Macaulay it was felt necessary
to invent Mrs L——n, for there can be little doubt that they were
one and the same person. It could have been an attempt to inform
the reader without laying the author open to charges of libel.
Described as having 'not only read the History of England, but
the History of Europe', of having 'understood the inestimable
value of the great charter as perfectly as she could trim the
balance of power', this Mrs L——n 'could reason upon the Bill
of Rights with as much precision, as she could descant upon the
golden bull. Machiavel and Puffendorf were quite familiar to her,
and Locke on government was at her finger-ends.' She is further
described as 'a widow about forty'—Mrs Macaulay's exact age at
the time. Wilson, it suggested, appeared 'literally to doat upon
her, which is no way irreconcilable with his age'. This 'paragon of
female politics' surely can only have been Catharine Macaulay.
What the article seems to confirm is that her friendship with
Wilson had started much earlier than Mrs Macaulay's move to
Bath, and before the death of Wilson's wife.[17]

Some time in the early years of her residence in Bath, Thomas

Gainsborough painted her. Unfortunately the painting is lost (but see Pls. 3–4 for two portraits completed at this time). It was included in an exhibition of Gainsborough's works at the Grosvenor Gallery in 1885. 'Exhibit 206. Mrs. Catharine Macaulay' was described as 'a canvas of 30 × 25"'. The subject was 'a friend of Gainsborough and Dr. Johnson'. The painting had been lent by one E. P. Roberts. Yet when in 1899, *Notes and Queries* published a letter from Catharine Macaulay's great-nephew, J. J. G. Graham, he held he knew of only two authentic portraits of her. 'One I possess', he wrote, 'either a Romney or a Gainsborough'. The other had been 'bought at a sale of Mrs D. Arnold's effects' by a Mr E. P. Roberts, 'whose address', Graham wrote, 'I should be glad to obtain'. Mrs Arnold was the sister of William Graham, Catharine's second husband. The following year the appeal in *Notes and Queries* was repeated.[18] But if as seems likely Roberts was still in possession of the portrait he had bought, there had only been one Gainsborough painting, and whatever portrait Graham owned, it could not have been a Gainsborough. It is curious that Graham was unaware of whether the portrait he possessed was 'a Romney or a Gainsborough'. There is certainly no evidence of a Romney portrait of Mrs Macaulay. Most probably Catharine Macaulay had bequeathed the Gainsborough portrait to her sister-in-law and close friend Mrs Arnold. On her death it was sold to Roberts. Behind Graham's inquiry was a desire to find the Gainsborough without perhaps revealing to anyone, other than the owner, the identity of the painter.

Of Catharine Macaulay's daughter, Catherine Sophia, we hear but little. 'In April 1775', we are told, she 'was formally adopted by' Wilson, 'in the presence of five or six witnesses'.[19] Joseph Wright (1734–97), pioneer painter of the industrial revolution, in 1776 wrote to his brother from Bath that he was engaged in painting 'a half-length of Dr. Wilson and his adopted daughter, Miss Macauley' (see Pl. 10). Two years earlier Gainsborough had left Bath, and Wright, thinking there might now be an opening

---

[18] A. Birabeau, *Life and Letters at Bath in the Eighteenth Century* (1904), 290; *Catalogue of the Grosvenor Gallery Exhibition of the Works of Thomas Gainsborough, R.A.* (1885), 93–4; *Notes and Queries*, 9th ser., 4 (1899), 238.

[19] Samuel Pegge, *Anonymiana: Or, Ten Centuries of Observations on Various Authors and Subjects* (1809), 329.

there for a portrait painter, had moved south from Derby. He
had undertaken the portrait, he wrote, 'for reputation only' but
added that Dr Wilson was 'a very popular man', thought Wright
'ill-treated' and was 'fighting . . . stoutly' in his cause.[20] In the
portrait Sophia and the Doctor are sitting at a table together. In
front of them is an open book. It is a volume of Catharine
Macaulay's *History*. With a plain but intelligent face, Sophia is
looking at her adoptive father for guidance, her finger pointing
to a line of the book before them. Wilson looks out at us. It is
the face of a kindly old man with a hint of weakness, even of
petulance in it. It fits with the accounts of his growing irritability
and truculence in old age. Apart from this portrait the only proof
we have that Sophia read her mother's *History* or sympathized
with her anti-monarchist ideas comes from Hannah More, and as
she was far from a friend of Catharine Macaulay's, the story
may well be apocryphal. She had come across Catherine Sophia
reading Shakespeare and 'asked her if she was not delighted with
many parts of King John'. 'I never read the Kings, ma'am' was the
response.[21]

In Bath Catharine Macaulay was said to have attracted many
admirers and 'made herself the centre of a little circle of politicians to whom she was accustomed to give lessons on general
politics and English constitutional history'.[22] She was not merely
a woman of great conversational wit and intelligence but, as
Elizabeth Carter had remarked much earlier, a woman of some
beauty and grace. Edmund Rack, the Quaker writer, who retired to Bath, and 'having cultivated a taste for literature, was
patronised by . . . Mrs Macaulay, and Dr. Wilson', was bowled
over by her.[23] 'I have seen Mrs. Macaulay' he wrote in 1778, 'she
is handsome, she is elegantly formed; and her *tout ensemble* the
object of admiration.'[24] At Alfred House she frequently gave
elegant dinner parties, and entertained a stream of visitors. Most
came to admire her. One of her later, and severest, critics was to

---

[20] William Bemrose, *Life and Works of Joseph Wright* (1885), 45.

[21] *The Letters of Hannah More*, ed. R. Brimley Johnson (1925), 80, in a letter to Mrs
Boscawen.

[22] Revd Joseph Hunter, *The Connection of Bath with the Literature and Science of
England* (1853), 56–7.

[23] *European Magazine*, 1 (1782), 360–1.

[24] George Monkland, *The Literature and Literati of Bath* (1854), supplement, 84–5,
in a letter from Edmund Rack to Polwhele dated 29 Dec. 1778.

write how 'while affecting unbounded admiration for the rigid simplicity of Republicanism, she exacted as much homage as her coteries of slavish admirers were willing to pay her in her petty *regal court* which she set up.'[25] Unfortunately the account of how she celebrated her 46th birthday did little to dispel such a view.

Although she devoted time to study and writing she progressed no further with her eight-volume *History*. Before he died in 1776, Hume had commented to a friend how 'her Muse now seems to be mute'.[26] Why was it that her time in Bath coincided with this significant pause between Volume V, which appeared in 1771 when she was still resident in London, and Volume VI, which only appeared ten years later, and after she had left Bath for good? Intriguingly there is evidence she had started on Volume VI well before her move to Bath. Augustus Toplady wrote to her in October 1773 of his pleasure at hearing from their mutual friend Mr N. (presumably Mr Northcote, Toplady's neighbour and friend) that her sixth volume would 'appear early in the spring'.[27] It suggests that it was already near completion. Ill health intervened in the winter of 1773 to postpone further work on the volume until her move to Bath. In fact publication was delayed until 1781, three years after she left Bath.

Before she moved into Alfred House, she produced two pamphlets. *A Modest Plea for the Property of Copyright* appeared in 1774. She referred to it as 'this hasty performance' which had been written under 'a heavy oppression of sickness and languor of body, at a great distance from the capital'. But for the encouragement given her by Dr Wilson she would not have had 'the spirits and resolution to attempt it'.[28] Horace Walpole confirmed her low state of health in a letter to the Revd William Mason where he referred to her 'very bad pamphlet'. 'It marks', he was to add, 'dejection and sickness'.[29] What provoked her to write the pamphlet was the case brought against the Scot Alexander Donaldson, who pioneered popular reprints, for reprinting James Thomson's

[25] R. E. Peach, *Historic Houses in Bath* (1883), 117.

[26] *The Letters of Hume*, ii. 321.

[27] *The Works of Augustus Toplady*, 851; see also the letter to Catharine Macaulay from Henry Marchant, Oct. 1774, in Marchant Papers, Rhode Island Historical Society.

[28] Catharine Macaulay, *A Modest Plea for the Property of Copyright* (1774), pp. v–vii.

[29] *Horace Walpole's Correspondence*, xxviii. 142.

The Seasons. He lost the case but, much to the anger of the London booksellers, on appealing to the House of Lords obtained a majority decision in his favour. The booksellers unsuccessfully tried to bring in a Bill to make copyright perpetual. It was passed in the Commons but thrown out in the Lords. The question Mrs Macaulay addressed was whether 'rendering literary property common' was 'advantageous or disadvantageous to the state of literature'? She argued that the result would be that authors would either have to have independent means or have their work sponsored by a patron. Could work completed by such dependent authors be edifying when written 'merely to earn the favour of a patron'? She claimed that many of the best authors were 'so little read', that it hardly paid to reprint them. Rendering literary property common would greatly increase the evil for new editions of works which failed to promise 'a quick return' would not be made. She seems to have been almost alone among authors in supporting the booksellers. When Parliament was petitioned on their behalf, it was John Sawbridge who seconded the motion asking for some relief to be granted them. He was a member of the committee set up to consider the petition and instrumental in getting agreement of the recommendation that a Bill be brought in to give the booksellers some relief, at least for a time.[30] The *Gentleman's Magazine* reviewed the pamphlet at length but uncritically. The *Monthly Miscellany*, in a comprehensive review, thought it a valuable defence against the attack on literary property. It appealed to 'the republic of letters' to remember that when the 'iron hand of power was extended totally to crush learning, genius, and science . . . a generous *female* stood forth . . . to combat the insulting giant'. 'Mrs . . . Macaulay, in her late spirited Apology for Authors', wrote William Enfield, 'has shown that they *may* receive the profitable as well as honorary fruits of their labour, without any degradation of their character.' A poem under the pseudonym of 'Stella' opposed Mrs Macaulay's pamphlet making the point that besides the interests of booksellers and authors, there was also one other interest to be considered:

---

[30] Colin Clair, *A History of Printing in Britain* (1965), 172; A. S. Collins, *Authorship in the Days of Johnson, 1726–1780* (1927), ch. 2, esp. 102–3; Macaulay, *A Modest Plea*, 33–4 n., 37, 42; *Public Advertiser*, 2 and 25 Mar., 1774.

Macaulay humble, modest in her plea;
How comes she, then, to be attack'd by me?
Obvious the reason, think but for a minute,
She writes, I read—that's all the diff'rence in it.[31]

In 1775 Catharine Macaulay published her *Address to the People of England, Scotland, and Ireland on the Present Important Crisis of Affairs*, which was concerned with avoiding the outbreak of war with the American colonies (see Ch. 9). The only work that appeared in her time at Alfred House was the first volume of the *History of England from the Revolution to the Present Time in a Series of Letters to a Friend*, published in 1778. The friend was Wilson. The promised second volume never appeared, although she may have started work on it. Only when later the same year she left Bath did she return again to her original *History* and resume work on Volume VI. So while one account describes her as writing 'a great part of her once famous *History of England* in Bath', in fact she seems to have neglected it during her stay in Alfred House.[32] If Thomas Wilson had an extensive library it is doubtful whether it contained the sort of books and pamphlets that would have helped in the writing of her *History*. She must have missed regular access to the British Museum on which her previous work so much depended. It may have been partly for these reasons she gave up her eight-volume *History*. More important was her continued ill health, combined with dejection at the reception with which her last two volumes had met, and the accusations some critics had made against her. Increasingly aware how fame, as quickly as it had come to her, was now receding, she can have felt little encouragement to continue the *History*. She plunged into the writing of a more recent period of history, adopting a new and less scholarly tone.

If she wrote little of her *History* in Bath, Catharine Macaulay continued to receive there 'extraordinary ovations' from admirers of her work already in print.[33] The poet Mary Scott (*fl.* 1774–88) in 1774 wrote an answer to John Duncombe's *Feminead* in which

[31] *Gentleman's Magazine*, 44 (1774), 125–6; *Monthly Miscellany*, 1 (1774), 198–201, at p. 201; William Enfield, *Observations on Literary Property* (1774), 8; 'Stella', 'Modest Exceptions from the Court of Parnassus to Mrs. Macaulay's Modest Plea', By the Author of *The Doctor Dissected: A Poem* (1774), 4.

[32] Birabeau, *Life and Letters at Bath*, 171 n. 4.

[33] Ibid.

she praised learned and talented women. Catharine Macaulay was singled out for particular attention:

> But thou MACAULAY, say canst thou excuse
> The fond presumption of a youthful Muse?
> A Muse, that raptur'd with thy growing fame,
> Wishes (at least) to celebrate thy name;
> A name, to ev'ry son of freedom dear,
> Which patriots yet unborn shall long revere.[34]

Was such praise any comfort to Catharine Macaulay? Did Bath represent for her a haven, where 'in this little world of fashion she found herself duly flattered and sought after as a literary celebrity'?[35] Two years later, on her 46th birthday, the flattery and adulation was to reach a peak.

One of her correspondents and close friends was the Revd Augustus Toplady. From being converted to Wesleyanism as a student, he totally rejected it two years later to become an extreme Calvinist. Ordained in 1764, he moved from London to Hungerford, and thence to the west country, where, in 1768, he became vicar of Broad Hembury in Devon. He was an eloquent preacher and while still in London 'so highly was he esteemed . . . that the churches in which he preached there could not contain the immense multitudes that crowded to hear him'. Toplady 'mixed freely with men of all denominations'; it may have been through dissenting clerical and radical friends in London that Catharine Macaulay came to meet him. Among them, not only Thomas Hollis but Edward and Charles Dilly, the Dissenting publishers and booksellers, were well known to Toplady. In London he dined with the Dillys in company that included Dr Johnson and Oliver Goldsmith. He had certainly known Mrs Macaulay several years before she moved to Bath. Soon after her arrival there, aware perhaps how few were her friends in the town, he wrote introducing her to a Mrs Derham, the wife of a wine merchant, who had 'a lovely daughter, nearly the same age as yours'.[36]

---

[34] Mary Scott, *The Female Advocate* (1774), 27.
[35] Daisy L. Hobman, 'Mrs Macaulay', *The Fortnightly*, 171 (1952), 116–21 at p. 117.
[36] *Memoirs of the Life and Writings of the Rev. A. M. Toplady B.A. 1740–78*, ed. W. Winters (1872), 31, 51, 46; *The Works of Augustus Toplady*, 855.

Toplady knew Catharine Macaulay well enough to have invited her to visit several times, and was the centre of a small group of people known to her in Devon. In 1774 she spent three months there. Her hosts were a Mr and Mrs Northcote, Toplady's near neighbours. She had first visited them some time before 1773 when they pressed her to come again. Toplady wrote reassuring her that they could provide most of the books she would require 'relative to the period on which you are now employed'. Both 'looked forward to it so much'.[37] It was the following year, after her move to Bath, before that visit was made. What is interesting about Toplady's friendship with Catharine Macaulay is not only that it was close and of some duration, but that while her admirer he was also prepared to criticize her, and said what he thought about her interpretation of history, raising points with which he disagreed. Described by his biographer as having 'a very capacious and soaring mind enclosed in a very weak and delicate body', this had not 'retarded his intense application to study'.[38] In 1775, consumption forced him to move to London. He died three years later.

In Bath she also saw a great deal of Clement Cruttwell (1743–1808), formerly Wilson's physician, who was editor of the *Bath Chronicle*. He had started his career as a surgeon, had then taken orders, and finally turned publisher. Very much a protégé of Wilson's, he seems to have spent much of his time at Alfred House. Richard Polwhele (1760–1838) was another of Mrs Macaulay's acquaintances. He submitted a poem for her 46th-birthday celebrations, and Wilson wrote to assure him that Catharine had read and liked it, and had given him 'her ready permission to dedicate it to her'. Wilson wrote suggesting Polwhele should call on them and be introduced to 'my great and worthy friend Mrs Macaulay'.[39] When Polwhele visited Bath, he was still only a schoolboy and was accompanied by his mother. Later he was introduced to Mrs Macaulay and Wilson. He also met Hannah More, 'the young dramatic poetess of Bristol', who 'whilst Catharine was receiving homage at Bath from greybeards and from boys, was herself enthroned amidst a crowd of boarding

---

[37] Eugene Charlton Black, *The Association* (1963), 194; *Works of Augustus Toplady*, 844.

[38] *Memoirs of the Life and Writings of A. M. Toplady B.A. 1740–78*, 51.

[39] Revd R. Polwhele, *Reminiscences in Prose and Verse*, 3 vols. (1836), i. 22.

school misses, tutored to lisp, in soothing accents, her dramas and her praises'.[40] Polwhele had begun to write poetry at the age of 12. Perhaps encouraged too early to think himself a poet, his early promise failed to mature. Later when asked why he had failed to win more academic honours, he was to blame his 'Bath and Bristol friends, Mrs Macaulay and Dr. Wilson . . . Mrs. Hannah More, Mr. Rack and the Rev. Mr. Towgood' who had 'flattered the Schoolboy's Muse'. In August 1778, it is true, Catharine Macaulay wrote to him that his 'merits as a poet' were 'much applauded by better judges' than herself. She thought the poem, 'Henry and Rosamond', which he had sent for her criticism, would be 'a valuable addition' to her *Miscellaneous Works*. Intriguingly it is the only reference to such a work. Apparently a quarto volume had been planned. 'Its republican principles', according to Polwhele, 'induced her friends to advise her to suppress' it. She must have heeded the advice.[41] What else, one wonders, was she intending to publish in it?

John Wilkes and his daughter Polly were frequent visitors to Bath. On Christmas Day, 1776, they dined with Mrs Macaulay at Alfred House. Among the other guests was a Dr James Graham (1745–94). Born in Edinburgh, the son of a saddler, he studied medicine at Edinburgh under distinguished teachers, but it is doubtful whether he ever qualified. He was later to write how he 'became exceedingly dissatisfied at the trifling absurdities and feebleness of what is called the regular practice of Physic'.[42] When he left university he moved to Pontefract, where, in 1770, he married. Soon after he went to America where he practised as a doctor specializing as an oculist and aurist. In Philadelphia, he became acquainted with the discoveries of Benjamin Franklin. They profoundly influenced his ideas on medicine.

In 1774 he returned to England, where he at first practised in Bristol. The following year after spending a short time in Bath, he moved to London and set up house in Pall Mall, but early in 1775 he began to practise in Bath. There he must have met and started to treat Catharine Macaulay. Later, in his book *The General State of Medical and Chirurgical Practice Exhibited*, he was to

---

[40] Id., *Traditions and Recollections*, 2 vols. (1826), i. 42–3.
[41] Ibid. 86–7; and see also pp. 98–9 (letter from Catharine Macaulay, 23 Aug. 1778).
[42] Dr James Graham, *The Guardian Goddess of Health* (1780), 34.

acknowledge his debt to her in giving him a start and publicizing his remedies. When he first published his 'valuable discoveries and improvements. . . . in the cure of diseases', nobody had taken much notice. But when Catharine Macaulay read the pamphlet, she was impressed by how 'at once powerful, safe, and rational' were Graham's methods and decided to try them.[43] According to him she was the first 'to make trial of them'. The result was that 'the complicated and obstinate maladies' with which her 'very delicate frame was afflicted' were dispersed. Exactly what were the symptoms of her illness? Graham described them as those that 'accompany a relaxed system, and an irritable state of nerves, viz. pains in the stomach, indigestion, trembling of the nerves, shivering fits, repeated pains in her ears and throat, and continual agitations of body and mind'. Together they had reduced a constitution 'originally delicate, to an almost insupportable degree of weakness and debility'. They were the consequence of 'a seven years' severe application' in writing her *History*. Enthusiastically she wrote to thank him and recommended his methods to others. She had been, Graham said, 'the fair foundation and grand pillar' of his 'fame and fortune'.[44] She was not the only one to recommend Graham's methods and cures. One thing Edmund Rack shared with Catharine Macaulay in these years was bad health, and he too was impressed by Graham's methods. Rack believed his own cure from 'a severe asthmatic and consumptive complaint' was entirely due to Graham, 'whose abilities and knowledge in the medical art' were 'only to be equalled by his politeness and generosity'.[45] Thomas Wilson, who 'had laboured, for many years, under an oppression of the lungs . . . with a troublesome and tormenting cough' was another who, in a letter to Graham, acknowledged his debt after having no recurrence of the complaint for nearly a year.[46]

Described as a handsome but rather heavy man, James Graham was broad-shouldered and tall. He chose always to dress in black. He was a 'quack' doctor, but given the state of medical knowledge

---

[43] *Six Odes Presented to the Justly-Celebrated Historian, Mrs. Catharine Macaulay, on her Birthday* (1777), pp. ix–x.

[44] *An Abstract from a Book Just Published Intituled 'Medical Transactions at the Temple of Health in London, in the course of the year 1780'* (1781), 4.

[45] *Six Odes*, p. xi.

[46] *An Abstract*, 5.

in the eighteenth century, his remedies were no more absurd than those of many others. John Taylor (1757–1832), journalist and writer for the stage, described him as 'a sensible and, as far as I could judge, an extremely well-informed man both generally and professionally'. He thought him handsome, his conversation 'grave and intelligent, and his manners easy and polite'. Taylor considered him 'a remarkably well-bred man, with most polished manners', but added one proviso—'when sober'. If he had remained in Pall Mall, where apparently 'he was successful in practice as a regular physician', Taylor believed 'he would have held a respectable rank'. His weakness was 'being too fond of notoriety'.[47] He was an accomplished showman and for a time in London had a large and fashionable audience. In 1779, some time after treating Catharine Macaulay, he opened his 'Temple of Health' on the Royal Terrace, Adelphi, where he lectured on the advantages to health of electricity and magnetism. His patients were placed either on a magnetic throne or in a bath through which electric currents were passed. He believed great benefits were to be had from taking frequent mud baths. And in order that he could 'be observed to practice what he preached he was to be seen on stated occasions, immersed to the chin; accompanied by a lady to whom he gave the name of Vestina, Goddess of Health'.[48] The lady was Emma Lyon, who became Lady Hamilton, and later, Nelson's mistress. When he moved from the Adelphi to Pall Mall, he introduced a celestial bed, 'a gorgeous structure'—said to have cost him £60,000—as a cure for sterility. For a fee of £100 a night, it was claimed, many hitherto childless had become prolific. He seems always to have been short of money and perhaps for this reason 'adopted expedients for support of a licentious description', as some of the accounts of Pall Mall suggest.[49]

An interesting sidelight on Graham is that in 1783, when he was giving a number of lectures in his London house, his contribution was preceded by a Mrs Curtis, the younger sister of Mrs Siddons, who talked on the state and influence of woman in society. It might suggest he had some sympathy with women's

---

[47] John Taylor, *Records of My Life*, 2 vols. (1832), i. 209–10.
[48] Robert Chambers, *The Book of Days*, 2 vols. (1863–4), i. 511.
[49] Edith Sitwell, *English Eccentrics* (1933), 89; Taylor, *Records of My Life*, i. 210.

position—a factor which may have played its part in endearing him to Catharine Macaulay.[50]

Was it so extraordinary that Mrs Macaulay turned to James Graham for a cure? Her enthusiasm for his methods, as we have seen, was shared by others. As someone suffering from a chronic illness for several years, was it in desperation that she turned to him in the hope that less orthodox medicine might provide an answer? Ill health had dogged her ever since 1768—perhaps even earlier. In January 1769 the *London Chronicle* reported her return to London from Bath, 'whither she has been for the restoration of her health since concluding the fourth volume of her history'. In August of the same year, for reasons of health, she set out for Tunbridge Wells and then on to visit her brother at Olantigh in Kent. She had 'been some time labouring under a bad state of health owing to the severe application in completing her fourth volume'. Three weeks later she returned 'much recovered from her late indisposition'.[51] When she was still living in London in June 1773, Augustus Toplady visited her. He was concerned at her appearance. 'I saw with pain', he was later to write to her, 'that the closeness of that over-grown town, your want of exercise, and your intense literary application, appear to have had an unfavourable effect on your health'. He begged her to visit once more her friends in Devon. A month later he wrote to her again. He was sorry to hear 'her health had not improved'. In October there were signs that she was better but when she published her pamphlet on copyright she was again ill. Not long after her move to Bath in 1774, Toplady wrote hoping the move would have a good effect on her health.[52] When Toplady visited her in May he found her 'very weak and languid'. That summer she visited Devon, where she 'wisely intermitted her historical pursuits, for the sake of pursuing that, without which the former would soon come to a final period; namely, health'. John Collett Ryland, the Baptist friend of Toplady's at Northampton, was another concerned with her health. He expressed the hope that when in Devon she would be 'a perfect idiot once in every twenty-four hours, and incapable of writing, reading, thinking, or convalesc-

---

[50] *Dictionary of National Biography.*
[51] *London Chronicle,* 25 (1769), 26, 216.
[52] *The Works of Augustus Toplady,* 844, 846, 850, 855.

ing, viz. from ten at night, until six or seven in the morning', so
that she would not damage her health by sitting up late.[53] By the
time she met James Graham in Bath, Catharine Macaulay must
have been seriously worried by her almost perpetual ill health. But
it was not only for his cures that she was indebted to James
Graham. Through him she was to meet William Graham, his
brother, who in 1778 became her second husband.

Of her relations with Thomas Wilson we have little evidence,
but in the opening letter of her *History of England from the Revolution to the Present Time* there is a eulogy on his character, parts of
which are revealing. She praised him for his 'moderation in
every circumstance of indulgence which regards yourself' while
'lavishing thousands on the public cause'; she admired 'the
exemplary regularity' of his life, and the 'patience and fortitude'
he displayed in the face of a 'weak and tender constitution'. She
commented on this 'singular instance of warm patriotism united to
the clerical character' for 'love of your country, and the welfare of
the human race' was the 'only ruling passion' she had ever found
in his character. Finally, one is left in no doubt of her gratitude to
him for 'the munificent favours' he had conferred on her, enough,
she wrote, 'to animate the dullest writer'.[54] Her respect and
admiration—and even affection—for him are clear but that there
was anything more to their relationship is doubtful. Praise for
Wilson's 'moderation' and 'exemplary regularity' is hardly the
language of love.

Wilson, however, was besotted by her. On 2 April 1777
Catharine Macaulay celebrated her 46th birthday. A collection
of six odes had been prepared—almost certainly at Wilson's
suggestion—which were presented to her on the day. The collection, under the title '*Six Odes* presented to that justly-celebrated
Historian, Mrs. Catherine Macaulay, on her Birthday, and publicly read to a polite and brilliant audience, Assembled April the
Second, at Alfred House, Bath, To congratulate that Lady on the
happy Occasion', was printed by Edward Dilly and priced at 1*s.*
6*d.* The collection was dedicated to Dr Wilson. Who—other than
Wilson himself—can have been the editor who wrote: 'To reside
under the same roof with the most accomplished Lady of the age;

---

[53] *The Works of Augustus Toplady*, 860, 857.
[54] Catharine Macaulay, *History from the Revolution*, i (1778), 2.

to stand in the honourable relation to her of an intimate friend; to have the felicity of enjoying her social and improving converse, in the hours of relaxation from arduous study, must, to a mind like your's, afford inexpressible happiness'?[55]

The day 'was ushered in by ringing of bells, and other public demonstrations of the general joy felt for an event so pleasing to the true friends of literature and liberty in these kingdoms'. In the evening 'an elegant entertainment was prepared'. Catharine, 'very elegantly dressed, was seated in a conspicuous elevated situation in front of the company' and the six odes read aloud to her by 'six Gentlemen selected out of the company'. Afterwards 'the pious, learned, and patriotic Dr. Wilson advanced, and presented to MRS. MACAULAY a large and curious gold medal . . . which he accompanied with a speech strongly expressive of her merit, and of his friendship and veneration.' He was followed by 'the ingenious Dr. Graham, to whom the world is so much indebted for restoring health to the Guardian of our Liberties', who 'presented her with a copy of his works, containing his surprising discoveries and cures' prefaced by a long dedication full of extravagant praise of her. She possessed a 'comprehensive and most penetrating genius'. He had had 'the honour of attending a Lady' of 'unique character' which was 'so strongly marked by learning and liberality, and so sweetly distinguished for philanthropy, and the most diffusive benevolence'. Hers was 'the first and most eloquent pen in the universe'. Attending her was 'the happiest and most honourable incident' of his life.[56] Both the third and the fifth odes made reference to Graham and the result of his healing powers. The third was written 'On reading Mrs. Macaulay's Letter to Dr. Graham'. The 'HISTORIC MUSE' approaches the throne of Apollo and asks:

> O! is there not some potent charm,
> The cruel spoiler to disarm,
> That health again may bloom?

In the sixth stanza the God replies:

> To stop the ravage of the foe,
> My Graham instantly shall go,
> And set thy Fav'rite free;

---

[55] *Six Odes*, p. iii.
[56] Ibid., pp. vii–xii.

> No more let sorrow fill thine eye,—
> On Graham's skill secure rely,
> For he was taught by me.

The fifth ode, entitled 'A Vision', contains the lines:

> Yet let not Graham unnotic'd pass away,
> Who, in her health, adds lustre to the day;
> Who, to the noon of aeth'ral knowledge run
> Its influence pours, diffusive like the sun
> To *all* its *subtle, genial* heat displays,
> Within the circle of its *fluid* rays;*
> New-strung her frame unnerv'd by sickness' reign,
> And gave elastic genius force to shine;
> Health to her body, vigour to her mind,
> With manly sense, and resolution join'd.

The other odes made reference to her history:

> Whose learned page, impartial, dares explain
> Each vice, or virtue, of each diff'rent reign

and again:

> Our annals thro' each varied line to trace,
> The Tudor, Norman, and the Saxon race;[57]

Perhaps the best of them was that written by Edmund Rack, who was described by Philip Thicknesse, author of the *New Prose Bath Guide* and no friend, as 'one of the creatures of Dr. Wilson, as well as one of the flatterers of Mrs. Macaulay'.[58] It was called 'An Irregular Ode':

> While in the mirror of th' historic page,
> Of BRITONS's woes she trac'd the springs,
> When haughty Stuarts scourg'd a venal age,
> Or Justice triumph'd o'er despotic Kings

It continues:

> To her capacious mind
> The clue of government unravel'd lies

---

* A philosophical, tho' figurative, disquisition of the qualities of Æther.

[57] Ibid., 29–30, 36–7, 18–19.
[58] *European Magazine*, 1 (1782), 361; *A Letter from Philip Thickskull, Esq. to Edmund Rack, A Quaker* (n.d.), 11.

In all its varying forms;
She explores its secret springs;
Tears off the mask, and brands with infamy
Those *self-created* powers usurp'd by Kings,
And *titled slaves of Kings*.

The evening ended with an ode beginning:

'Tis She, 'tis She, 'tis She!
The Child of Liberty!
To whom *Britannia* gave the prize,
Oh! Sound her triumph thro' the skies![59]

News of the celebrations soon spread. It did little to endear her to her real friends and provided just the ammunition her enemies wanted. Augustus Toplady heard from the Revd Dr Baker of St Martin's, Sarum, of 'the extravagant and ridiculous manner in which' her birthday was celebrated. It gave him, he wrote back, 'extreme disgust' and 'contributed to reduce my opinion of her magnanimity and good sense'. He thought 'such contemptible vanity, and such childish affectation of mock majesty, would have disgraced a much inferior understanding'. He vowed if he ever saw her again to 'rally her handsomely'.[60] 'Surely nothing ever equalled that farcical parade of foolery with which she suffered herself to be flattered, and almost worshipped by that poor old wrong-headed firebrand of party,' Elizabeth Carter wrote to Mrs Montagu. 'I think one never heard of anybody, above the degree of an idiot', she continued, 'who took pleasure in being so dressed out with the very rags and ribbons of vanity, like a queen in a puppet show.'[61] (See Pl. 11 for a satirical comment on her love of fashionable clothes and elaborate coiffures, and her habit of 'painting'.) Were the birthday celebrations the cause of Eliza Draper's comments in a letter to Miss Strange in 1777? 'I do not envy the Society of the celebrated Mrs. McCauley,' she wrote, 'for I begin to think that learned People are never seen to advantage but in their Works'.[62] Thicknesse, in *The New Prose Bath*

[59] *Six Odes*, 22, 25, 45.
[60] *The Works of Augustus Toplady*, 877.
[61] *Letters from Mrs. Elizabeth Carter to Mrs. Montagu*, ed. Revd Montagu Pennington, 3 vols. (1817), iii. 98.
[62] W. L. Sclater, 'Letters Addressed by Eliza Draper to the Strange Family, 1776–1778', *Notes and Queries*, 187 (1944), 27–33, at p. 32.

Guide for 1778, with smug self-righteousness, wrote that 'there is a certain Line beyond which, if Ridicule attempts to go, it becomes itself ridiculous', and again: 'if the Critic plays his Batteries on contemptible Objects, he must unavoidably depart from his proper Dignity, and must himself become an Object of the Raillery he would convey.' Yet Thicknesse could not resist giving a detailed account of the whole day's proceedings.[63]

How are we to explain Catharine's acceptance of 'that farcical parade of foolery'? For an intelligent and rational woman such behaviour seems curiously out of character. The initiative clearly came from Dr Wilson, but she was a passive if not eager participant, knew of the planned celebrations in advance, and apparently offered no resistance to the form they took. Rather then, as Elizabeth Carter expressed it, Wilson merely 'aided and abetted her eccentricities'.[64] But eccentricities they undoubtedly were. It was a depressing time for English radicals. The efforts they had made to persuade the administration to change its policies towards the American colonists had not prevented the outbreak of war. Americans' recognition of that failure had led to a turning away from any dependence on English radicalism. After the war broke out English radicals were left in sad disarray. Wilkes's gradual withdrawal from radical politics was disillusioning. It would be hardly surprising if Catharine Macaulay was depressed and suffering from 'dejection'. She must also have been aware that her period of fame was coming to an end. The preface to Volume VI of her *History* suggests how bitterly she felt her rejection by those who had earlier so enthusiastically praised her. There is a hint too of some personal hurt she had earlier received from a 'Mr. ——'s ingratitude and injustice' in a letter to her from Toplady in February 1774. Toplady had been amazed at her story and admitted had he heard it from anyone else, he would have 'questioned the reality of the fact'. Of the 'incident of which you so justly complain', he wrote advising her to 'forget it all, and, as you are more than female in understanding, be more than masculine in fortitude'. To let it prey on her mind was 'to do too much honour to the remembrance of a social delinquent'. He talked of 'the irritating savageness of the cynicism which has

---

[63] Philip Thicknesse, *The New Prose Bath Guide for the Year 1778* (1778), 65.
[64] *Letters from Mrs. Elizabeth Carter to Mrs. Montagu*, iii. 98.

requited you so ill', and suggested she oppose to it 'the iron apathy of the portico'.[65] From her willingness to confide in Toplady, it seems more likely to have been something to do with politics than an emotional involvement. What is revealed is how vulnerable this seemingly powerful and austere woman was to criticism. Behind a confident, indeed somewhat daunting, exterior was a very different, softer character. Surprisingly unsure of herself, she desperately needed encouragement and acceptance. It is a sign of her *naïveté* that rejection came to her as a surprise. Her shrewdness about the true nature of present-day Whigs did not extend to her abandonment by them after the use they had made of her earlier. She certainly felt this rejection keenly. Part of her constant illness in this period almost certainly reflected dejection of spirits. In such a situation even the petty acclaim of a handful of second-rate poets could have seemed preferable to none. She was too intelligent not to have seen it in retrospect for what it was, and despised herself for the role she had played. Part of her problem was that of all eighteenth-century women who won fame. They were ill prepared to cope with it, and the tension between their private and public lives must have imposed intolerable strain on them. The very nature of the apparent acclaim given to women was always ambivalent, the qualified praise barely concealing other far less attractive attitudes.

On 8 September 1777, Wilson was responsible for the erection of 'a superb white marble statue' of her 'in the chancel of the church of St. Stephen's, Walbrooke' (see Pl. 9).[66] Although Monkland attributed it to Bacon, the sculpture was the work of J. F. Moore. Earlier Wilson had employed him to make 'a monument to the memory of his wife'. Also placed in the chancel of his church at Walbrook, it is uncertain whether it was removed before the statue of Catharine was erected. One newspaper report described the later work as depicting her 'in the character of history, in a singular and pleasing antique style, and judged to be a good likeness; has a pen in her right hand apparently as if she had just finished some lines written on a scrole she holds in her left on which arm she leans on her five volumes of the *History of England*'. The lines ran:

---

[65] *The Works of Augustus Toplady*, 855.
[66] *Gentleman's Magazine*, 47 (1777), 458.

Government is a Power delegated for the Happiness of Mankind, when conducted by Wisdom, Justice and Mercy.

But the statue alone had not satisfied Dr. Wilson. Beneath the stone on which the statue stood was a white marble table, on one side of which was written in capitals:

You speak of Mrs. Macaulay;
She is a kind of prodigy.
I revere her abilities;
I cannot bear to hear her voice sarcastically mentioned;
I would have her taste the exalted pleasure of universal applause;
I would have statues erected to her memory;
And once in every age I could wish such a woman to appear
As a proof that genius is not confined to sex;
But at the same time—you will pardon me—
We want no more than
One Mrs. Macaulay.

This inscription, Wilson claimed, was an 'extract from the late Lord Lyttelton's letter to Mrs. Peach'.[67] Indeed, even the page-reference was given. Thomas Lyttelton (1744–79) had the reputation of a libertine. He married Mrs Peach in 1772 but soon deserted her for a barmaid. He is known to have written verses to Mrs Peach, but as he did not die until 1779 there does seem to have been some confusion in Wilson's reference to him.

The claim raised a furore of protest. A letter in the *Gentleman's Magazine* was 'confident that no such work exists'. Some letters had appeared earlier which were ascribed to him but 'their authenticity was positively disavowed ... by his Lordship's executors'. The writer was indignant at Wilson's claim 'especially as some passages in them [the letters] are very unworthy of his principles, and inconsistent with his known virtuous and religious principles'.[68] If Dr Wilson chose to erect a statue of Mrs Macaulay 'as high as that which Nebuchadnezzar placed on the plains of Dura', Elizabeth Carter told Mrs Montagu, 'nobody has any thing to do with it'. But, she went on, 'to choose his inscription from a book written by two nameless writers and then call these two

---

[67] George Monkland, *Supplement to the 'Literature and Literati of Bath'* (1885), 84; *The Gazetteer and New Daily Advertiser*, 10 Sept. 1777; John Thomas Smith, *Nollekens and His Times*, 2 vols. (1828), ii. 204.
[68] *Gentleman's Magazine*, 47 (1777), 470.

writers Lord Lyttelton and Mrs. Peach is such an instance of
absurdity and impertinence as one shall not often meet with'.[69]
But whatever doubt was thrown on the source of the inscription, it
remained. On the other side of the marble table was written
'Erected by Thomas Wilson, D.D. Rector of this Parish, as a
Testimony of the high Esteem he bears to the distinguished Merit
of his Friend, Catharine Macaulay. A.D. 1777.'[70]

The statue was erected in Wilson's church, it was later held, 'to
the scandal of the devout, the astonishment of the learned, and
the disgust of the Royalists among his congregation'.[71] Not
surprisingly the churchwardens were anything but pleased and the
'inhabitants of the parish thought the church was not a proper
place for *enthusiastic Party and politicks*'.[72] They must also have
felt their church was getting rather cluttered up with sculptures.
They sought legal advice on Wilson's right to erect the statue
within the church. It hinged on whether or not the area occupied
by it was, or was not, Wilson's freehold. The legal advice favoured
the Vestry, who in November, 1777, proceeded to write demanding that Wilson remove the statue 'on or before the 19th Day of
December next, Mrs. Macaulay never having been an inhabitant
of the parish'. When on 24 December no answer had come, a
further letter was sent warning Wilson that unless a satisfactory
answer was received within a month, the churchwardens would
'commence a suit' against him.[73] Still no answer was received.
The following July the Vestry Clerk was ordered to write to the
sculptor 'to know whether he had received instructions from
Wilson to move the statue'.[74] A month later the statue had not
been moved. The vestry minutes made no further reference to it.
In its obituary for Wilson in 1784, the *Gentleman's Magazine*
claimed it had been 'boarded up till her death by authority of the
spiritual court'.[75] Mrs Macaulay—it was reported—had wished to

[69] *Letters from Mrs. Elizabeth Carter to Mrs. Montagu*, iii. 40.
[70] *The Gazetteer and New Daily Advertiser*, 10 Sept. 1777.
[71] *Catalogue of the Grosvenor Gallery Exhibition of the Works of Thomas Gainsborough R.A.*, 93–4.
[72] *Gentleman's Magazine*, 61 (1791), 618.
[73] Robert Pierpoint, *Catharine Macaulay 'History': The Marble Statue in the Entrance Hall of Warrington Town Hall*, 2 parts (1908–10).
[74] *The Diaries of Thomas Wilson D.D.* (1964), 20n. 19.
[75] *Gentleman's Magazine*, 54 (1784), 317, but see below, p. 110, for a later counter-claim. The statue passed into the possession of Colonel John Wilson-Patten, afterwards Lord Winmarleigh (1802–92), MP for North Lancs., of Bank Hall,

return the compliment paid to her and planned to erect a statue of Wilson.[76] If such was her wish it was never fulfilled—or, wisely, she may have had second thoughts about it.

Despite the 'cure' of her ailments by Graham, Catharine Macaulay was still unwell. Her visit to France at the end of 1777, according to her own account, was undertaken because of ill health. The letter she wrote to Lord Harcourt on her return is that of a very sick woman obsessed by continued ill health. Three months after her return from Paris, Wilkes dined at Alfred House and found 'poor Kitty Macaulay, the grave, dull, Catharine' looking ill.[77] Edmund Rack in a letter dated 2 May 1778 wrote that 'Mrs Macaulay's health is but indifferent'.[78] 'Poor Mrs. Macaulay, like General Burgoyne', wrote the *St. James's Chronicle* three months later, 'hallooed before she was out of the wood, for all her Complaints are returned as bad as ever.'[79]

Her time at Alfred House had been brief. It was in October 1776 at the earliest that she moved there; less than two years later she had left Bath for good. In that time, it was said, Dr Wilson had 'rendered himself, and afterwards the lady truly ridiculous, by the unaccountable frolicks of his attachment'.[80] In the light of subsequent happenings it is interesting to find that before she ever came to share Wilson's house, Catharine Macaulay had received a warning about her relations with the 'doctor'. It came from Augustus Toplady, in a letter dated 18 February 1774. 'Let me submit a single caution to your candour,' he wrote, 'be careful not to renew your acquaintance with the dapper doctor; and above all, beware of being seen with him in public.' Toplady was not content to let the subject rest there. He went on to spell out his fears for her. 'He would derive lustre from you,' he wrote, 'but,

Warrington. Dr Wilson had married Mary Patten, his first cousin. When he died, Wilson's property was inherited by Thomas Patten (1770–1827), a child at the time. The statue seems to have been sent to Bank Hall, at that time the home of Colonel Wilson-Patten's grandfather. When in 1872 he sold Bank Hall to the corporation to be converted into the Town Hall, he gave the statue to the town. For years it stood in the entrance to the Town Hall, but in 1964 was moved to outside the public library, where it can still be seen. See Pierpoint, *Catharine Macaulay 'History'*.

[76] *The Gazetteer and New Daily Advertiser*, 10 Sept. 1777.

[77] *Letters from the Year 1774 to the Year 1796 of John Wilkes, Esq., Addressed to His Daughter, the Late Miss Wilkes*, 4 vols. (1804), ii. 93.

[78] Polwhele, *Traditions and Recollections*, i. 115.

[79] *St. James's Chronicle*, No. 2720 (20 Aug. 1778).

[80] *European Magazine and London Review*, 4 (1783), 332.

like a piece of black cloth, he would absorb the rays, without reflecting any of them back'.[81] He went on to warn her that the world was malicious and as her fame had made her conspicuous she should be careful to avoid any behaviour likely to attract attention. There has been some uncertainty over the identification of the 'doctor'. Toplady's description could fit either Dr Wilson or Dr Graham. Graham, we know, habitually dressed in black. He was certainly interested in using Catharine Macaulay's fame for purposes of self-promotion. But Professor Donnelly assumed it was Dr Wilson, and the date of the letter from Toplady supports such a thesis.[82] For as far as we know James Graham only returned from America in 1774 and only started practising in Bath in 1777. After his return to England there would have been very little time—if any—for him to have met Catharine Macaulay and for his acquaintance with her to have been known to Toplady. Toplady was warning her against Wilson. As we shall see in the next chapter the warning was timely, but, alas, Catharine Macaulay failed to heed it until too late.

Postscript

There are times when biographers wish they could ignore part of their subjects' lives. Some of them of course do. But many today tend rather to lay bare every aspect, however unsavoury or belittling, of the lives of their subjects, to reveal all the dirty washing, leaving no bone of a skeleton in the cupboard. Nobody suggests because a man is an insufferable, arrogant, mean bastard, he cannot also be a great poet. Where Catharine Macaulay is concerned there is a strong temptation to gloss over events of the Bath period, more particularly the 46th-birthday charade. In an attempt to have Catharine Macaulay, her history, republicanism, and radicalism taken seriously, why does she have to frustrate her biographer's designs by behaving in such a manner? It would be wrong to give in to the temptation of skipping certain episodes of her life. If she is to attract serious study and gain historians' respect she has to be seen as a whole, however embarrassing some

---

[81] *Works of Augustus Toplady*, 855.

[82] Lucy Martin Donnelly, 'The Celebrated Mrs. Macaulay', *William and Mary Quarterly*, 3rd ser., 6(ii) (1949), 172–207, at p. 184; Daisy Hobman, 'Mrs Macaulay', *The Fortnightly*, 171 (1952), 116–21, at p. 117.

parts may be, and made sense of. Yet a nagging doubt lingers that while the private lives of men are rarely allowed to interfere with their public worth, where women are concerned it is different. Today it may be less different than it was in the eighteenth century but the fact that it is a woman writing history or political polemic is never lost sight of. Consciously or unconsciously it comes between what she writes and the male reader, reviewer, or critic. If being a woman affects the judgement of her work, it is difficult to imagine incidents in her life will be ignored and will not also intrude in any evaluation of her importance and influence.

5. *After the Second Marriage, 1778–1791*

Last week was married at Leicester, the celebrated
Historian, Mrs. Catharine Macaulay, to the younger brother
of the still more celebrated Dr. Graham.

(Extract from a letter from Bath, 27 November, in *The
London Evening-Post*, Saturday, 28 November to Tuesday,
1 December 1778)

IF, after her marriage to William Graham, Catharine Macaulay
ever returned to Bath, it is not recorded. It seems unlikely. She
may have turned her back on what had been, both in her personal
and public life, a disastrous period. What first persuaded her
to accept Dr Wilson's offer to share his house? Although later
Wilson hinted that she was after his money, it is impossible to
accept that this was her motive. It was not as though she had
nowhere to live. On her move to Bath in 1774, she had set up
house at St James's Parade. Nothing of what we know of her way
of life in London suggests she was in anything but very comfortable circumstances. Her brother, with whom she had close relations, was very rich. In seeking to explain her acceptance of
Wilson's offer, it is perhaps relevant that her first marriage had
been to a man fifteen years older than herself. Motherless from
infancy, and with a father who had little interest in his children,
her life as a child and young woman must have been singularly
lonely. George Macaulay may have provided the father-figure she
sought. To be deprived of his devoted, kindly, and encouraging
presence in 1766 left her after only six years of marriage facing
the same dilemma again. The role of a widow, and a widow with a
comfortable fortune, cannot have been without its problems. She
was ill-prepared to face them. Her daughter was still a child.
Was she besieged by predatory male admirers anxious to marry
her? Did she feel a need to protect herself from them, while at
the same time providing a substitute father for her daughter—
someone to share the responsibilities of parenthood? If she had
such feelings they almost certainly increased when she moved to
Bath. Continued ill health exacerbated them.

When Wilson made his offer it may have seemed like a miraculous answer to her problems. She, and her brother John, had known him for some time. Indeed one report suggested it was her brother who was responsible for introducing Wilson to her.[1] Catharine and John shared political sympathies, and were active participants in London radical and Wilkite politics. After the split between Sawbridge and Wilkes in 1771, despite a later reconciliation, relations between them were never again to be close. Sawbridge may have had reservations about Wilson's continued loyalty to Wilkes, and viewed with misgiving his growing friendship with Catharine. Both could have contributed to a certain cooling of relations between brother and sister, at least for a time.

References to Polly Wilkes in Wilson's letters to her father suggest an avuncular, playful character genuinely fond of children.[2] His only child, a boy, had died of smallpox when barely 1 year old. It had been the great tragedy in what appears to have been a happy marriage until the death of his wife in 1772.[3] He seemed ideally suited to Catharine's needs. Naïvely, she gratefully accepted his offer without considering its implications and inherent dangers.

Given the outcry against her behaviour when she married Graham, it is extraordinary there was not more gossip about her relations with Wilson when she moved into Alfred House. But there was no suggestion of any impropriety in her behaviour except retrospectively, and particularly after her marriage to William Graham. How is this to be explained? Was it the great discrepancy in their ages, or was Wilson seen as so old and senile he could not occupy the role of lover? When first she woke up to the situation she was in we do not know. By the time she left for Paris in the autumn of 1777, only a few months after the charade of her 46th birthday, she was very well aware of her problem. Was the illness that provoked her journey to France entirely divorced from that awareness? Almost certainly not. By that time the

---

[1] Mary Hays, *Female Biography*, 6 vols. (1803), v. 304.

[2] See e.g. *The Correspondence of the Late John Wilkes with His Friends*, ed. J. Almon, 5 vols. (1805), iv. 47, 52.

[3] *The Diaries of Thomas Wilson D.D.*, ed. C. L. S. Linnell (1964), 10. Together with the diaries, which cover the periods 1731–7 and 1750, there were also four volumes of Wilson's correspondence, potentially a most valuable source, in the possession of Keble College, Oxford, but unfortunately those covering the relevant period have been lost.

possessive protectiveness of Wilson could have become stifling. Wilson's extravagant worship of her may have begun to cloy. If this was the cost of protection, might it be better to turn her back on the haven of Alfred House? Whatever she found in William Graham, it was not a father-figure. Her absence from Bath for two months after her return from France was perhaps the only way she saw of escaping from an intolerable situation. The dedication of the *History of England from the Revolution to the Present Time* (1778) to Wilson did not help. When it was reviewed, the *Critical Review* could not resist mentioning 'the mutual sympathy so conspicuous between these Platonic lovers', and quoted the dedication in order that 'readers may judge of Mrs. Macaulay's impartiality and discernment, qualifications so essentially requisite in a faithful writer of history'.[4] The public did not forget the exaggerated nature of Wilson's attachment to her. There was more charade to come: the birthday celebrations were followed by Wilson's placing of her statue in St Stephen's Church, Walbrook.

As Wilson grew increasingly besotted with her, Alfred House became 'our little Tusculum which is honoured with the visits of all the Literary Persons who frequent this place; and forreigners particularly, for she is known and admired abroad more than at home'. To his friend Philip Moore, Wilson wrote of 'the *great* Mrs. Macaulay—I talk of her to everybody in raptures. The brilliancy of her eyes is gone in a great measure, but her mind is as elevated as ever.' He described her as 'my *great* woman—the *first* woman in Europe for Virtues and Shining Literary Abilities.' He was daily becoming more senile. Frequently ill, he 'was inclined to be hypochondriacal, and, as the years increased upon him, not a little cantankerous.' For the last ten years of his life he was 'more or less an invalid the whole of the time'.[5] In April 1778 Wilkes described him as 'half gone . . . it would scarcely be a sin to bury him as he is'.[6]

The *Gentleman's Magazine* of the 17 December 1778 recorded the marriage of 'the celebrated historian Mrs. Macaulay, to the younger brother of Dr. Graham'.[7] Significantly, the name of her

[4] *The Critical Review*, 45 (1778), 131.
[5] *The Diaries of Thomas Wilson*, 6, 17, 18, 19.
[6] *Letters from the Year 1774 to the Year 1796 of John Wilkes, Esq., Addressed to His Daughter, the Late Miss Wilkes*, ed. Sir W. Rough, 4 vols. (1804), ii. 84.
[7] *The Gentleman's Magazine*, 48 (1778), 606.

husband was omitted. He was, after all, a nonentity whose only claim to a mention lay in the two celebrities with whom he was connected. At the time of their marriage William Graham was described as a 'surgeon's mate'.[8] He was 21 while Catharine Macaulay was 47. (See Pl. 8 for a satirical comment on the marriage.) Was the marriage the result of a sudden decision on her part? Dr Wilson certainly thought so. 'To the great surprise of the world', he wrote, 'Mrs. Macaulay without giving me the slightest notice at the age of 52 married a YOUNG SCOTCH LOON of 21 whom she had not seen for above a month before the fatal knot was tied.' Although he had been the organizer of her 46th-birthday celebrations the previous year, he had either forgotten her age or deliberately exaggerated it. She had left Alfred House at the beginning of October 1778 'on the pretence of the health of her sister at Leicester whose Husband keeps a mad house'.[9] This 'sister' was Mrs Arnold, Catharine Macaulay's future sister-in-law. Even before Catharine married her brother, a close friendship had developed between them. Mrs Arnold accompanied her to France in 1777. After the marriage the friendship continued until Catharine Macaulay's death. Mrs Arnold was the wife of a distinguished physician and writer on insanity, Dr Thomas Arnold (1742–94). Born in Leicester, he was educated in Edinburgh. He became a fellow of the Royal College of Physicians, and of the Royal Medical Society of Edinburgh. At first he practised in Leicester, where he was described as 'deservedly popular' and later became the owner and director of a large lunatic asylum there.[10] Significantly, at this stage Dr Wilson made no mention of Dr James Graham.

Wilson emphasized in his diary and correspondence that Catharine had married beneath her. Graham was only 'a mate to an East India Ship without clothes on his back'. The Grahams were 'a most beggarly Family in Edinburgh. How are the mighty fallen.'[11] In the *St James's Chronicle* there appeared a letter from Bath suggesting that by the marriage the bridegroom 'has now got, *he thinks, a better Birth*'.[12] But if William Graham was so

[8] *Dictionary of National Biography.*
[9] *The Diaries of Thomas Wilson*, 19.
[10] *Gentleman's Magazine*, 86 (1816), 378.
[11] *The Diaries of Thomas Wilson*, 19.
[12] *St James's Chronicle*, No. 2763 (28 Nov. 1778).

'beggarly', Catharine Macaulay was seemingly indifferent to his
fortune. Whatever her reason for marrying him it was not for
money.

The marriage was the focus of a scandal that reverberated far
beyond Bath. Accounts in the press make it difficult to get at the
truth. Most relied on reports from Bath and only repeated current
rumours. Shortly after Catharine Macaulay's return from Paris,
Wilkes confided to his daughter that it was his opinion and
'that of the generality of Mrs. M——'s friends, that her head is
affected'. This and 'some indiscretion with Dr. G—— are the
common topics of conversation'. Just after her marriage he wrote
that Dr Wilson was now 'thoroughly convinced *from facts* of
the lady's former intimacy with Dr. ——, and he thinks her a
monster'. A few days later he writes again of a letter 'from Mr.
S—— [presumably her brother John Sawbridge] to the Doctor, in
which he gives an account of finding his sister and Dr. —— at
breakfast, at Canterbury, in a matrimonial way'. According to
Wilkes's informant, Mr S—— seized the Doctor 'by the collar,
turned him down stairs, and told him that if he did not immediately return to London, he would shoot him through the
head'. Sawbridge accused his sister of being 'so abandoned a
woman, Miss —— [presumably her daughter, Catherine Sophia]
should not stay with her, and that he would take care of her'.
Wilkes added that Sawbridge 'had forgiven her at that time'.[13]
'She consulted the noted Dr. Graham upon the state of her
health', wrote John Taylor, 'and the doctor, who knew that she
had money, contrived to introduce his brother to her as a better
adviser than himself.'[14] Philip Thicknesse in 1780 suggested that
she had 'married out of gratitude to the doctor for health, and
other favours'.[15]

Through all the rumpus that followed her departure from
Alfred House Catharine Macaulay remained silent. She cannot
have been unaware of the rumours circulating about her relations
with Dr James Graham and Wilson, but she made no attempt to
answer them. In April 1778 Wilkes had written of a new caricature 'of her and the Doctor' which had 'vexed her to the heart'

[13] *Letters from the Year 1774 to the Year 1796 of John Wilkes Esq.*, ii. 76, 115, 126, 127.
[14] John Taylor, *Records of My Life*, 2 vols. (1832), i. 209.
[15] Philip Thicknesse, *The Valetudinarian's Bath Guide* (1780), 7.

(see Darly's cartoon, Pl. 11).[16] Wilson vowed she would never again be given entrance to Alfred House.[17] According to the poem 'The Female Patriot' published in 1779, soon after the marriage she announced her intention of bringing her new husband to visit Wilson.[18] It could be seen as evidence of her *naïveté* that she ever proposed such a visit. On 28 November it was reported that 'the late Mrs. Catherine Macaulay (now Mrs. Graham) with her *Spousy*, is expected at the Door of Dr. Wilson tomorrow at Ten'.[19] But such a visit 'was so far from being acceptable to Wilson, that immediately the brazen plate of her name was removed from the door, and the Doctor substituted in its place'.[20]

After all the vain attempts of his parishioners to get Wilson to take the statue of Catharine from their church, now he immediately removed it and sold the vault intended for her remains. A correspondent of the *Gentleman's Magazine* in 1791 was unwilling to commit himself as to 'whether the Doctor was instigated to do so from motives of revenge, because she married Dr. Graham, or whether from fear, because the vestry was just upon citing him in the commons'.[21] According to Wilkes, Wilson busied himself removing every trace of Mrs Macaulay's former presence. All the servants she had recommended to him were discharged, while 'the old servant, whom she hated, and ineffectually often urged him to discharge is now in high favour'. Wilson admitted Alfred House was legally her property. But, Wilkes wrote, he 'detains it by the advice of *three* lawyers, till she reimburses him the immense sums he had paid on her account'. 'During about two months absence from Bath', one story went, 'this Lady drew Bills on her Friend, the old Doctor, for the Benefit of the young one, to the amount of Six Hundred Pounds.'[22] It was rumoured that 'a suit in Chancery' was 'commenced between the parties'. According to Wilson the sums she owed him amounted to 'twice

---

[16] *Letters from the Year 1774 to the Year 1796 of John Wilkes Esq.*, ii. 93. The caricaturist was Matthew Darly (*fl.* 1778), who for a time lived in Bath.

[17] *The Diaries of Thomas Wilson*, 19.

[18] *The Female Patriot: An Epistle from C—t—e M—c—y to the Reverend Dr. W—l—n on Her Late Marriage* (1779), 6 n.

[19] *St. James's Chronicle*, No. 2764 (1 Dec. 1778).   [20] *The Female Patriot*, 6 n.

[21] *Gentleman's Magazine*, 61 (1791), 618.

[22] *Letters from the Year 1774 to the Year 1796 of John Wilkes Esq.*, ii. 115–16.

the value of the house'.[23] Such debts had been incurred through her use of 'paper, pins, pomatum, and parchment'.[24] She must have gone through a lot if its value was what Wilson claimed! In May 1779 Wilson's legacy to her of £15,000 was cancelled, and 'a new will revoking all gifts, etc. to "Catherine Graham, formerly Macaulay"' was made.[25]

In January 1779, No. 2 Alfred Street, according to Wilkes, was in a state of considerable disorder. 'Mrs. ——'s woman' had returned to fetch her mistress's clothes and other possessions. The old Doctor 'with the aid of a patriotic bookseller' was occupied in sorting out his own books from hers, while his male servants looked out her clothes. No letter had come for the Doctor from Mrs Macaulay—merely a written order for her clothes and books. The Doctor had even refused to see Mrs Macaulay's woman. She went away with all Mrs Macaulay's clothes, but the books remained at Alfred House 'packed in four large boxes to be sent by the next waggon'.[26]

When a few days after her marriage Wilkes visited Alfred House, Wilson had read aloud 'her *long* letter' to him, which according to Wilkes contained 'every variety of style, it is indecent, insolent, mean, fawning, threatening, coaxing, menacing, and declamatory. Such words I believe never escaped a female pen.'[27] 'To explain to Wilson why she married the Scotchman', a later comment suggested, was 'the most foolish thing she did'.[28] Thicknesse talked of a letter she had written to Wilson—'her dear friend'—in which she 'assigned her reasons (and they were very strong ones) for the *slip* she had taken'.[29] Five years after the event, the *European Magazine* reported a rumour that 'some attempt had been made by her to defend the step she had taken' and that 'she entered into a formal vindication of herself'.[30] On Christmas Day, 1778, Wilkes told Polly there was still hope of this

[23] Ibid. 116.
[24] *The Female Patriot*, 6 n.
[25] Robert Pierpoint, *Catharine Macaulay 'History': The Statue in the Warrington Town Hall*, 2 parts (1908–10), ii. 10.
[26] *Letters from the Year 1774 to the Year 1796 of John Wilkes, Esq.*, ii. 142.
[27] Ibid. 115.
[28] R. E. Peach, *Historic Houses in Bath* (1883), 118.
[29] Thicknesse, *The Valetudinarian's Bath Guide*, 7.
[30] *The European Magazine and London Review*, 4 (1783), 334.

letter being published. He added that 'as she complains loudly of the Doctor as having treated her unkindly' he had pressed Wilson to 'let her tell her own story to the world, which would be his full justification'.[31] In September 1779 he confirmed that Mrs Macaulay's Bath publisher, Cruttwell, under Wilson's directions, had agreed to publish 'several letters of Mrs. M—— to the doctor and Dr. G.——' including 'her celebrated letter to the Doctor just before her marriage'. He thought some passages of her letter to Dr Graham 'too gross for the public eye'. Whether or not Wilkes intended to draw a distinction between the public and private eye, it was an extraordinary accusation coming from the distributor of *An Essay on Woman*; he seems to have had no such qualms about publishing the 'indecent' letter Catharine Macaulay is said to have written to Wilson. It is even more extraordinary since the letter referred to was published by James Graham in 1781 and is merely an account of the symptoms of her illness and their response to Graham's cure (see Ch. 4). Was it her reference to stomach pains he found offensive? All these letters, Wilkes claimed, had been saved from the fire by a maid.[32]

On 1 January 1780 Polly Wilkes, perhaps with more sympathy than her father for the situation of her friend, wrote of Dr Wilson's determination 'to publish the letters'. She expressed the hope that those 'in which Mrs. M. is mentioned could be omitted', for, as she added 'there would remain quite enough to answer his purpose'.[33] What was his purpose? The letters had been advertised, presumably on Wilson's initiative, as 'An authentic narrative of the conduct and behaviour of Mrs. M——y now Mrs. M——y G——m during her residence at A——d house, B—h; containing a succinct and faithful history of the extraordinary means made use of by that lady to obtain such a profusion of expensive gifts from her benevolent patron the Rev. Dr. W——n.' The advertisement claimed that from the time of 'her acquaintance with Dr. James G——m' her behaviour had changed. Also to be included in this threatened publication was an account of 'her intimacy and friendship for Mrs. A., sister to the empiric, her journey to Paris with occurrences there, her journey to Leicester and her marriage . . . with all the original letters, notes

---

[31] *Letters from the Year 1774 to the Year 1796 of John Wilkes Esq.*, ii. 122.
[32] Ibid. 165–6.
[33] *The Correspondence of the late John Wilkes with his Friends*, iv. 294.

and anecdotes'. To this narrative was to be joined 'a dissertation on swindling'.

Wilson's determination to publish such a document is revealing. His reaction to her marriage has been compared to that of Johnson on Mrs Thrale's marriage to Gabriel Piozzi. An earlier incident in his life suggests he was capable of passionate and uncontrolled resentment. In 1758 a quarrel broke out between Wilson and the headmaster of Westminster school. Earlier, Wilson had bought a house adjoining the Old Dormitory, intending to repair and live in it. He had also purchased two other houses nearby with the intention of demolishing them and creating a garden for himself. The headmaster, however, wanted to use the site for extending the school accommodation. Although the Dean and Chapter had approved the headmaster's plans, Wilson was 'almost apoplectic with rage', and went to law over the business.[34] He claimed, although with what justice it is difficult to say, that by the decision 'many hundred *innocent* and *industrious* Families' would lose their homes and their work. Only as an apparent afterthought does he ask 'what Amends can be made to any Gentleman who has laid out his Money on a favourite Spot of Ground ... who has been at a great additional Expence in removing every Incumbrance about it; and ... fitted up every Part of his Habitation to his own peculiar Taste'.[35] He lost the case, but before it ever came to law he wrote a pamphlet on the subject. It was prefaced by the text from Micah 2: 2: 'And they covet Fields, and take them by Violence; and Houses, and take them away: So they oppress a Man and his House, even a Man and his Heritage.' On one copy he had written in his own hand that it was an 'instance of Cruelty, Bribery, Lying, and Corruption'. The petitioners had been solely motivated by personal gain.[36] It is an example of his growing truculence as age and ill health overtook him. 'His love', wrote Wilkes of his feelings for Catharine Macaulay, 'seems turned to rage and hatred.' Wilson now referred to her as the 'modern Messalina' and claimed she had seriously planned for Dr James Graham to keep house for the happy couple, adding that 'it could not have lasted long, for she would

---

[34] *The Diaries of Thomas Wilson*, 13–14, 17.
[35] Thomas Wilson, *A Review of the Project for Building a New Square at Westminster* (1757), vii, 43.
[36] Ibid., preface; *The Diaries of Thomas Wilson*, 14 n. 9.

have *poisoned* him . . . and forged a will in her own favour'. Three years after her marriage, Wilkes found Wilson still 'so full of vexation' he was thinking 'of selling everything and settling in America for a time'.[37]

In December 1779 Wilkes told Polly of how a 'Mr. B——' some time before had written 'an abusive letter to Dr. ——'. 'Mr. B' was the Revd Dr Baker, Vicar of St Martin's, Sarum, a close friend and correspondent of Augustus Toplady. There is no doubt that Wilson was the recipient of Baker's letter. In it Baker accused 'the Doctor with being the cause of all the misconduct of Mrs. ——', and as Wilkes made clear, it was to Catharine Macaulay that Baker referred. The Doctor, Wilkes added, 'did not deign to reply', although the letter was to have been included in the correspondence Wilson intended to publish.[38] It is an interesting sequel to Toplady's earlier warnings to Mrs Macaulay against 'the dapper doctor'.[39] At the time of the marriage, Wilson had been annoyed that newspapers had been 'very free' with his character. But, he insisted, those that knew him ('the better part of mankind'), and everyone at Bath, took his side. If Catharine had as much as shown her face in Bath, she would have been mobbed 'for her ingratitude' to him. He had taken her into his 'protection upon her Publick Character, and it could not be for any other motive'. He may have felt safe making such a claim retrospectively, but at the same time and quite gratuitously he added that a certain Sir Richard Brooke decided not to remarry when his wife died: 'I am sure it will be the better for him, for the women are all gone stark staring MADD and when I see such a woman as Mrs. Macaulay make one of the number, with the finest tongue and greatest mental faculties, what must we think? We must call it EPIDEMICAL.'[40]

'He would derive lustre from you', Toplady had written to Catharine Macaulay earlier.[41] If Wilson never considered marrying her, he may have wanted the distinction of sheltering such a woman under his roof. Once the marriage had taken place the only way to preserve his pride—and 'the doctor's vanity . . . is

[37] *Letters from the Year 1774 to the Year 1796 of John Wilkes Esq.*, ii. 116, 130, 135, 229.
[38] Ibid. 184.
[39] *The Works of Augustus Toplady* (1853), 855.
[40] *The Diaries of Thomas Wilson*, 19.
[41] *The Works of Augustus Toplady*, 855.

1. 'Catharina Macaulay', engraving by G. B. Cipriani after
J. Basire, 1767. Used as the frontispiece of Volume III of
her *History*.

2. 'Catharine Macaulay', mezzotint by
J. Spilsbury after C. Read, 1764.

3. 'Catharine Macaulay', oil-painting now attributed to Robert Edge Pine, *c.*1774.

opposite page:
(*above*) 4. 'Catharine Macaulay', by or after Mason Chamberlain, *c.*1774.

(*below*) 5. 'The Nine Living Muses of Great Britain', oil-painting by Richard Samuel. Catharine Macaulay is seated below the statue holding a scroll.

MME. MACAULAY

Histoire d'Angleterre. Gravé par Marais le jeune

(*above*) 6. 'Mme Macaulay, Histoire d'Angleterre', engraving by Marais le jeune.

(*below*) 7. 'Olanteigh', engraving from W. S. Morris, *History and Topography of Wye* (1842), facing p. 42.

Opposite page:
(*above*) 8. 'The *Auspicious* Marriage!', *Town and Country Magazine,* 10 (1778), 623.

(*below*) 9. Statue of Catharine Macaulay as 'History' by J. F. Moore, 1778. Now standing outside the public library at Warrington.

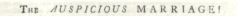

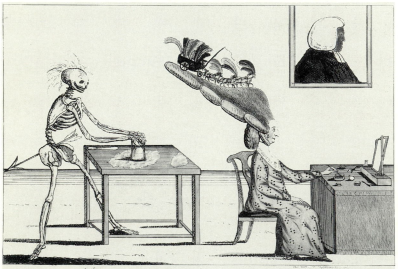

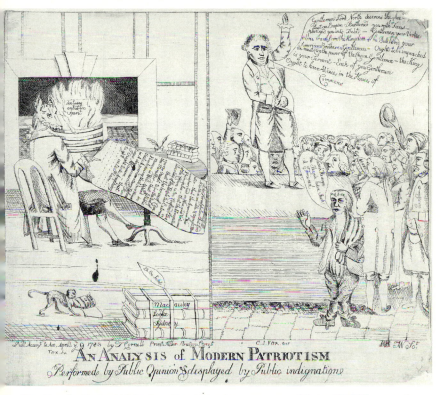

12. 'An Analysis of Modern Patriotism', a cartoon of 9 April 1783, a week after the formation of a coalition between Fox and North, illustrating how the attitude of Charles James Fox to Catharine Macaulay's writings and reform changed according as he was in or out of office. Once in office reform is rejected and her works, together with those of Locke and Sidney, are tied up for sale.

opposite page:
(*above*) 10. 'The Revd. Thomas Wilson and his adopted daughter Miss Macaulay, daughter of Catharine Macaulay', oil-painting by Joseph Wright, 1776. The incorrect identification above the girl's head is a later addition.

(*below*) 11. 'A Speedy Effectual Preparation for the Next World', cartoon by Matthew Darly, 1777.

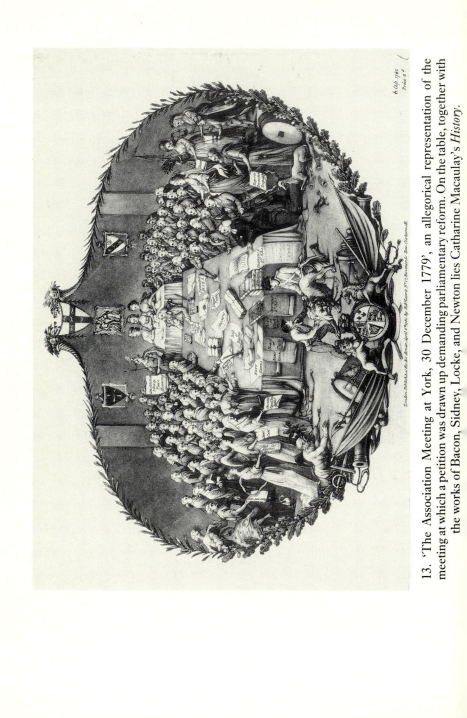

13. 'The Association Meeting at York, 30 December 1779', an allegorical representation of the meeting at which a petition was drawn up demanding parliamentary reform. On the table, together with the works of Bacon, Sidney, Locke, and Newton lies Catharine Macaulay's *History*.

among ... his prevailing passions'—was to show that Catharine Macaulay had never been distinguished, and her 'Publick Character' was undeserved. This presented Wilson with no problems. By early January 1779, he had had 'time to find out, that her late History' was 'very false and incorrect'![42] There was almost certainly some truth in the *Town and Country Magazine*'s claim that with increasing age Wilson had some difficulty in 'keeping pace with her in all her operations and researches'. He was 'frequently obliged to have recourse to his library, through a failure of memory'.[43]

If such a 'performance' as Wilson threatened to make public ever existed, it was suppressed. In December 1779 Wilkes wrote that publication had been held up for 'S—— [Sawbridge] is expected to propose terms to stop the intended publication of certain letters'. Yet a few days later he mentioned that 'part is already printed'.[44] Whether or not any such letters appeared in print, apart from Catharine Macaulay's letter to James Graham none have survived although, as the *European Magazine* admitted, such a publication 'would probably excite the public curiosity as much as anything which has fallen from her pen'. It was 'the prudence of friends' which had 'influenced the conduct of both parties, much to the credit of each'.[45] Nevertheless it did not prevent the publication in 1779 of three scurrilous, satirical pamphlets—two of them based on the letter it was rumoured she had written to Wilson.[46] *A Remarkable Moving Letter* claimed she wrote it 'to combat the prejudices of a respectable and reverend Friend'.[47] Both assume her relationship with Wilson was only one of friendship and mutual respect; in both she addresses Wilson as 'my parent' or 'my honour'd parent'.[48] In *The Female Patriot* she appeals to Wilson to remember

> Our correspondent sympathy of breast;
> Where friendship's flame unsullied by desire

[42] *Letters from the Year 1774 to the year 1796 of John Wilkes, Esq.*, ii. 125.
[43] *Town and Country Magazine*, 3 (1771), 683.
[44] *Letters from the Year 1774 to the Year 1796 of John Wilkes, Esq.*, ii. 178, 184.
[45] *European Magazine*, 4 (1783), 334.
[46] *The Female Patriot* (1779); *A Remarkable Moving Letter, which was Suggested by an Extraordinary Epistle Sent by Her on Her Second Marriage to Her Clerical Admirer* (1779); *A Bridal Ode on the Marriage of Catherine and Petruchio* (1779).
[47] *A Remarkable Moving Letter*, 4, prefatory advertisement.
[48] *The Female Patriot*, 7; *A Remarkable Moving Letter*, 5, 6.

> Shone holy lambent with seraphick fire;
> Nor e'er that boist'rous tyrant dar'd to thrust,
> Which maids call Love, but which Immortals, Lust.

In *A Remarkable Moving Letter*, she is insistent that

> Parent thou wert,—A widow's wants denied
> Thy feeble Holiness should call me bride.—

but had Wilson been younger their political sympathies might have led to love:

> Hadst thou possess'd (shame checks my falt'ring pen)
> The pow'rs that Heav'n allots to younger men,
> My frailer nature had not dar'd to rove,
> But politics had paved the road of love.[49]

Both pamphlets assumed the marriage signalled the end of her career as historian and politician:

> Let Hamden, Sidney, Sawbridge, be forgot!
> Let patriotick thunders cease to roll,
> And tune to metre my Historick soul.[50]

The same view was taken by the author of the *Bridal Ode*, who saw the marriage as marking the end of her writing:

> Farewell the plumed Pen and Ink!
> Which made *Taxation's Champion* shrink;
>   Here faithful *Hist'ry* ends.
> *Britain* must to her *Centre* shake!
> For such a Loss, how can Love make
>   Poor *Dilly's* Types Amends?
>
> Our *Grievances* who can express
> With equal Nerve? With like Address
>   Paint all a Lady's Fears?
> The Edge of *Opposition* whet?
> Who with such glowing Diction set
>   Three kingdoms by the Ears?[51]

Wilson was uncertain. 'Whether she will exercise her Talents any more', he wrote, 'is impossible to tell.'[52]

---

[49] *The Female Patriot*, 7; *A Remarkable Moving Letter*, 6.
[50] *The Female Patriot*, 8.
[51] *A Bridal Ode* (1779), 7.
[52] *The Diaries of Thomas Wilson*, 19.

A successful farce *A Widow—No Widow* was staged at the Haymarket in July 1779, in which both Dr Wilson and Catharine Macaulay figured. The playwright was Richard Paul Jodrell, almost certainly the author of *The Female Patriot*. The heroine, Mrs Sharp, posing as a rich widow, attempts to extort money from her several admirers in order to go off on the proceeds to 'a safe harbour' with a Captain O'Kite. One of her admirers is Dr Alfred, referred to as Mrs Sharp's 'politician'. Mrs Sharp expresses her fear that he is 'one of those gay old gentlemen, who, the older they grow, the more wicked they are'. Once married, he 'will keep a naughty girl'. Did he not 'maintain Mrs. Roundhead—keep her a coach, and treat her as [his] wife'?

> *Doctor* That was only to be popular.
> *Mrs. Sharp* And most probably you will be popular again.
> *Doctor* No, no:——she has chang'd her Doctor now . . . Indeed, she wou'd never have done for me—she talked so furiously about a change of men and measures, that she quite overcame me.—So, my dear widow, I have given her up. . . . She wanted to turn me out of my own house . . . she never thought of any thing but the Revolution.[53]

What most scandalized people about her marriage to William Graham was not only that she had married beneath her, but the discrepancy in their ages. 'It is said the young Gentleman is near one and twenty Years of Age', reported the *St. James's Chronicle*, 'the Bride is some Years older than her Brother the Patriot'. She had married 'a young Stripling School-Boy', and by so doing 'was considered to have lowered herself in public estimation'.[54] Later Robert Chambers remarked how 'the disparity of their years exposed her to much ridicule'.[55] *A Bridal Ode* of 1779 made a point of emphasizing her age and the risks involved in older women marrying young lads. 'I should not have thought it strange if Mrs. Macaulay had crossed the Atlantic to marry some arch rebel or even the descendant of a regicide,' wrote Mrs Montagu to Elizabeth Carter, 'but to unite herself with a boy and a Scotch boy is quite out of the path of such a comet.' To Mrs Thrale she

---

[53] Richard Paul Jodrell, *A Widow—No Widow* (1780), 58, 60. The poem *The Female Patriot* was included in *The Poetical Works of P. R. P. Jodrell* (1814).

[54] *St. James's Chronicle*, No. 2673 (28 Nov. 1778); George Monkland, *The Literature and Literati of Bath* (1854), 33.

[55] Robert Chambers, *The Book of Days*, 2 vols. (1863–4), i. 810.

wrote that by choosing 'a surgeon's mate aged 22' Mrs Macaulay had substituted Venus for the chaste Minerva. It was 'both passing strange & wondrous pittiful!'[56] Horace Walpole told the Countess of Ossory that 'Dame Thucydides' had 'made but an uncouth match'.[57] 'Poor Mrs. Macaulay!', Edmund Rack wrote to Polwhele. 'She is irrecoverably fallen. *Frailty thy name is woman*'. 'Her passions, even at 52, were too strong for her reason; and she has taken to bed a stout brawny Scotchman of 21. For shame!'[58] John Taylor thought she married Graham 'at a time of life when she ought to have been wiser, and then lost all her historical reputation.'[59] Such critics forgot, or chose to ignore, that the difference in age between Graham and Catharine (Catharine was in fact 47) was less than that between her and Wilson. But for a woman to marry a man much younger than herself was quite different from a man marrying a much younger woman—just as a woman marrying beneath her was very different from a man doing the same.[60]

Much later, a voice from the other side of the Atlantic was raised in defence of Catharine Macaulay's second marriage. It belonged to Mercy Warren. Her intervention was provoked by a letter from John Adams in which he hoped 'the World would spread a Vail of Candour over a Circumstance' she had mentioned. He implied some criticism of Catharine Macaulay's behaviour. Indignantly Mercy Warren replied that it was probable that Mrs Macaulay's 'Independency of spirit led her to suppose she might associate for the remainder of her life, with an inoffensive, obliging youth, with the same impunity a Gentleman of three score and ten might marry a Damsel of fifteen!'[61] For what exactly was the 'crime' Catharine Macaulay had committed? Present-day practice makes a nonsense of the affair. A widow for twelve years, at the age of 47 she remarried. Her new husband was a young man of 21. For barely two years, with her daughter,

---

[56] *Mrs. Montagu—'Queen of the Blues': Her Letters and Friendships from 1762 to 1800*, ed. Reginald Blunt, 2 vols. (1923), ii. 64; Elizabeth Montagu's Letters to Hester Thrale, Manchester University, John Rylands Library, Eng. MS 551, 30.

[57] *Horace Walpole's Correspondence*, ed. W. S. Lewis, 48 vols. (1937–83), xxxiii. 84.

[58] Revd R. Polwhele, *Traditions and Recollections*, 2 vols. (1826), i. 122–3.

[59] Taylor, *Records of My Life*, i. 209.

[60] See e.g. Samuel Richardson, *Pamela or Virtue Rewarded*.

[61] *Warren–Adams Letters*, 2 vols. (Massachusetts Historical Society Collections; 72, 73, 1917–25), ii. 254.

she had shared the house of an elderly cleric generally admitted to be senile. There is no hint they were more than friends. Not one of her many critics, who would have loved a more salacious story, dared suggest they had been lovers. If Wilson ever proposed marriage to her it is surprising he never told one of the many friends and acquaintances who frequented Alfred House. That her behaviour with Wilson was foolish there is no denying, but that she had acted innocently and in good faith with no idea of the morass she was to find herself in is equally clear. The real source of her crime lay in her sex. It was doubly ironic that accusations of indecency should be levelled at her by, of all people, Wilkes.

Wilkes's role in the scandal deserves attention. He remained a regular visitor to Alfred House in the years after Catharine Macaulay's second marriage. Wilson, it is true, had been a very loyal and devoted disciple. Wilkes may have felt the least he could do was to provide support in this difficult period. Earlier, it is claimed, he had been concerned, 'that Catharine Macaulay was ruining the happiness of his old friend Dr. Wilson'.[62] But there is another aspect to his apparent devotion to Wilson. In December 1778 he had mentioned to Polly that when at Alfred House he was treated 'as the declared favourite', and a few days later that Wilson 'inquired kindly after' her. On another visit he had been treated 'with a kind distinction the whole day'. Later the same month he sent Wilson some game. Early in 1779 he repeated meaningfully that he was 'still first favourite' and added 'if it holds, *tant mieux pour une certaine demoiselle*'. By December 1779 Wilson was 'greatly out of order'. Wilkes meant 'to revisit the good old Dr. at Alfred House' and, he added, 'shall not fail, as he kindly desires, to pay him almost daily visits'. In the same letter to Polly he mentioned that Wilson was 'regularly attended by physician, surgeon and apothecary'. 'He cannot long survive', he concluded. But despite Wilkes's belief that the Doctor was 'declining very rapidly', Wilson survived another three years. By April 1783 Wilkes cannot 'muster courage sufficient to accept a second dinner invitation from Alfred House' and sends his excuses. A year later Wilson died. Almost immediately the letters of Wilkes to his daughter reveal a preoccupation with 'Dr. Wilson's legacy to us both'. In his obituary notice in the

---

[62] Horace Bleackley, *Life of John Wilkes* (1917), 332.

Gentleman's Magazine it was reported that he had left £20,000 to Wilkes, but the magazine admitted it could not vouch for the report. In the event the legacies included in Wilson's will were modest in the extreme. Wilkes had been left £50, while Polly was to receive a gold ring of the same value. In June 1784, it was announced that the legacy would be paid within six months. The following May the bombshell fell; Wilson had 'left in legacies many thousands more than he was worth'. The will had been put into Chancery and nobody was paid. 'I believe you and I', Wilkes wrote to Polly, 'shall scarcely seek a remedy by throwing our guinea after the Doctor's.'[63]

Wilkes's involvement in, and obvious enjoyment of, the scandal that was so effectively to destroy Catharine Macaulay's reputation may have had other motives. We can only guess at how much, in Wilkes's eyes, the errors of her brother were visited on Catharine. But from the time she moved to Bath, despite his friendship with Wilson, Wilkes's comments on her become more critical, almost always less than kind, and often spiteful. Apart from a growing diversion in their political ideas, there is another possible motive for Wilkes's pleasure in her fall from fame—jealousy. A little over ten years earlier, when an exile in Paris, Wilkes had seen himself as a historian in the making. He had a contract with John Almon for a *History of England from the Revolution to the Accession of the House of Brunswick*. The manuscript of the first volume was to have been finished by January 1768. All that ever appeared was a 39-page Introduction to the first volume which ended with an advertisement for the forthcoming 'Reigns of King William and Queen Anne', apparently, or so it was claimed, already in the press.[64] But events intervened and the *History* was put aside never to be resumed. Did he later resent the success with which Catharine Macaulay's *History* was greeted? Criticism of her became stronger as his political ideas diverged from those of Catharine and her brother. Wilkes's attitude to the Revolution of 1688, as expressed in the Introduction of 1768, makes it clear that their interpretations differed, and explains his dislike of her attack on William III in her volume of 1778.

[63] *Letters from the Year 1774 to the Year 1796 of John Wilkes, Esq.*, ii. 115, 120, 126, 134, 143, 178, 181, 184, 261; iii. 59, 125; *The Diaries of Thomas Wilson*, 24.
[64] John Almon, *Memoirs of a Late Eminent Bookseller* (1790), 42; John Wilkes, introduction to *The History of England from the Revolution to the Accession of the Brunswick Line* (1768), i, advertisement at end of text.

In 1779 Catharine Macaulay's fame and favour in the eyes of the world was at an end. 'Her enemies' triumph is now complete,' wrote Edmund Rack, 'her friends can say nothing in her favour. O, poor Catharine—never canst thou emerge from the abyss into which thou art fallen.'[65] Rack was not alone in seeing her second marriage as the main or even the sole cause of her fall from public favour. Yet the turning-point in her fortunes was already long passed. 'Certain it is', wrote the *European Magazine* in 1774, 'that the respect in which she had been held, as an author, began manifestly to decline.' Her *History* was 'no longer a popular performance, nor did the booksellers contend for the publication of the remainder of it'.[66] When she died in 1791 the *Annual Register* published a short obituary of 'this lady' who 'had the misfortune ... in a great degree to outlive the respect of the public'.[67] If her fall from fame was not the result of her second marriage why was it? The answer lies in two closely related factors: the nature of her *History*, and the changing nature of opposition politics.

When she started her *History* the Whigs were in need of an effective response to Hume's version of events of the seventeenth century. Catharine Macaulay must have seemed a godsend. Briefly she became their spokeswoman. No wonder her first volumes were greeted with such enthusiasm. Her 'eloquent republicanism', one author has written, 'catapulted her into the waiting arms of the Whigs'.[68] But it is doubtful whether at first they realized just how much of a republican she was. Soon those 'waiting arms' were to be abruptly removed. The first volumes of her *History* had dealt with the relatively safe period before 1640. There was little in them to dismay even the most conservative of Whigs. But as new volumes appeared, the original fulsome praise became muted. Even reviewers of her first volume had tempered their admiration with the suggestion that hers was not an entirely impartial *History*. 'An exuberance of zeal, even in the glorious cause of liberty', wrote the *Monthly Review* in 1763, 'may tempt an historian to represent facts in a partial view, and to suppress circumstances which do not admit of a favourite[*sic*: favourable?]

[65] Polwhele, *Traditions and Recollections*, i. 123.

[66] *European Magazine*, 4 (1783), 333.

[67] *Annual Register for the Year 1791* (1810), Chronicle 26.

[68] David S. Lovejoy, 'Henry Marchant and the Mistress of the World', *William and Mary Quarterly*, 3rd ser., 12 (1955), 375–98, at p. 391.

gloss'. Or again, 'she seems studiously to have selected only such parts of the *History* as might afford an opportunity of indulging her favourite propensity'.[69] But it was when she reached Volumes IV and V, and the far more controversial period of 1643–60, that she provoked most hostile criticism. 'We cannot think', the *Monthly Review* wrote of Volume IV, 'that . . . she has discharged the duty of a judicious and candid historian.' In reviewing the first volume had it not cautioned her 'against an exuberance of zeal'? Now she appeared 'inflamed to such a high degree of party enthusiasm, as to lose sight of that earlier candour' it had 'with so much pleasure commended'.[70] In 1774 the *Gentleman's Magazine* published a number of letters attacking her fourth volume. One correspondent criticized it under the heading 'Gross Misrepresentations in Mrs. Macaulay's *History of England*'. The publication of *A Modest Plea for the Property of Copyright* in the same year did little to save her reputation. There was a suggestion from one correspondent that in the inaccuracy of some of her examples, she had been led astray 'by her *very good and worthy friend Dr. Wilson*'.[71]

The cooling of Whig enthusiasm for her and her *History* was made clear in 1770 when Burke as spokesman for the Rockingham Whigs published his *Thoughts on the Cause of the Present Discontents*. It marked the abandonment of her as Whig propagandist. By the time her fifth volume appeared in 1771, if 'the Writer's bias' was not already clear from her *History*, there was more practical evidence of her radical politics and of her republicanism.[72] In her open and enthusiastic support of Wilkes, and her active defence of the American colonists, she was increasingly labelled 'the patriot historian'. Along with other consistent supporters of the Americans she almost certainly suffered from the sharp decline of sympathy with the rebels once war broke out.

Thus long before 1778 and the publication of her ill-fated volume of history dedicated to Wilson, she had ceased to be acceptable to many of those who in the 1760s had been loudest in her praise. Her view of the 'Glorious Revolution' expressed in this volume had already been made clear eight years earlier in her

[69] *Monthly Review*, 29 (1763), 374, 380.
[70] Ibid. 40 (1769), 353.
[71] *Gentleman's Magazine*, 44 (1774), 303, 125, 557.
[72] *Monthly Review*, 40 (1769), 359.

reply to Burke's *Thoughts on the Cause of the Present Discontents*. It was an interpretation far from acceptable to many Whigs—or even to all her former political allies. Wilkes in 1777 had had a preview of the one-volume *History*. 'I find she has attacked the memory of King William with such acrimony', he wrote in a letter to his daughter, 'which will please all the tory wretches of the kingdom. Even Shebbeare and Johnson will quote Mrs. Macaulay against King William.'[73] Her portrayal of William, as we shall see later, was also responsible for alienating Lord Harcourt.[74] The fact that some of those who earlier had shared her political sympathies were now having doubts about her *History* is indicative of a change in their attitudes rather than in hers.

Trying to account for the plummeting of her reputation, the *European Magazine* was later to ponder 'whether the world was really disgusted with the acrimony of her treatment of some characters, whether it revolted against the violence of her republican principles, or whether some of the absurd conduct of her reverend patron has been imputed to her'.[75] Perhaps all three contributed, but the last, like her second marriage, was less a cause of her declining reputation than an excuse for her critics to distance themselves from views with which they had long found themselves out of sympathy. Her *History* and her republicanism cannot be separated, but it was only when she reached that period of seventeenth-century history when her republicanism clearly revealed itself that the combination became a threat to her reputation.

In at least one respect her critics were proved wrong. Her second marriage did not mark the end of her career as a historian or as a political polemicist. Very rapidly she resumed her eight-volume *History*. In 1781 she produced Volumes VI and VII. In February of that year Walpole wrote to the Revd William Mason that 'Kate Macgraham [Mrs Macaulay] has published two more; yet does not advance beyond the death of Algernon Sidney. I believe England will be finished before her *History*'.[76] He too was wrong, for two years later the final volume was completed. It is true she never fulfilled her original design for the eight-volume

[73] *Letters from the Year 1774 to the Year 1796 of John Wilkes, Esq.*, ii. 55.
[74] *The Harcourt Papers*, ed. E. W. Harcourt, 14 vols. (1876–1905), viii. 113–14.
[75] *European Magazine*, 4 (1783), 333.
[76] *Horace Walpole's Correspondence*, xxix. 102.

History, for it ended with James II's reign. But the completion of the last three volumes of her *History* were not all she accomplished. In 1783 she produced a *Treatise on the Immutability of Moral Truth*. In the year before her death she published not only her *Letters on Education with Observations on Religious and Metaphysical Matters* but an answer to Burke's *Reflections on the Revolution in France*.

The prophecy of Colonel Whitmore, friend of Wilkes, echoed by Wilson, that she would poison William Graham 'in a month' proved false.[77] The fear expressed that the 'disparity of their ages and stations, the contrast of their political notions, and prior pursuits in life' made them 'almost incompatible' was unjustified. The evidence—scant although it is—suggests a happy marriage. 'With congenial tastes and dispositions', it was said, 'they passed their time in literary avocations and pursuits'.[78] The only hint of criticism of William Graham came in 1876, when it was claimed that he shared his brother's eccentricities.[79] So vague a criticism made at such a late date cannot carry much weight. However unsuitable a mother her brother may have once thought her, her daughter remained with them. Far from being irresponsible she seems to have experienced all the anxiety of a devoted mother. Earlier she had talked to Ezra Stiles of that 'maternal tenderness [one] feels for an only child'.[80] In 1785 when about to leave America at the end of her visit she told Mercy Warren that it was 'the calls of maternal affection' that prevented her staying longer.[81] 'She now returns', Martha Washington wrote to Mercy Warren, 'to make happy those whom she left.'[82] Most of her letters to Mercy Warren include news of her daughter. She was enjoying 'a perfect state of health'; she joined with her mother in sending her best wishes to the Warren family.[83] In June 1787 a marriage at Marylebone Church was recorded between Charles Gregory and the 'daughter and heiress of the late Dr. George

---

[77] *Letters from the Year 1774 to the Year 1796 of John Wilkes, Esq.*, ii. 124, 135.
[78] *Town and Country Magazine*, 10 (1778), 623–4; Hays, *Female Biography*, v. 304.
[79] *Notes and Queries*, 5th ser., 6 (1876), 545.
[80] Mildred Chaffee Beckwith, 'Catharine Macaulay: Eighteenth-Century Rebel'. Ph.D. thesis (Ohio State University, 1953), 49.
[81] *Warren–Adams Letters*, ii. 258.
[82] Ibid. 257.
[83] Ibid. 284–5, 300.

Macaulay, and of the female Historian of England'.[84] Mr Gregory was captain of an East Indian ship. It was a 'Match', Mrs Macaulay told Mercy Warren, 'very much to mine and the rest of her friends' liking'. In October of the following year, in the last letter Mercy Warren received from her, Catharine Macaulay proudly reported that Mrs Gregory had 'got a Daughter and that the Mother and the Child are both well'.[85]

Her movements in the last ten years are obscure. Absence of reports on her in this period is particularly galling. So many unanswered questions remain; what were her relations with her brother and other radicals in the 1780s? Who were the friends—if any—who stood by her? One longs to know more of her friendship with Mrs Arnold, and of how she and William Graham spent these eleven to twelve years. Only occasionally is she mentioned in a letter or newspaper report. One understands why John Taylor in his memoirs could note: 'what became of Mrs. Macaulay... I never heard'.[86] 'Since her second marriage', the *European Magazine* reported, 'Mrs. Macaulay has lived retired from the world'.[87] Although she married in Leicester and was rumoured to have 'retired to a cottage in Leicestershire' with her husband, by 1781 she was once more back in London at Laurence Street, Chelsea.[88] Some time in the spring of 1780 Wilkes wrote to Polly from Bath 'I have seen Dr. —— a second time but not Mrs M–ca–l–y'. In March of the following year he reported that Mrs Molineux was 'with great reason anxious about the fate of *little Kitty*'.[89] There were rumours. It was said that after her marriage to 'Dr Graham' she and 'other champions of democracy' had emigrated to America, where she had died.[90] The truth was that when finally she finished her *History* she left England for her long promised visit to America.

During that visit, which lasted over a year, we can follow her movements in some detail. If her reputation in England was destroyed there were still many in America who were enthusiastic

[84] *Warren–Adams Letters*, ii. 300 n.
[85] *Warren–Adams Letters*, ii. 300, 304.
[86] Taylor, *Records of My Life*, i. 211.
[87] *European Magazine*, 4 (1783), 334.
[88] *Gentleman's Magazine*, 61 (1791), 589.
[89] *Letters from the Year 1774 to the Year 1796 of John Wilkes Esq.*, ii. 229, 241.
[90] Polwhele, *Traditions and Recollections*, i. 43 n.

in their admiration of her. Her earlier contribution to the American cause was not forgotten. In 1784, less than ten years after her *Address to the People of England, Scotland, and Ireland on the Present Important Crisis of Affairs*, almost all she had predicted had come about. She was the first English radical to visit that 'empire of freemen . . . on the other side of the Atlantic', since recognition of American independence.[91] In May the *Gentleman's Magazine* reported 'a few days ago the celebrated Mrs Macaulay Graham and her husband embarked on board a ship in the Downs, bound for North America. Whether she is gone to frame a code of laws for that continent, or not', it added, 'we have not heard'.[92] It was October 1785 when the *Annual Register* recorded that 'the celebrated democratic historian, Mrs. Catharine McAulay Graham sailed for Europe the middle of July last'.[93] Her friend and correspondent, Ezra Stiles followed her itinerary. 'She landed at Boston July 15, 1784. Travelled to Piscataqua, spent the winter at Boston. In May passed thro' Newport to New York; thence to Philad. & so on to G. Washington's Seat at Mt. Vernon in Virginia. Returned to New York and embarkt there July 17, 1785 for Port L'Orient in France'.[94]

It is from Mercy Otis Warren, wife of James Warren and sister of James Otis, and one of the two most remarkable American women of the revolutionary years, that we hear most about the visit. The two women shared both interests and political sympathies. Catharine Macaulay is said to have had 'a more profound influence on Mercy than had any other woman of her era'.[95] Perhaps inspired by Catharine's example Mercy turned historian and in 1805 produced her *History of the American Revolution*. John Adams assumed they 'compared Notes of the History of Liberty on both sides of the Atlantic'.[96] She reported to her son on the arrival of Catharine Macaulay at their home. 'She is a lady whose Resources of knowledge seem to be almost inexhaustible', she

[91] Catharine Macaulay, *An Address to the People of England, Scotland and Ireland on the Present Important Crisis of Affairs* (1775), 26.

[92] *Gentleman's Magazine*, 54 (1784), 378.

[93] *Annual Register for the Years 1784 and 1785* (1787), Chronicle, 243.

[94] *The Literary Diary of Ezra Stiles*, ed. Franklin Bowditch Dexter, 3 vols. (1901), iii. 172.

[95] Katharine Anthony, *First Lady of the Revolution: The Life of Mercy Otis Warren* (1958), 123.

[96] *Warren–Adams Letters*, ii. 251.

wrote. To John Adams she confided that she thought her 'a Lady of most Extraordinary talent, a Commanding Genius and Brilliance of thought'.[97]

Leaving Mercy Warren, Catharine Macaulay moved briefly to New York, where she had an introduction to Richard Henry Lee, at that time President of the Continental Congress. After she left he thanked Samuel Adams for introducing him to 'this excellent Lady'.[98] With Henry Knox he had written to Washington asking that Catharine Macaulay be allowed to pay her respects to him for, he believed, 'this had been her only motive for going so far South as Virginia'. Her 'reputation in the learned world, and among the friends to the rights of human nature is very high indeed. Her merit as an historian is very great, and places her as an author in the foremost rank of writers'.[99] By return there came an invitation to spend ten days at Mount Vernon, where she was 'received . . . with the usual hospitality and with the delicate attentions due to a woman of literary distinction'.[100] To Lee, Washington wrote of his pleasure in meeting 'a Lady . . . whose principles are so much and so justly admired by the friends of liberty and mankind'. On her return to England she continued to correspond with her American friends.

In April 1785 Mercy Warren wrote to John Adams of a subscription out for an American edition of Mrs Macaulay's *History of England from the Revolution to the Present Time in a Series of Letters to a Friend*. 'It fills very fast', she told him, 'and I dare say will succeed to her wishes.' But three months later Catharine Macaulay decided not to pursue the idea. 'A variety of reasons' had persuaded her to 'give up all thoughts of' it. In part, the decision was the result of the poor state of her health, which, she wrote, 'inclined me to take the advantage of two or three years' residence in the mild and steady climate of the South of France'. In part, she claimed, it was 'the delicacy' of her sentiment which urged her to leave her visit to America 'free and unclogged with any consideration of interest'.[101] Was it also perhaps because of the hostile reviews the work had received from some quarters, and

[97] Alice Brown, *Mercy Otis Warren* (1896), 58; *Warren–Adams Letters*, ii. 254.
[98] *Letters of Richard Henry Lee*, ed. J. C. Ballagh, 2 vols. (1911–14), ii. 359.
[99] Ibid. 352.
[100] Douglas Southall Freeman, *George Washington*, 7 vols. (1948–57), vi. 39.
[101] *Warren–Adams Letters*, ii. 254, 258.

above all, its close associations with Wilson, which persuaded her not to sanction the reprinting of it in America?

On 25 March 1786 *Jackson's Oxford Journal* carried a report that 'after having visited several Parts of America, and received many Tokens of Esteem from the principal Characters in the United States', she had 'now retired, on account of her health, to the south of France; and lives with her husband . . . at a beautiful villa in the environs of Marseilles, where she is employed in writing a history of the American revolution'.[102] If they did move to France they did not stay there long, for by October 1786 if not earlier she was back in London. But there is other evidence suggesting that at one time she intended to write a history of the American Revolution. Mary Hays claimed that for this purpose 'she had been furnished by general Washington with many materials', but that 'she was, by the infirm state of her health . . . prevented from the execution of her plan'.[103] In a letter to Mercy of 6 March 1787, Catharine Macaulay confirmed that she had thought of writing such a history. 'Tho' the History of your late glorious revolution is what I should certainly undertake were I again young,' she wrote, 'yet as things are I must for many reasons decline such a task.'[104] Twenty years later Mercy Warren was to complete her own *History of the American Revolution*.

When exactly Catharine Macaulay left London for Binfield near Reading is unclear but by March 1788 the move was already made. A letter to Mercy Warren described her new home as 'a small Villa in Berkshire' where she intended 'chiefly' to reside. The reason for the move was her 'being quite tired of the absurdities of the Capital'. In November 1787, in response to a request to tell Mercy Warren on what work she was employed, she had replied that she was still writing her *Letters on Education*. 'When I have finished this work,' she added, 'I propose to resume my pen on a political subject which I have in view.' What the subject of this work could have been we can only guess, but she was convinced it would 'close' her 'sublunary labors'.[105] In fact within two years, the French Revolution intervened to change her plans. The publication of Burke's *Reflections on the French Revolution* in

---

[102] *Jackson's Oxford Journal*, No. 1717.
[103] Hays, *Female Biography*, v. 303.
[104] *Warren–Adams Letters*, ii. 284.
[105] Ibid. 305, 300.

October 1790 persuaded her to devote all her dwindling energies to a spirited reply. Her death at Binfield in Berkshire on 22 June 1791, came 'after a long and very painful illness'.[106] It was 'attended by much suffering, which she supported with exemplary patience and fortitude'.[107] After her death William Graham placed a medallion in the porch of Binfield Church in memory of 'Catharine Macaulay Graham'. There—still to be seen—is her head in profile surrounded by a wreath, and at the top an owl, symbol of wisdom, in relief.[108]

[106] *Gentleman's Magazine*, 61 (1791), 589.
[107] Hays, *Female Biography*, v. 303–4.
[108] Pierpoint, *Catharine Macaulay 'History'*, ii (1910), 9.

6. *A Woman in a Man's World*

Woman has everything against her.

> (Catharine Macaulay, *Letters on Education* (1790), 212)

...'the Men being the Historians, they seldom condescend to record the great and the good Actions of Women; and when they take notice of them, 'tis with this wise Remark, That such Women *acted above their Sex*. By which one must suppose they wou'd have their Readers understand, That they were not Women who did those Great Actions, but that they were Men in Petticoats'.

> (Mary Astell, *The Christian Religion* (1705), 293)

THE situation of women of any education in the eighteenth century was, at best, frustrating and restrictive. Even for those fully prepared to act out the role allotted to them by society, willingly submissive, and sometimes almost conniving at their own subordination, there must have been times of painful awareness of the confines of their world, of the limits to their participation in it, and of the uselessness of the little education they had acquired. That there were women who led relatively happy lives, achieving a degree of self-fulfilment remains true—and astonishing. For those few who attempted to use their education, to think independently, to invade spheres of activity monopolized by men, the path was fraught with dangers. As a historian, a political polemicist, a 'learned lady' with scholarly pretensions, an independent and fearless critic of all she thought wrong, Catharine Macaulay broke every rule in the eighteenth-century book on how a woman should conduct herself and the role she should occupy. Her second marriage to a man twenty-six years her junior and socially inferior was further proof of her rejection of acceptable standards of behaviour.

Like other writers of her sex she was acutely aware of just how rare it was for a woman to enter the realms of literary expression, let alone the writing of history. What first aroused the American Abigail Adams's curiosity about Catharine Macaulay and her *History* was her discovery of 'one of my own sex so eminent in a tract so uncommon'.[1] There were no other English female historians in her field—or indeed outside it—with whom she could discuss history. One thing that later endeared Mercy Warren to her was the interest they shared in history. The 'blue-stockings' with whom she was associated (see Pl. 5), had little sympathy for her republicanism. In consequence her life as a historian must have been curiously isolated from contact with other women. It was not that she failed to discuss her history with other historians. As we have seen, there were lengthy exchanges with Hume, Hollis, Toplady, and friends in America, who were prepared to argue over her interpretation. But, with the exception of Mercy Warren, there was no woman among them.

Almost certainly underestimated is the effect on women writers of the sheer weight of prejudice directed against them. It is impossible to read any female author writing between the late seventeenth and the late eighteenth century without becoming aware of just what it cost them to break out of the mould to which society confined them. When she commenced her *History* Catharine Macaulay was conscious of the uniqueness in her position, and of 'the invidious censures which may ensue from striking into a path of literature rarely trodden by my sex'. She refused, she wrote, to allow such considerations to keep her 'mute in the cause of liberty and virtue'.[2] But in the preface to the first volume she wrote nervously of 'the inaccuracies of style' that might be found in her work, which she hoped the readers would overlook as 'the defects of a female historian' not to be 'weighed in the balance of severe criticism'.[3] For some women fear of the response to such 'defects' dictated their remaining silent. When in 1818 it was suggested to Abigail Adams that she publish her letters, she retorted 'No. No. . . . Heedless and Inaccurate as I am, I have too much vanity to risk my reputation before the public'.[4] Appeals for leniency in judging their work on the grounds of their sex is found in many women writers from the seventeenth to the nineteenth century. Even Mercy Warren, when attacked by John

---

[1] Letter from Abigail Adams to Isaac Smith Jr., 20 Apr. 1771, *Adams Family Correspondence*, ed. L. H. Butterfield, 4 vols. (1963–73), i. 77.

[2] Catharine Macaulay, *History of England*, 8 vols. (1763–83), i, p. x.

[3] Ibid. p. xviii.

[4] As quoted Edith B. Gelles, 'The Abigail Industry', *William and Mary Quarterly*, 3rd ser., 45 (1988), 656–83, at p. 656.

Adams for what he saw as the inadequacies of her history of the American revolution, fell back on such an appeal. She was, she wrote, 'a writer whose sex alone ought to have protected her from the grossness' of his invectives.[5] Such an appeal might seem out of character in Catharine Macaulay. It is notable that after the appearance of her first volume it was never repeated. She might be forced on to the defensive—as in the preface to Volume VI of her *History*—but she did not ask for leniency on account of her sex. To protect themselves against the prejudices of male readers many women writers wrote anonymously or under a pseudonym. Most of Catharine Macaulay's polemical pamphlets were so published. Anonymity, while protecting women writers against attacks based on their sex, also deprived them of any identity. It was difficult enough for those who published under their own names to establish such an identity. When Catharine Macaulay's first volume was reviewed by the *Gentleman's Magazine* it referred to its author as 'Mrs. Macaulay, Dr. Macaulay's wife'.[6]

'Learned ladies' in the eighteenth century were considered unnatural. Richard Polwhele, despite the considerable debt he owed women for their encouragement and help as a young poet, in later life wrote a poem, '*The Unsex'd Females*', against women writers. It included the lines

> Survey with me, what ne'er our fathers saw,
> A female band despising nature's law,
> As 'proud defiance' flashes from their arms,
> And vengeance smothers all their softer charms.[7]

Was it male expectations of the appearance of learned women that, at least in part, lay behind Richard Baron's early description of her as 'a woman without passions' with a face as 'abstract as the print of Mr. Locke'?[8] Baron was not alone in being terrified of learned women. Given the powerful social stigma attached to them it was difficult for any man to view learning in women objectively. If a woman had learning it was better for her if she concealed the fact. Learning was seen as a masculine attribute so

---

[5] *Warren–Adams Letters* (Massachusetts Historical Society, *Collections*, 5th ser., 4; 1878), 455 in a letter to John Adams dated 15 Aug. 1807.
[6] *Gentleman's Magazine*, 36 (1766), 439.
[7] *The Unsex'd Females* (1798), repr. Revd R. Polwhele, *Poems*, 5 vols. (1810), ii. 36.
[8] See Ch. 1, n. 52.

that a 'learned lady' must be unwomanly, suffering either from too little or too much sex. For a woman to appear as an author, Delarivière Manley, the novelist and playwright, argued, 'bodes impotence'.[9] There was a tendency to associate learning with unmarried women. If by some accident learned women were married this boded ill for husband, children, and home. In 1765, in a review of her second volume, when Catharine Macaulay was discovered to be married, the *Monthly Review* expressed itself 'glad... to find, that the woman is not lost in the historian'.[10] When Thomas Coombe, a relative of Benjamin Rush, met Catharine Macaulay at the dinner table of the Dilly brothers, he was flattered to be shown a copy of the pamphlet she was about to publish. But in a letter to Rush he asked whether 'if this Lady was yours "to have and to hold", would you not be apt to recommend the Discontents of a Husband as a fitter Subject for her Meditations than the Politics of a Kingdom?'[11] For the great majority of women, one reviewer of her *History* argued, it was 'wisest' and 'safest' to remain in the background and to flee 'the applauding multitude'.[12]

Many were the accusations made against 'women of masculine minds', who were assumed to have 'masculine manners'. Because 'Queen Elizabeth understood Latin and Greek, swore with the fluency of a sailor, and boxed the ears of her courtiers' she was said to have had a 'masculine mind'. Knowledge of Latin and Greek, swearing, and the boxing of ears were seen as confined to men. But the same accusation of possessing 'a masculine mind' was made of Mrs Macaulay, 'the author of a dull democratic history', because 'at a tolerably advanced age' she 'married a boy'.[13] Mrs Montagu thought the whole cause of her second marriage came 'from Mrs. Macaulay's adopting Masculine opinions & masculine manners'.[14] By marrying a man twenty-six

[9] Delarivière Manley, *The Lost Lover* (1696), Prologue.
[10] *Monthly Review*, 32 (1765), 275.
[11] As quoted L. H. Butterfield, 'The American Interests of the Firm of E. and C. Dilly, with Their Letters to Benjamin Rush, 1770–1795', *Papers of the Bibliographical Society of America*, 45 (1951), 283–332, at pp. 287–8.
[12] *The Repository or Treasury of Politics and Literature for 1770*, 2 vols. (1771), ii. 290, a reprint of *The London Chronicle*, 28 (1770), 109.
[13] From *Mercury and the New England Palladium*, 18 Sept. 1801, as quoted Linda K. Kerber, *Women of the Republic* (1980), 279–80.
[14] Elizabeth Montagu's Letters to Hester Thrale, Manchester University, John Rylands Library, Eng. MS 551, No. 29.

years her junior she was held to betray sexual passions only recognized as existing in men. Remarrying widows, always suspect in the eighteenth century, were unable to control their lusts. Widowhood should not be 'sully'd with the Remembrances of past Enjoyments, nor with the present Desires of a second Bed'.[15]

Ideas about the domestic shortcomings of writing women were not confined to men. As the young Hannah More observed

> The ladies too their well-meant censure give.
> What!—does she write? A slattern, as I live.[16]

'What a pity', wrote Sarah Vaughan to Catharine Livingston of Mrs Macaulay when, on her tour of America, she visited Philadelphia, 'that superior understanding & superior cultivation in our sex should so often root out those amiable domestic, and useful qualities that ever will be most praiseworthy in us.' She refused to accompany her parents when they called on Mrs Macaulay.[17] Many women deprived of any education themselves were frightened of educated women, and readily accepted the prejudices of men. When Gertrude Meredith, the Philadelphian novelist and essayist, visited Baltimore, she found that some of the readers of her satirical essays were terrified to meet her. 'Mrs. Cole', she recorded, 'says she should not have been more distressed at visiting Mrs. Macaulay the authoress than myself as she had heard *I was so sensible*, but she was glad to find I was so free and easy'.[18] Unmarried women took to learning, it was assumed, because they could not get themselves a husband. It went with the assumption that all spinsters were ugly. By a curious logic, learned women whether married or not were assumed to be ungainly and ugly creatures. 'She is deformed', one account of Catharine Macaulay claimed, 'she is unfortunately ugly, she despairs of distinction and admiration as a woman, she seeks therefore, to encroach on the province of man'.[19] It is reminiscent of the newssheet description of Charlotte Corday when she was

---

[15] *The ladies library*, 3 vols. (1714), i. 156.
[16] From Hannah More, epilogue to *The Search after Happiness: A Pastoral Drama* (1774), as quoted *Eighteenth-Century Women Poets: An Oxford Anthology*, ed. Roger Lonsdale (1989), 325.
[17] Kerber, *Women of the Republic*, 227 and n. 68.
[18] Ibid. 196.
[19] As quoted Mary Hays, *Female Biography*, 6 vols. (1803), v. 292.

waiting to go to the guillotine. 'Cette femme, qu'on dit fort jolie, n'était point jolie; c'était une *virago* plus charnue que fraîche, sans grâce, malpropre, comme le sont tous les philosophes et beaux esprits femelles ... cette femme s'était jetée absolument hors de son sexe'.[20]

Rarely did a woman writer win acclaim from men. Often those that did never questioned the role assigned to them. Some avoided publishing their writings. Posing no threat to men they were more easily accepted. The first works of Catharine Macaulay were exceptional in meeting with approval. In the sort of criticism a woman writer could expect to receive, at best there was condescension, at worst a constant reminder that women were not fitted for the author's trade. What is less appreciated is just how damning could be the nature of their critics' approval, even their praise. Reviews that were favourable or even enthusiastic were frequently as insidious as those that were not. Like the words of courtly love, behind the praise there lay malice, envy, and a deep sexism. Sometimes the implications of being accepted were almost worse than those of being censured. Take for example the review of the first volume of her *History* in *The Monthly Review*. 'The fair Macaulay', 'our fair Historian', is indeed praised for 'collecting and digesting the political fragments which have escaped the researches of so many learned and ingenious men', but 'many, perhaps, will be inclined to wish the same degree of genius and application had been exerted in *more suitable pursuits*' (my emphasis). If her *History* was proof that 'the fair sex have powers to keep pace with, if not to outstrip us, in the more arduous paths of literature', the reviewer writes, 'yet we would by no means recommend such a laborious competition to the practice of our lovely countrywomen'. He goes on to argue that 'each sex has its characteristical excellence, and the soft and delicate texture of a female frame, was no more intended for severe study, than the laborious drudge, Man, was formed for working of catgut'. What did Catharine Macaulay feel when she read that 'intense thought spoils a lady's features; it banishes *les ris et les grâces*, which form all the enchantment of a female face'?[21] How did she react to

---

[20] As quoted Claire Tomalin, *The Life and Death of Mary Wollstonecraft* (1974), 152, from *Répertoire du Tribunal révolutionnaire*.

[21] *Monthly Review*, 29 (1763), 373.

David Hume's recommendation that women study history because, among other reasons, 'they were debarred the severer studies, by the tenderness of their complexion'?[22] When the *Monthly Review*, having acknowledged the 'unquestionable merit' of her work, with the same hand took back its praise, and concluded that 'some critics may dispute the propriety of calling it a History', how did she respond?[23] The writing of history was a male preserve. The result of her efforts, commendable although it might be, was not history but some curious and undefined feminine thing.

For even the most enthusiastic of her reviewers she was seen not as a historian, but as a *female* historian. Her work was never judged on its merits alone but always inseparably linked with the fact that she was a woman. In reviewing the fourth volume of her *History*, the *Monthly Review*, while acknowledging that 'in the literary republic, there are no distinctions of rank or sex', nevertheless added 'what critic is there so hardy as not to be impressed with a partial veneration when a fair writer brandishes her crow quill.'[24] It is reminiscent of the story of Professor Clapham at an economic history conference greeting Eileen Power: 'Eileen you look like Semiramis'. To which she replied 'I thought I looked like a Professor of Economic History.'[25] Often it is not just what is said by reviewers but the tone of condescension in which they say it that is so offensive. Reactions to her non-historical works were no different. Even Samuel Badcock (1747–88), the literary critic, in his favourable review of *The Immutability of Moral Truth* in 1789, wrote that it was 'really wonderful considering her sex'. And lest he should be thought 'impolite' he appealed to the ladies to acknowledge that in general 'their talents are not adapted to abstract speculations'.[26]

There were topics in history that it was thought indecent for a woman to consider. In her fourth volume she analysed in some detail the character of Charles I and considered the question of his chastity, which had been 'called in question by an author

---

[22] David Hume, *Essays Moral, Political and Literary* (1903), 560.
[23] *Monthly Review*, 29 (1763), 373.
[24] Ibid. 40 (1769), 353.
[25] As quoted Maxine Berg, 'The First Women Economic Historians: The LSE Connection', a paper given in 1989. *Economic History Review*, forthcoming.
[26] *Gentleman's Magazine*, 59 (1789), 777.

of the highest repute'—Milton.[27] This was forbidden territory. 'Since kings have the feelings common to human nature, what if the amorous Charles was tempted to rumple a tucker?' It was 'surely invidious now to reproach his memory with such an idle piece of dalliance'. While Mrs Macaulay might be offended by 'such a wanton liberty', it was 'beneath the dignity of the historian to record, or even to allude to the frailty of certain moments, when it is scarce possible for a man, under the like temptations, to keep his hands to himself.'[28] In her first volume she had talked of the friendships of James I as 'directed by so puerile a fancy, and so absurd a caprice, that the objects of it were ever contemptible'.[29] One reviewer picked out these remarks for comment. He admired 'the nice touch by which the fair Writer' had referred to 'the odious vice imputed to James'. It showed 'a chastity becoming history and a delicacy becoming her sex'.[30] Such comments recall the anecdote told of Catharine Macaulay visiting the British Museum in the course of writing the early volumes of her *History*, and asking to see the letters which passed between James I and his favourite the Duke of Buckingham. 'Dr Birch, whose duty was to take care of these papers, and knew many of them to be very obscene,' we are told, 'requested that she would permit him to select a certain portion for her perusal, observing that many of them were wholly unfit for the inspection of any one of her sex. "Phoo," said she, "a historian is of no sex", and then deliberately read through all'.[31] It is a story which, from all we know of her, has the ring of truth.

One of Catharine Macaulay's most fervent admirers in France was Madame Roland. Although highly intelligent and with a gift for writing, she published very little. On the consequences of a woman becoming author she had 'perceived very early in life that a woman who gained this title, lost a great deal more than she acquired. The men do not love her; and her own sex criticise her: if her works be bad, she is ridiculed, and not without reason; if good her right to them is disputed'.[32] Despite her admiration for

[27] Macaulay, *History of England*, 8 vols. (1763–83), iv. 422.
[28] *Monthly Review*, 40 (1769), 361–2.
[29] Macaulay, *History of England*, i. 266.
[30] *Monthly Review*, 29 (1763), 380–1.
[31] John Taylor, *Records of My Life*, 2 vols. (1832), i. 209.
[32] *The Works of Jeanne-Marie Phlipon Roland, Translated from the French*, ed. L. A. Chapagneux (1800), p. iv.

Catharine Macaulay, it angered her 'to see women disputing privileges which ill befit them'. The 'name of author' when applied to women she found 'ridiculous'. 'No matter what their facility may be in some respects, they should never show their learning or talents in public'.[33] When her correspondence with Brissot was published in the *Patriote Francais* she insisted on remaining anonymous.

In accounting for the work of a woman writer meeting with praise it was often assumed a masculine hand must lie behind it. 'The World will hardly allow a Woman to say anything well,' wrote Mary Astell, one of the first women to express feminist ideas, 'unless as she borrows it from Men, or is assisted by them'.[34] A review of Catharine Macaulay's first volume of *History* contained a hint of such an accusation. The style in which her *History* was written was 'so correct, bold, and nervous, that we can discover no traces of a female pen ... and were we at liberty to suppose Mrs. Macaulay married, we might suspect that her husband and she were joint Historians'.[35] The accusation, it was said, came from 'an envious cabal' who claimed the *History* was 'too capital a work for any Woman in the World to write'. Dr Macaulay, who was 'a man of openness, sincerity, and generosity of soul, scorned to deprive his lady of her reputation', and categorically denied the charge.[36] He insisted he never saw any of her work until it appeared in print. Unfortunately for those who continued to believe him the author, he inconveniently died when only two volumes of her *History* had appeared.

When an alternative mentor was needed, he was found in her friend and adviser, Thomas Hollis, who after the death of Dr Macaulay was said to have 'assisted his widow in composing her *History*'. Hollis, as we have seen, was the source of many of those 'curious, important, and authentic materials' on which she drew, but as his biographer insisted 'Mr. Hollis never attempted history as an author' nor was he 'ambitious of the reputation of assisting her in her history'.[37] In the *St. James's Chronicle* a letter appeared defending Mrs Macaulay, and while acknowledging great respect

---

[33] As quoted Gita May, *Madame Roland and the Age of Revolution* (1970), 116.
[34] Mary Astell, *Reflections upon Marriage* (1706), preface.
[35] *Monthly Review*, 29 (1763), 375.
[36] *St. James's Chronicle*, No. 2733 (19 Sept. 1778).
[37] *Memoirs of Thomas Hollis*, ed. Francis Blackburne, 2 vols. (1780), i. 478.

for Hollis, curtly dismissed the possibility of his being the author of the history, for 'his abilities were inferior, far inferior to Mrs. Macaulay's *History of England*'.[38] It was a phrase that Hollis's biographer immediately took exception to and on which he challenged the author of the letter. But whether or not Hollis's abilities were inferior to those of Catharine Macaulay, Hollis died before the last three volumes had appeared. James Burgh, author of *Political Disquisitions* and described as 'the intimate acquaintance and friend of Mrs. Macaulay', was said to be the author of her *History of England from the Revolution to the Present Time*. At his death in 1775 it was claimed that all his papers became her property, and during his lifetime 'all his writings were open to her inspection and use, for he never published anything under his own name'.[39] As this was untrue, the rest of the claim is suspect. A final proof that she was incapable of writing the history that appeared under her name, it was argued, lay in her letter to Dr James Graham. There was said to be no signature to the letter but her accuser vouched for it being in her handwriting. The excerpts quoted make clear it was the letter written to Graham by Catharine Macaulay—and signed by her—which, with her agreement, was later published by the doctor. But the reason for concluding that she was not the author of the history was that no author could have been capable of writing so 'ludicrous' a letter![40] Much later Brissot de Warville was to describe this attempt to deprive her of authorship of the history as 'calomnie ordinaire a l'envie quand l'éclat de la gloire d'une femme l'éblouit', and to add 'cette injustice venge l'amour-propre des autres'.[41] That she was aware of the scepticism among some of her readers about her authorship is clear. When Benjamin Rush 'took the liberty of telling her that some grammatical errors had been made by the printers of her history', she denied the charge. 'No (said she), they are my errors, and not the printers. I have constantly refused to have them corrected, lest it should be suspected that my history was not altogether my own'.[42]

It was quite impossible for any woman in the eighteenth century

---

[38] *St. James's Chronicle*, No. 2733 (19 Sept. 1778).
[39] Ibid., No. 2723, letter of 27 Aug. 1778.
[40] Ibid.
[41] *Mémoires de Brissot*, ed. M. F. de Montrol, 4 vols. (1830), ii. 231.
[42] *The Autobiography of Benjamin Rush*, ed. George Corner (1948), 61.

to associate with a man, share his political views, or merely enjoy
his company, without its being assumed that it was not politics
or intellectual interest which drew them together but that the
relationship was sexual. This goes some way to accounting for the
large number of men to whom Catharine Macaulay was reported
married or about to be married. When in 1767, as a recently
widowed woman, she drank tea with Thomas Hollis, there was
gossip about their relations.[43] Hollis, we are told, was very
annoyed about the gossip—but how did Catharine Macaulay feel?
When in 1769 she was rumoured to have put her house at the
disposal of the Corsican exile Pasquale Paoli, it was said she was
to marry him.[44] Because of her support for Wilkes, it was
assumed that her relations with him must be sexual. In a Political
Alphabet published 4 August 1769, reputedly written by Mrs
Thrale, 'W. was a Widow would make Wilkes a Wife'; the widow
was Catharine Macaulay. When General Lee, an Englishman
formerly in the British army, joined the Americans, he achieved
high command, but was subsequently court-martialled for disobedience. No doubt intending to make a political joke, Mrs
Montagu suggested he should be sentenced to hanging, but that
Catharine Macaulay should save his life by marrying him under
the gallows.[45] Such an attitude may explain why her choice of
doctor and her declared admiration for his methods led Wilkes
and others to talk of 'some indiscretions' with Dr Graham.[46]

How far do her writings reflect any awareness of the position of
women? Her *History* is far from being a history of women. But if
not directed specifically at women, frequently in it she reveals a
sympathy for her sex, and she never omits any 'anecdote which
does honour to the female sex'. When at the trial of John
Hampden in the Ship Money case Mr Justice Crook (Sir George
Croke), was called on to give his verdict, he was so much in fear
of the ministry he had decided 'to give judgement for the king',
but his wife, 'a woman of true virtue', persuaded him not to 'err

[43] Caroline Robbins, 'The Strenuous Whig: Thomas Hollis of Lincoln's Inn',
William and Mary Quarterly, 3rd ser., 7 (1950), 406–53, at p. 420.

[44] *Horace Walpole's Correspondence*, ed. W. S. Lewis, 48 vols. (1937–83), xxiii.
145–6.

[45] *Thraliana: The Diary of Mrs H. L. Thrale, Later Mrs Piozzi, 1776–1809*, ed. K. C.
Balderston, 2nd edn., 2 vols. (1951), i. 121, 123.

[46] *Letters from the Year 1774 to the Year 1796 of John Wilkes, Esq. Addressed to His
Daughter, the Late Miss Wilkes*, 4 vols. (1804), ii. 76.

against his conscience and his honour' whatever it cost him. 'Struck with the exalted sentiments, and strengthened with the further encouragements, of so dear and persuasive a friend', Crook changed his mind and—although it did not alter the condemnation of Hampden—'argued with a noble boldness and firmness on the side of Law and Liberty'. It was an example that gave her 'infinite pleasure', for 'were the principles of the generality of the sex as just and as well founded as were those of this respectable woman, it would have a very happy effect on the conduct of society'.[47] Her comment did not go unnoticed. For women 'to give such a bias to the morals and manners of men', one reviewer agreed, would be 'a happiness to society'. But unfortunately the present state of feminine education was such that it was difficult 'for a man of sense and worth to make any impression on a woman's mind, without first debasing his own'.[48]

Among various petitions to the House of Commons against 'the cruelty and persecution of Papists, prelates and their adherents' in 1641, she noted that 'from gentlewomen, tradesmen's wives, etc.' They had felt it necessary to apologize 'for this their uncommon act' but, as they pointed out, they too were 'sharers in the common calamities which oppression produced'. They presented their petition 'not regarding the reproaches which may and are by many cast upon us'. It was done, they said, 'not out of any self-conceit or pride of heart, as seeking to equal ourselves with men, either in authority or in wisdom, but according to our places, to discharge that duty we owe to God, and the cause of the Church'.[49] Later she notes that the petition signed by 10,000 demanding an end to the illegal persecution of Lilburne and three other Leveller leaders for publication of *England's Second Chains*, was 'seconded by a female petition of the same tendency'.[50] One of her few comments on what marriage meant for many women was provoked by the view of Charles II as 'a civil and obliging husband'. 'Setting aside the advantages of affluence, and the splendour of rank', she wrote, 'the queen's situation must be considered as equally mortifying to that in which every other

---

[47] Macaulay, *History of England*, ii (1765), 217–18.
[48] *Monthly Review*, 32 (1765), 271.
[49] Macaulay, *History of England*, iii (1767), 186–7.
[50] Ibid. v. 196.

female is involved, whom a severe fate united in the indissoluble bonds of matrimony with a profligate rake.'[51]

Even in her philosophical work injustices to women are never far from her thoughts. Lord Bolingbroke was chastized for the view that 'restraining men from the practice of polygamy is an unjust and an unnecessary restraint on the natural prerogative of the male species'—a view, she wrote, that did not extend to 'the inferior creature, woman'. That part of Jewish law that deprived women of property 'for the sake of preserving the opulence of families in the male species' Bolingbroke thought admirable. He was prepared to approve an amendment of the law to make all female children choose husbands 'out of the males of their own race', arguing that 'if in many cases it be agreeable to the law of nature to extend the bonds of society by a prohibition of marriages between persons too near a-kin, it is, in many cases, at least, as agreeable to this law to preserve possessions and wealth in the families to which they belong, and not to suffer them to be carried away by any female caprice into others'. Thus, she comments, he would have denied women 'the right of choice in their domestic tyranny'. If there were those who believed that God, having made 'two species of creatures of equal intelligence and similar feelings, and consequently capable of an equal degree of suffering under injuries', was content to consign 'one of those species as a kind of property to a different species of their fellow-creatures', it was little wonder that justice was so little considered or understood.[52]

Of all Catharine Macaulay's work that which had most to say about women, their weaknesses and strengths, and, above all, their education was her *Letters on Education* (1790). Even in this work the subject of women was by no means her sole pre-occupation. If in her earlier work references to women are rare, it was not from unawareness of their situation. But by 1790 her own experience had made her painfully aware of the vulnerability of her sex. A woman who rebelled against all the rules took immense risks. Catharine Macaulay knew how easily women's reputations could be destroyed, their characters defamed, and their work ignored. If the position of women was better than it had been under slavery, she wrote, 'we ... have no great reason to boast of

---

[51] Macaulay, *History of England*, viii. 62–3; see also vii. 196 n.
[52] Ead., *Treatise on the Immutability of Moral Truth* (1783), 138, 156–7.

our privileges, or of the candour and indulgence of the men towards us'. Compared with men she admitted women 'in point of corporal strength' demonstrated 'some degree of inferiority' but this advantage had been so abused and exploited by men 'in the barbarous ages of mankind' as 'to destroy all the *natural* rights of the female species and reduce them to a state of abject slavery'. There were no sexual differences in the human character. The source of all women's so-called 'foibles and vices' originated in 'situation and education only'. The advantages men had over women had led to a 'more consistent picture of excellence' in them. She was critical of women's passive acceptance of the idea of men's natural superiority. If 'the difference that does subsist between the sexes, is too flattering for men to be willingly imputed to accident', she wrote, 'mark how readily they are yielded to by the women; not from humility I assure you, but merely to preserve with character those fond vanities on which they set their hearts'. All too willingly they joined 'in the sentence of their own degradation'.[53]

Shrewdly she recognized how often the assumption of male superiority was behind the compliments she received. If women's writing was good it was because they wrote like men. For 'when we compliment the appearance of a more than ordinary energy in the female mind, we call it masculine'.[54] If she read Mary Wollstonecraft's review of her *Letters* in the *Analytical Review* of 1790 she would have found herself described as 'this masculine and fervid writer'. Yet two years later Mary Wollstonecraft deliberately avoided the use of the phrase 'masculine understanding' because, as she emphasized, she did not admit 'of such an arrogant assumption of reason'.[55] But most of Catharine Macaulay's admirers and critics agreed in describing her work as 'untinctured with the weakness of a female pen'.[56] As we have seen her friend Toplady described her as 'more than female in understanding'.[57]

[53] Ead., *Letters on Education with Observations on Religious and Metaphysical Subjects*, (1790), 204–6, 210.
[54] Ibid. 204.
[55] *Analytical Review*, 8 (Sept.–Dec. 1790), 241–54, at p. 241; Mary Wollstonecraft, *Vindication of the Rights of Woman*, ed. Miriam Kramnick (1978), 206.
[56] *The European Magazine and London Review*, 4 (1783), 330.
[57] *The Works of Augustus Toplady* (1853), 855.

But in the eighteenth century there were few women of Mary Wollstonecraft's way of thinking. Catharine Macaulay was made painfully aware that if men constituted the main opposition to women achieving equality, all too often her own sex subscribed to the efforts to undermine women's confidence in their own ability and achievement. Such criticism was doubly hurtful, for women are more aware of the areas of vulnerability in their own sex. 'This woman', wrote Hannah More to Mrs Boscawen, 'is far from being any criterion by which to judge of the whole sex; she was not feminine either in her writings or her manners; she was only a tolerably clever man.'[58] Richard Polwhele, who knew them both, was not unperceptive when it came to Hannah More's comments on Catharine. He wrote that Hannah More more than once talked of her 'in a language that betrayed her envy'. Hannah More could 'bear no rival near the throne'. 'The vast superiority of Mrs. Macaulay', he went on, 'she could not but feel: and in the expression of that feeling, her eyes often sparkled with "resentful fire"'.[59] Hannah More not only disliked Catharine Macaulay's politics but had a horror of 'female politicians' and those who meddled in practical politics. She boasted that the title of Mary Wollstonecraft's *A Vindication of the Rights of Woman* was enough to put her off ever reading it.[60] If the rest of the blue stocking coterie were less vindictive in their prejudices, they too shared the belief that politics was not an area in which women should interfere—particularly when it was Catharine Macaulay's brand of politics. Mrs Montagu refused to read any of Mrs Macaulay's works.

Hannah More must have been delighted at the rumours that circulated at the time of Catharine Macaulay's second marriage. 'I feel extremely scandalized at her conduct', she wrote in 1782, but lest this demonstrated too much interest she added: 'yet I did not esteem her, I knew her to be absurd, vain, and affected'. But what confirmed her in her rightness in scorning Catharine Macaulay was the 'profligate turn which her late actions and letters have betrayed'.[61] In her opinion any woman who broke the rules of

---

[58] *The Letters of Hannah More*, ed. R. Brimley Johnson (1925), 80.

[59] R. Polwhele, *Reminiscences in Prose and Verse*, 3 vols. (1836), ii. 167.

[60] Hannah More, *Strictures on the Modern System of Female Education*, 2 vols. (1799), 6.

[61] *The Letters of Hannah More*, 80.

strict morality as she, Hannah More, interpreted them must be shunned. Sarah Vaughan of Philadelphia would have agreed. She felt, she wrote of Mrs Macaulay's visit, only scorn for a woman who 'carried with her a living monument of her want of common understanding and delicacy'. The 'living monument' was poor William Graham.[62] At the end of the century it was Mary Wollstonecraft's 'direct vindication of adultery' that was used to justify Hannah More's rejection of all she wrote.[63] For all Polwhele's criticism of Hannah More, he would have agreed with her in this rejection of Mary Wollstonecraft,

> ... whom no decorum checks,
> Arise, the intrepid champion of her sex;
> O'er humbled man assert the sovereign claim,
> And slight the timid blush of virgin fame.[64]

'To give girls such an idea of chastity as shall arm their reason and their sentiments on the side of this virtue' Mrs Macaulay regarded as 'the most difficult part of female education'. She can have had no illusions of the hypocrisy and double standards behind society's 'morality'. 'The great difference ... in the external consequences' following 'the deviations from chastity in the two sexes' probably arose 'from women having been considered as the mere property of the men' who therefore 'had no right to dispose of their own persons'. She wrote of how 'there is but one fault which a woman of honour may not commit with impunity; let her only take care that she is not caught in a love intrigue, and she may lie, she may deceive, she may defame, she may ruin her own family with gaming, and the peace of twenty others with her coquettry, and yet preserve both her reputation and her peace'.[65] She had lost both through the 'profligacy' of marrying a man twenty-six years her junior—proof of the unnatural lusts of widows.

Was it her experience of those last twelve years that led her to write that 'Woman has everything against her, as well our faults, as her own timidity and weakness'? All she had in her favour was 'her subtlety and her beauty'. 'Was it not very reasonable', she

---

[62] Kerber, *Women of the Republic*, 227 n. 68.
[63] More, *Strictures on the Modern System of Female Education*, 44.
[64] *The Unsex'd Females*, in Polwhele, *Poems*, ii. 38.
[65] Macaulay, *Letters on Education*, 210–11, 218–20.

added ironically, that 'she should cultivate both'? But she deplored 'false notions of beauty and delicacy' that tended only 'to corrupt and debilitate both powers of mind and body'. From such ideas originated the 'nervous diseases' and 'feebleness of constitution' with which so many women were burdened. Male children were allowed to act on impulse, but if a female child 'is inclined to show her locomotive tricks in a manner not entirely agreeable to the trammels of custom, she is reproved with a sharpness which gives her a consciousness of having highly transgressed the laws of decorum'. She called on parents to reject 'the absurd notion, that the education of females should be of an opposite kind to that of males'. They should give the same education to both. 'Let your children be brought up together; let their sports and studies be the same; let them enjoy, in the constant presence of those who are set over them, all that freedom which innocence renders harmless, and in which Nature rejoices'. The meaning of vice and virtue, she insisted, was the same for both sexes, for there was 'but one rule of right for the conduct of all rational beings'.[66]

One reason why she said little of women's situation in marriage was that in both of her marriages, she had been exceptional in finding happiness—a rare achievement in her time. Marriage had been no hindrance to her development. Rather, both husbands gave her every encouragement in her career. She was convinced the education of women was essential if happiness in marriage was to be achieved. For this reason 'true wisdom' was 'as useful to women as to men; because it is necessary to the highest degree of happiness, which can never exist with ignorance'. She saw 'the happiness and perfection of the two sexes' as 'so reciprocally dependent on one another that, till both are reformed, there is no expecting excellence in either.'[67]

For all her enlightened views on women's education, the double standard of morality that operated to women's cost, and the basis of happy marriages, Catharine Macaulay was not primarily concerned with the position of women, whether political or sexual. It needs emphasizing that only in her *Letters on Education*,

---

[66] Ibid. 47, 50, 201–2, 207, 212.
[67] Ibid. 201, 216.

published in 1790, did she focus attention on women. There is no doubt she was sympathetic to women, and that that sympathy increased with age, but neither her *History* nor her political polemic was primarily concerned with them. And when it came to her demand for reform of the system of parliamentary representation and an extension of the electorate, women's rights apparently had no place in her scheme of things. That she had thought of them—at least by 1790—is clear from her *Letters on Education*. She recognized that women suffered 'a total and absolute exclusion' from 'every political right'.[68] In such exclusion they shared the position of the great majority of the population. But reform of women's representation was not one of her priorities. In so far as she believed in an extension of the franchise she thought true political equality was impossible of achievement without more education of those as yet disenfranchized. Like the Levellers before her, and indeed her radical contemporaries, where women were concerned she seems not to have contemplated the possibility of change. She had read the works of the Levellers and she never questioned their limited objective of an extension of the electorate confined to men only.

Was Catharine Macaulay a feminist? It is doubtful whether in her ideas she would qualify in any modern sense of the word. Her priorities would have put women's position in society, bad although she recognized it as being, far down the list. Yet in the unwritten assumptions behind her behaviour there is much worthy of the name. All the obstacles and hindrances that most other women found insuperable she chose to ignore. She knew there was no real equality in the society in which she lived, but often she acted as though equality already existed. She did not hesitate to embark on a career that hitherto had been a virtual monopoly of men, and in her exchanges with her fellow historians she assumed her ideas were at least as worthy of consideration as theirs. One might question whether, despite her early achievement of fame, the idea of a scholarly woman historian was ever really accepted. But Catharine Macaulay acted always as though it was. In her determination to let no social convention interfere with what she wanted to do and say she was unique. The

---

[68] Ibid. 210.

Revd Joseph Price, a near neighbour and friend of John Sawbridge, noted on dining at Olantigh that 'Mrs. Macaulay does not retire after dinner with the ladies, but stays with the men'.[69] She was sometimes foolhardy, rash, emotionally innocent—even naïve—but consistently she behaved as an equal of men.

[69] *A Kentish Parson. Selections from the Private Papers of the Reverend Joseph Price, Vicar of Brabourne, 1767–86* ed. G. M. Ditchfield and Bryan Keith-Lucas (1991), 141.

7. *Religion, Ethics, and Education*

> She confirmed the reality of her prepossession in favour of the christian revelation, by the most diligent cultivation of benevolence towards mankind, and the most exact moral rectitude in every action of her life.
>
> (Mary Hays, *Female Biography*, 6 vols. (1806), v. 299)

> Every work published on education that affords one new idea which may be found useful in practice, is worthy the attention of the public.
>
> (Catharine Macaulay, *Letters on Education* (1790), preface p. iii)

IN the last ten years of her life Catharine Macaulay not only published three volumes of her *History* and a reply to Burke on the French Revolution, but ventured into two new fields. In 1783, the year the last volume of her *History* appeared, she published her *Treatise on the Immutability of Moral Truth*. Seven years later she produced *Letters on Education with Observations on Religious and Metaphysical Subjects*. Both represented a marked break with her earlier writings.

Until the publication of her *Treatise* we hear little of her religious beliefs. Catharine Macaulay was a member of the Church of England, and remained so all her life. Yet the nature of her friendships suggests she was anything but orthodox in her beliefs. Meeting her in the 1770s, Polwhele thought her 'abominably profane' and that 'she betrayed the sceptic when talking on religious subjects'. He had been horrified by her 'bold attack on St. Paul'—'very injudicious, certainly in conversation with a boy'. She had not only criticized several of the 'finest passages' in 'that sublime and beautiful chapter' (1 Cor. 15), but had censured St Paul for being, in his own words, 'all things to all men', a versatility she considered 'highly reprehensible'. She recognized his 'human literature and his supernatural intelligence', but thought him superstitious and mocked at the attention he paid to 'the ceremonies of the Jews in the case

of Timothy's circumcision'.[1] 'With a mind too enlightened for
bigotry, and an enemy to mere forms of devotion, often absurd,
and always spiritless,' wrote Mary Hays, 'the freedom with which
she delivered her sentiments on these subjects, drew upon her the
imputation of scepticism and infidelity.'[2] Catharine Macaulay was
later to condemn both.

How much or little religion meant to her in her early life is
uncertain. By the end of her life it had become important. She
had lost fame, reputation, and friends. She now demanded of
religion not merely consolation but some unchanging certainty.
'The thoughts of a fatherless universe, and a set of beings let
loose by chance or fate on one another, without other law than
power dictates and opportunity gives a right to exact,' she was to
write, 'chills the sensibility of the feeling mind into indifference
and despair'.[3]

She was liberal in her attitude to other religious sects. She
had 'never gone out of her way to attack the religious opinion
of others'.[4] Her close friendships with Dissenters and others
of diverse affiliations make this clear. They were formed with
religious men like Augustus Toplady, a liberal and radical clergyman of the Establishment; Thomas Wilson, a devoted Wilkite
but also rector of St Stephen's, Walbrook, and St Margaret's,
Westminster; Theophilus Lindsey, a convert to Unitarianism; and
in America, Ezra Stiles, a Congregationalist. With Stiles she
believed that reason should 'be allowed free play to propagate
both truth and error'. The trouble with established creeds and
orthodoxies was that they 'prevented other interpretations and
compelled the acceptance, as truth, of what was quite probably
only the erroneous opinion of man'.[5] In the 1760s she knew a
number of the Dissenters who moved inside the Club of Honest
Whigs: Thomas Hollis, Richard Baron, Caleb Fleming, James
Burgh, Richard Price, and Joseph Priestley. What they all had in
common besides religion was radical political sympathies.

What persuaded her to embark on the *Treatise*? It was a belated

---

[1] R. Polwhele, *Reminiscences in Prose and Verse*, 3 vols. (1836), ii. 103.

[2] Mary Hays, *Female Biography*, 6 vols. (1803), v. 298–9.

[3] Catharine Macaulay, *Letters on Education with Observations on Religious and Metaphysical Subjects* (1790), 324.

[4] Ibid., p. iv.

[5] *Dictionary of National Biography*; Edmund S. Morgan, *The Gentle Puritan: A Life of Ezra Stiles, 1727–1795* (1962), 178.

response to Archbishop King (1650–1729), who on Lockian principles had written *De Origine Mali* (1702) in an attempt 'to reconcile the existence of evil, and particularly moral evil, with the idea of an omnipotent and beneficent deity'.[6] With those before her who had answered King, she agreed that all who attempted such reconciliation had 'miserably failed in the Attempt'. She wrote approvingly of Dr Samuel Clarke, who had earlier preached much the same doctrine as she was to outline. The *Treatise* is not her best work, but clearly it was very important to her. Having 'stripped the Deity of Wisdom, and reduced the attributes of God to those of a physical nature, accompanied with a kind of intelligent mechanical ability', King was accused of proceeding 'to establish good and evil on the footing of will, dependent on the pleasure of God and to be read by man through the medium of suffering and enjoyment'. If the 'moral colour of actions take their complexion solely from their consequence', she argued, it meant that without punishment there would be no vice. If the origin of right and wrong lay in the 'arbitrary determination of the divine will' it removed 'one regular, simple, and universal rule of action for all intelligent nature'. 'To call God good, and wise, and omnipotent', she wrote, 'without being able to comprehend the manner or the mode in which he is good, wise and omnipotent ... is not praising either with judgment or with knowledge'. Her own belief was that God was 'omnipotent in the largest sense of the word, and that his works and commands' were 'founded in righteousness and not in mere will'. With approval she quoted Clarke's belief that 'every moral action which man performs ... is free, and without any compulsion or natural necessity, and proceeds either from some good motive or some evil one'.[7]

She was dealing with an age-old problem and her answer is not original. But what it reveals is her optimism about man and society. She was convinced of the possibility, given the power of reason, of achieving perfection both in individuals and in society as a whole. But reason was insufficient without faith. She wrote of the need for the teaching of the Church to concentrate particularly 'on the practical doctrines of the Christian religion'. It 'should represent man as a creature endued with powers capable

[6] *Dictionary of National Biography*.

[7] Catharine Macaulay, *A Treatise on the Immutability of Moral Truth* (1783), pp. viii, x n., 8, 32, 36–7, 40, 69.

of ameliorating his own natural situation', for she believed the 'power of human reason' could 'never be so properly employed as when enlarging boundaries of good and narrowing the empire of evil'.[8] She believed in the 'inherent virtues of the human character' and rejected Hobbes's notion of its 'irreclaimable depravity'. Yet vice, she admitted, was 'a much more glaring feature in all societies, than virtue', and 'some causes, more powerful than mere depravity of will', accounted for this 'general perversion of human sentiments'. Foremost was the effect of commerce rather than 'any fixed and irreclaimable principle of vice in men'. She rejected the idea of 'natural propensities' and insisted that 'there is not a virtue or a vice that belongs to humanity, which we do not make ourselves'. Commerce not only spread 'the contagion of flagitious luxury' but it made people more selfish and thus militated against 'honesty, integrity, frugality, moderation, sobriety, and a conscientious regard to the interests of the community at large, and to the private good of individuals'.[9] As we shall see she identified virtue in a nation with a simple agricultural society of smallholders.

She questioned whether civilization had kept pace with material improvements. Could there be any real progress in the state of morals 'whilst men are fettered with illiberal prejudices?'[10] She pointed to the 'greatest evils and uncertainties' that resulted from making morals and religion submissive to governments. Tories with no belief in scripture were willing to quote it 'in support of tyranny'. In discussion with one, when she refuted all other arguments, he replied he believed 'the bible in what St. Paul' said. 'I believe it as well as you,' she replied, 'but what St. Paul says was calculated for the circumstances of the Christians at that time'. Tyranny was 'contrary to all our ideas of God'.[11] If there was greater toleration in the world it arose 'not from an improvement of religious principle, but from the total loss of it'. 'Are wars less frequent than they were of old', she asked, 'and does a sentiment of justice forbid the carnage of the human mind, when interest

---

[8] Ead., *Letters on Education*, 335.

[9] Ead., *A Treatise on the Immutability of Moral Truth*, 5, 6, 10, 14, 16; *Letters on Education*, 10–11.

[10] Ead., *A Treatise on the Immutability of Moral Truth*, vi, 12.

[11] G. M. Ditchfield, 'Some Literary and Political Views of Catherine Macaulay', *American Notes and Queries*, 12 (1974), 70–6, at p. 73.

prompts and opportunity gives the word?' 'Are public trusts less abused; are public offices held with greater integrity than in former times; has such an improvement in the laws, manners, and the police of modern societies taken place, as to spread those advantages of opulence and plenty which commerce furnishes in a manner as shall be sensibly felt by all citizens; is the right of property in the persons of our fellow-creatures given up; or are slaves less abused?'[12]

She was convinced of the 'truth of the christian revelation, and the recompence which its author promises to his disciples'.[13] Her idea of God was as 'the universal parent of the creation' by which she meant 'a relation more tender than what we commonly annex to our ideas of the author of nature'. Most Christian sects, she noted, 'in order to spur on the lazy virtue of their votaries, have represented the rigorous justice of God, in a light which confines his benevolence to a narrow sphere of action'.[14] She opposed all 'principles of religion' which represented God as 'partial in the distribution of reward and punishment'.[15] By barring the gates of Paradise to 'all but the elect', God was represented as damning 'to an eternity of torments the far greater number of the human race. Tremendous thought! It is thus indeed that the gift of eternal life is a dangerous pre-eminence, and the balance becomes more than equal between us and the brute creation.'[16] The idea that 'the sorrows of a certain portion of individuals are necessary to the rejoicing of others' she found abhorrent. 'I should have small hopes', she wrote, 'could I once suppose him [God] so partially benevolent, as to make the final happiness of one part of the creation his care, whilst he sacrificed the rest to the devouring jaws of death.'[17] Augustus Toplady made the arithmetic work out differently when he argued with Joseph Priestley that 'Calvin's notions' meant 'the far greater part of the human race are made for endless happiness', and only 'a very small portion, comparatively, of the human species, falls under the decree of preterition and non-redemption'.[18]

---

[12] Macaulay, *Immutability of Moral Truth*, 12–14.
[13] Hays, *Female Biography*, v. 300.
[14] Macaulay, *Letters on Education*, 2.
[15] Ibid., p. iv.
[16] Ibid. 2–3.
[17] Ead., *History of England*, 8 vols. (1763–83), viii. 69; *Letters on Education*, 6.
[18] *The Works of Augustus Toplady* (1853), 863.

Catharine Macaulay saw 'the *events* of human life' as 'but a series of *benevolent providences*'. Not always was the '*omnipotent will*' seen behind them, but when it was seen 'declaring itself in favour of the future *perfection* and *happiness* of the moral world', little wonder if men were transported by '*hope* and *gratitude*'. It was this, she wrote in 1790, that Burke failed to understand in men's reactions to the French Revolution. She questioned whether he had 'heard of any millenium [*sic*]' except 'that fanciful one which is supposed to exist in the kingdom of the saints'.[19] The view that the 'doctrine of post-millennialism was central to Macaulay's religious beliefs' is a valid one. Lynne Withey has shown how clearly Catharine Macaulay envisaged the nature of the millennium as 'a period of time when the *iron* sceptre of *arbitrary* sway shall be broken: when *righteousness shall prevail* over the whole earth, and a *correct* system of equity take place in the conduct of man'. It was towards such a millennium that all improvement in men and society tended. This was God's plan for the world but by co-operating with it men 'had the power to affect the course of history'.[20]

She was confident of an afterlife. On her journey to Paris in 1777, she became so ill that her companion had feared the worst. Death, she told her when recovering, had no fears for her. It was but 'a short separation between virtuous friends', after which they would be reunited 'in a more perfect state'.[21]

An intriguing discovery is that she read the works of Jonathan Edwards, the Congregational clergyman, theologian, and philosopher, and the inspiration behind the Great Awakening in America in the early 1740s. Her sympathy for some of his ideas is understandable. He too was concerned at the growth of irreligion under the impact of commercial values. He had viewed with concern the emergence of a 'dangerous materialism and self-satisfaction in America'.[22] While most ministers held to the belief that God's saving grace was arbitrary and unearnable, they had

[19] Catharine Macaulay, *Observations on the Reflections of the Rt. Hon. Edmund Burke, on the Revolution in France* (1790), 20–1.
[20] Lynne E. Withey, 'Catharine Macaulay and the Use of History: Ancient Rights, Perfectionism, and Propaganda', *Journal of British Studies*, 16 (1976), 59–83, at pp. 61, 63.
[21] Hays, *Female Biography*, v. 299.
[22] David S. Lovejoy, *Religious Enthusiasm in the New World* (Cambridge, Mass. 1985), 178.

shied away from emphasizing such an uncompromising doctrine to their congregations, suggesting good behaviour would be rewarded. What people lacked, he thought, was any real awareness of their sinfulness, compared with which 'all the virtuous acts that ever [a man] performs, are as nothing'. Through recognizing their sinfulness, 'despairing of any hope, they could look for no escape but to throw themselves on God's mercy'.[23] They were completely dependent on God's forgiveness for salvation. God was under no obligation then to give them his saving grace, but as Edwards emphasized, 'most often conversion followed conviction'.[24] Like Catharine Macaulay later, Edwards lamented the lack of any vitality in religion. 'Never did the Cause of Religion and Virtue', he wrote of his times, 'run so low.' He saw a purely rational approach to religion as 'tending to Arminianism and even deism'.[25] Behind Edwards's ideas also there lurked a millennialism, a belief that the Awakening foreshadowed 'a time when all nations and countries "shall be full of light and knowledge"'.[26] Like Catharine Macaulay he wanted to open the churches to all and not just the elect. Not only does Catharine Macaulay make reference to him and Dr Priestley, as together having attempted 'to clear the doctrine of moral necessity from the dark perplexity in which it lay involved by Hobbes and other mischievous writers', but we learn from Thomas Adams that Edwards was 'a favourite author with her'. He had found her reading 'Edwards on the Will'.[27]

Augustus Toplady shared this admiration for Edwards's ideas. It may have been he who was responsible for introducing her to 'the great and good Mr. Edwards'. He talked of Edwards as 'that deep and masterly reasoner' and emphasized 'how upright and valuable a man Mr. Edwards by all accounts proved himself, in every part of his conduct'.[28] An extreme Calvinist and an admirer of George Whitefield, Toplady welcomed signs of an evangelical revival, from whatever source. He too remained within the Established

[23] Norman Fiering, *Jonathan Edwards's Moral Thought and its British Context* (1981), 57; Lovejoy, *Religious Enthusiasm in the New World*, 180.
[24] Edmund S. Morgan, *The Gentle Puritan* (1962), 25.
[25] Fiering, *Jonathan Edwards's Moral Thought*, 60.
[26] Lovejoy, *Religious Enthusiasm in the New World*, 194.
[27] Macaulay, *Immutability of Moral Truth*, p. xiv; *Extracts from the Itineraries and Other Miscellanies of Ezra Stiles*, ed. F. B. Dexter (1916), 418.
[28] *The Works of Augustus Toplady*, 862, 864, 856–7.

church, but this did not prevent him having many Dissenting friends and correspondents. His correspondence throws light on the religious views he shared with Mrs Macaulay. He preached, he told the Countess of Huntingdon, 'of little else but of justification by faith only in the righteousness and atonement of Christ; and of that personal holiness, without which no man shall see the Lord'. In his account of meeting James Burgh, he wrote of how they had got into a debate on free will. Burgh had argued that 'God does all he possibly can . . . to hinder moral and natural evil, but he cannot prevail; men will not permit God to have his wish.' When Toplady retorted that if this was the case, 'the Deity must needs be very unhappy', Burgh brushed his answer aside. God knew 'he must be so disappointed and defeated, and that there' was 'no help for it: and therefore he submits to necessity'.[29] As Catharine Macaulay wrote later, the 'idea that God can ever act independent of the best motive, is a plain contradiction of his acknowledged perfection'. It was 'highly derogatory to God to represent him as forming the creation, not for . . . bestowing happiness on sensitive existence', but from 'a motive of a very inferior nature, a certain kind of self gratification arising from the exertion of infinite intelligence and power'.[30] Much earlier Thomas Hollis had recorded how 'in a visit to Mrs. Macaulay, the question, whether evil may be committed to a great sole public good' being debated between them, he had 'strenuously held the negative'.[31] But Mrs Macaulay thought otherwise. Evil as well as good depended on God's will but 'the omnipotent Disposer and Director of all human actions and events produces good out of evil, and often renders the prejudices and vicious affections of his creatures instrumental to public and private happiness'.[32]

Edwards's works seem to have been well known in England. His *Faithful Narrative of the Surprising Work of God* (1737), became a best-seller among English Dissenting clergymen. His works enjoyed something of a renaissance in the 1770s, when the Dilly brothers reprinted his *Treatise concerning Religious Affections.*[33]

[29] Ibid. 862.
[30] Macaulay, *Immutability of Moral Truth*, xiii, 37.
[31] *Memoirs of Thomas Hollis*, ed. Francis Blackburne, 2 vols. (1780), i. 307.
[32] Macaulay, *History of England*, ii. 55.
[33] L. H. Butterfield, 'The American Interests of the Firm of E. and C. Dilly, with their Letters to Benjamin Rush, 1770–1795', *Papers of the Bibliographical Society of America*, 45 (1951), 283–332, at p. 294 n. 29.

Whatever attracted Catharine Macaulay in Edwards, it was not his hell-fire sermons, for she disliked enthusiasm of any kind. But Edwards was far more than a tub-thumping preacher. He denied the charge of enthusiasm, arguing that the revival produced by the advocates of the Great Awakening was nothing but 'remarkable outpourings of God's grace'.[34] He wished to restate 'the Calvinist dogma', writes Patricia Tracy, 'so that its meaning would be clear and emotionally affecting'. The emotions—or 'affections' as he called them—'fear and sorrow, desire, love or joy' were '*bona fide* channels for transmission of religious truths'.[35]

Edwards has been described as 'the culminating thinker in early American moral philosophy ... both more profound and original, and more acute in philosophical reasoning, than any other American in the eighteenth century'.[36] Recently some historians have seen 'the new spirit of defiant individualism' that Edwards inspired in his congregations as 'playing a central part in preparing Americans for the revolution'.[37] His enemies saw the Awakening as generating 'the same spirit which had inspired the bloody fanatics at Münster and Ranters everywhere'.[38] It was attacked as a threat to orthodoxy in religion, social order, and political stability. In the years before the revolution the heirs of the Great Awakening were to stress that the coming revolution was as much a struggle for religious as political liberty. But what had started as a religious 'enthusiasm' became increasingly secularized as the century proceeded with attempts to extend the revolution into areas subversive of colonial tradition and custom, the issue of slavery, for example, and the treatment of the Indians. It raises interesting questions about Catharine Macaulay's familiarity with, and admiration for, Edwards's ideas. We know she shared Edwards's views on slavery—as did many of her American friends. They had more than religious beliefs in common. Did she also see the revolutionary potential of his teaching?

[34] Lovejoy, *Religious Enthusiasm in the New World*, 179.
[35] Patricia Tracy, *Jonathan Edwards, Pastor: Religion and Society in 18th-century Northampton* (1980), 4; Lovejoy, *Religious Enthusiasm in the New World*, 193.
[36] Fiering, *Jonathan Edwards' Moral Thought*, 13.
[37] Patricia U. Bonomi, '"A Just Opposition": The Great Awakening as a Radical Model', in Margaret and James Jacobs (eds.), *The Origins of Anglo-American Radicalism* (1984), 242–56, at pp. 251, 253.
[38] Lovejoy, *Religious Enthusiasm in the New World*, 188.

The *Gentleman's Magazine* of September 1789 contained a comment on the *Treatise* written by Samuel Badcock in 1784. He thought this 'metaphysical performance' was 'wonderful'. Catharine Macaulay was 'not only a bold and fervid writer, but a shrewd and acute reasoner'.[39] These words from 'a gentleman of uncommon celebrity in the literary world' delighted her and she reprinted the *Treatise* in another form at the end of her *Letters on Education with Observations on Religious and Metaphysical Subjects*.[40]

If by the use of reason men and women could co-operate in God's purpose of achieving perfection, education was essential. This was one reason for her attaching such importance to its extension and improvement. Her *Letters on Education* range over a wide variety of subjects; nursing and infant care, the upbringing, training, and education of children; slavery, capital punishment and public executions, the need for improved care of prisoners and the better management of prisons; the importance of personal cleanliness, the treatment of animals, and the conditions of slaughter-houses. The diversity of contents may reflect awareness that time was running out for her. She wanted to express her ideas on a host of questions before it was too late. There is also evidence of a new humility, a concern with the dispossessed and the underdog, and even with the injustices of social and economic inequality. Her own sufferings had made her more sensitive to those of others.

Her ideas on child-care and education were in advance of her time. Against the French habit of swaddling babies in layers of clothes, she was not entirely convinced of the wisdom of the Americans exposing the heads of infants in all seasons. Children should be fed with fruit, eggs, and vegetables, and only very occasionally with meat. 'The taste of flesh', she wrote, 'is not natural to the human palate'. Sugar in excess was bad. 'Nature never intended', she wrote, 'to deprive us of our teeth', and 'warm liquors, warm beds, and warm nightcaps' led to bad teeth. Such ideas were of a piece with the asceticism of her daily life. She favoured cold baths from infancy to adulthood—although not in excess. She thought children should be accustomed at an early age to 'hardy habits'. She advised mothers not to overdress them,

---

[39] *Gentleman's Magazine*, 59 (1789), 777.
[40] Macaulay, *Letters on Education*, p. vii.

never to put them in stays, and not to let them wear shoes or socks. Washing was a good thing and she favoured a daily bath for infants. She strongly disapproved of using baby language. Breast-feeding, she wrote, did 'more harm than good', but she seems to have been thinking only of women of the upper classes and to have been writing with her tongue firmly in her cheek. How could one expect 'a fine lady' to give up 'all her amusements and enter into the sober habits of domestic life', just to 'nourish her offspring with wholesome food'? She could not be expected to 'part with her luxuries'. And when she returned, 'her milk, overheated with midnight revels and with the passionate agitations of a gamester's mind, must have qualities rather injurious than beneficial to life'.[41]

Children, she believed, should be taught 'the practice of benevolence' by keeping pets. Although she admitted she 'did not give harbour to all animals', she never made them 'suffer for having taken shelter under' her roof. There were more humane ways of killing animals for food than those used in slaughter-houses. Anyone not using 'the least painful' should be penalized. Against capital punishment, she thought 'the examples of taking away life should be as few as the nature of things will admit'. But on no account should it be made the object of public spectacle. England's penal laws needed reforming, but she recognized that given the nature of contemporary society there were 'no hopes of amendment'. Conditions inside prisons and houses of correction were 'better adapted to the eradicating out of the mind every principle of virtue than to the correction of vice'. She called for a reformation, recommending the work of the philanthropist and prison reformer, Mr Howard. Finally and without elaboration she deplored the 'treatment given by some of our countrymen to their African slaves'.[42]

She was against extravagant display of any kind, despite the fact that her critics in the past had thought her guilty of precisely this fault. Time and money spent on the 'extremes of fashion' indicated 'a mind vain, trifling and ostentatious'. Keeping large trains of useless servants was a luxury which had 'a greater tendency to vitiate than to mend the morals of society'. Perhaps

[41] Ibid. 27, 28–9, 33, 38, 41.
[42] Ibid. 278, 279, 283, 285.

with Dr Wilson's ludicrous behaviour in mind she expressed the view that 'no statue, or monument, should be permitted a place in the church, but of those citizens who have been especially useful in the mitigating the woes attendant on animal life; or who have been the authors of any invention, by which the happiness of man, or brute, may be rationally improved.' Pews should be allotted to worshippers 'according to an exact rule of parity' and no 'private decorations, no distinctions' should be permitted to destroy 'that equality which ought to be felt whilst we are worshipping our common Father'. Churches should be kept well aired, but she believed in heating them 'in the rigorous season of the year'.[43]

There are a bewildering variety of ideas here but the main thrust is towards education. Political equality, she was convinced, was impossible without an educated electorate. Any progress for women, she implied, relied on their receiving more and a better education. Such was the 'wretched state of domestic education' and so frequent the neglect the rich showed for 'this first of their social duties', that she favoured a 'system of public education'. There was much to be said for that 'attitude of the ancients in regarding the education of youth as part of the business of government'. There should be 'public nurseries for infants of all ranks'. A public system would 'increase the happiness of society'. The cost should be borne by taxing people according to their 'rank and fortune'. Would such a system deprive parents of their rights? Domestic instruction at its best she recognized as superior to public education, but many were incapable of undertaking the responsibility. It was 'only the opulent' who could 'bring education to its utmost point of perfection'. The main drawback to public education was 'that corrupt and narrow spirit which pervades all governments'. She knew of no European government to which she would feel confident to trust the education of her children. While against 'indiscriminate indulgence' in the education of children, with Locke, Rousseau, and Madame Genlis she wanted all severe punishment of children abolished.[44]

While children should learn 'much of habit and principle', they should not be troubled with religious doctrine. Their minds were 'very little fit for the contemplation of religious subjects'. It was 'a

[43] Ibid. 173, 307, 332, 333, 336.
[44] Ibid. 15, 98–9.

great mistake in point of prudence' for children to be made to read the Bible, and the 'perusal of sacred writings' should be postponed until the age of 21. Nor did she think children should be made to attend church regularly. Her aim in the religious instruction of a child, was 'to make a true Christian, that is . . . on conviction, of which', she went on to comment drily, 'I believe there are very few in this age'. The method to be adopted was to provide 'the evidence for and against Christianity'. If the result was Christian faith it would have been reached by an 'unbiased judgment' if 'an infidel [one] on rational principles'. For religion to become 'a powerful engine in the great work of human civilization . . . the articles of its faith', she wrote, 'must be clear of every mystery . . . contrary to rational belief and purged of every corruption which is repugnant to human ideas of rectitude'.[45]

With Rousseau she believed in instructing young minds, for 'we were not born to play all our lives'. Boys and girls should early be taught dancing, music, and drawing but these should be viewed only as 'sources of elegant and innocent amusement'. Until they reached the age of 10 or 12 when they could co-operate with their teachers and think independently, it was best not to burden the young mind 'with ideas it cannot comprehend'. 'For opinions taken up on mere authority, must ever prevent original thinking'. She stressed 'inducing habits of independence' at an early age. She listed books suitable for the instruction of children at every age. At 12, apart from instruction in English grammar, *Plutarch's Lives*, Addison's *Spectator*, and Guthrie's *Geographical Grammar* were recommended. At 14 attention should be paid to Dr Johnson's practical precepts, to written composition in both Latin and English, together with reading in history: Rollin's *Ancient History* in French, then 'one of the best of English Histories in this language'. Roman history from Livy to Tacitus in Latin and 'leisurely pursued', was to follow, together with Ferguson and Gibbon in English. Reading should then be directed at Greek history, to be succeeded by the history of Modern Europe. At 15 and 16 she recommended a study of the Greek language, a course of moral lectures, and the reading of poetry. English poetry should be limited to Shakespeare's plays, Addison's *Cato*, Steele's *Conscious Lovers*, Milton, and Pope. Among French poets she

---

[45] Ibid. 89–91, 136–7, 139, 328.

recommended Boileau, and the plays of Corneille, Racine, Molière, and Voltaire. Before they reached 18 she advised instruction in ancient geography, astronomy, experimental philosophy, and natural history. Once 18, pupils 'of genius', should know enough Greek to be able to read Plato, Demosthenes, Homer, Euripides, and Sophocles, and should have started a course of logic and philosophy. At 19 their political education should commence with a study of Harrington, Sydney, Locke, and Hobbes. After studying some ancient mythology and metaphysics, at 21 they could start on sacred writings.[46]

It was a daunting list, perhaps reflecting awareness of the limitations of her own education. Mary Wollstonecraft was stunned. 'We should be almost afraid that the number mentioned are more than could be digested, unless by a youth of uncommon abilities, during the period specified'![47] Catharine Macaulay emphasized that her recommended reading was for female as well as male children. For the 'judicious reader' she advised the reading of Cervantes, Le Sage, Fielding, which would 'ever give delight', but was against indiscriminate novel-reading in youth. She considered Richardson wholly unsuitable for young people. Finally she cautioned parents that the happiness or misery of their 'posterity' depended on them. It was their 'natural virtues and vices' which 'commonly' descended to their children. She encouraged them to 'lay aside the air of the solemn dictator to their children' and 'enter into the familiarity of a companionable friendship' with them.[48]

Mary Wollstonecraft reviewed the work and warmly recommended it to parents. It added 'new lustre to Mrs Macaulay's character as an historian and a moralist'. It showed 'a degree of sound reason and profound thought which either through defective organs, or a mistaken education, seldom appears in female productions'.[49] That Catharine Macaulay devoted her last major work to education tells us something about how her outlook had changed. She was now convinced that progress, whether political or social, could only come about through the extension

---

[46] Ibid. 46, 62, 66, 129–30, 133–5.

[47] Mary Wollstonecraft's review of Catharine Macaulay's *Letters on Education* in the *Analytical Review*, 8 (Sept.–Dec. 1790), 241–54, at p. 245.

[48] Macaulay, *Letters on Education*, 144–5, 161, 154.

[49] *Analytical Review*, 8 (1790), 254.

and improvement of education. 'Of all the arts of life', she wrote, 'that of giving useful instruction to the human mind, and of rendering it the master of its affections, is the most important'.[50] Many of the questions with which she was concerned remain relevant today.

[50] Macaulay, *Letters on Education*, p. i.

8. The Sources and Nature of Catharine Macaulay's Republicanism

Sir, there is one Mrs. Macaulay in this town, a great republican.

(*Boswell's Life of Johnson*, ed. G. B. Hill, rev. L. F. Powell, 6 vols. (1934), i. 447)

WHEN Horace Walpole recalled events of 1768 he thought 'there was at this time an avowed, though very small republican party, the chiefs of which were Mrs. Macaulay, the historian, her brother Sawbridge, his brother-in-law, Stephenson, a rich merchant, and Thomas Hollis'.[1] It is an intriguing comment for it not only suggests her brother shared her republican ideas, but links together the Wilkites and the Society of the Supporters of the Bill of Rights which they formed, with the Real Whigs. It is said that Thomas Wilson invited Hollis to become a member of the Supporters of the Bill of Rights, but there is no evidence that he accepted.[2] He sought to avoid involvement in current political activity whether in England or America. Hollis is an extreme case, but all Real Whigs in the 1760s and 1770s, as we have seen, were concerned more with the theory of government than practical political activity. In the late nineteenth century Lecky wrote of the emergence of a new Radical party which was 'very weak in Parliament and not strong in the country'. According to him 'it included a few speculative republicans, the most prominent of whom were Mrs. Macaulay, the historian . . . and a wealthy and very excellent private gentleman named Hollis'.[3] It is worth remarking that it was Walpole, a shrewd contemporary, and Lecky, a far from insignificant historian of the eighteenth century, who picked out Mrs Macaulay as one of 'the chiefs' and 'the most prominent'

---

[1] Horace Walpole, *Memoirs of the Reign of George III*, ed. G. F. Russell Barker, 4 vols. (1894), iii. 220.

[2] Caroline Robbins, 'The Strenuous Whig: Thomas Hollis of Lincoln's Inn', *William and Mary Quarterly*, 3rd ser., 7 (1950), 406–53, at p. 448.

[3] W. E. H. Lecky, *A History of England in the Eighteenth Century*, 8 vols. (1878–90), iii. 375.

of the republicans. By bracketing the names of Macaulay and Hollis together, they indicate that one source of her republicanism was the group of commonwealthmen among whom both she and Hollis circulated. Within this group it was Hollis who influenced her most: first by providing material on the basis of which a republican history of the seventeenth century could be written; and secondly, by conveying to her something of his enthusiasm for the writings of his heroes of that century, in particular, Milton, Sidney, and Harrington.

For all the anecdotes related of Catharine Macaulay's hatred of monarchy it was her history which first won her the label of 'republican'. Hollis provides an important clue to that republicanism. She shared his belief that knowledge of the seventeenth century was crucial to an understanding of events in the eighteenth. There was a continuity between them. In their ideas of what was wrong with the constitution, and what reforms were needed, they went back to the writings of Milton and Marvell, the Levellers, Ludlow, Sidney, and Harrington. Catharine Macaulay delighted in the existence, in her own time, of 'a few enlightened citizens' who recognized that 'the works of Nevil, Sydney, and Harrington' were 'performances which excel even the antient classics in the science of policy'.[4] If she had been asked what above all else enabled her to write a republican history of the seventeenth century, she could hardly have failed to mention the help she received from Hollis. As we have seen, Hollis and his friend and collaborator, Richard Baron, played a vital role in collecting seventeenth-century material. They rediscovered, and made accessible, many texts and tracts of the period 1640–60 which had been mislaid or lost. They reprinted works of writers that, but for them, would have remained largely unknown to the eighteenth century.

Hollis's political position is well illustrated by the reply he sent to a letter from his steward when on his travels, that told him one of the livings in Hollis's gift had fallen vacant. His advice was sought on how the living should be filled. Hollis replied that the incumbent must possess the 'right qualities befitting a clergyman'. These included 'that he undoubtedly be a whig in its most extensive sense, that is an advocate for the civil and religious rights

---

[4] Catharine Macaulay, *The History of England*, 8 vols. (1763–83), v. 383 (*recte* 391).

of mankind, without being activated by the narrow views of a party'. Friends pressed him to become a parliamentary candidate. Hollis admitted privately he would have liked a political career but he was strongly opposed to any system of entering parliament which depended on favours or bribes. Finding these were essential to gaining entry, about 1754 he firmly turned his back on a career in politics, and began his collection of books, tracts, and medals 'for the purpose of illustrating and upholding liberty, and preserving the memory of its champions, to render tyranny and its abettors odious'. His considerable fortune made such collecting possible, but he was no mere antiquarian. His initial concern was with English writers on liberty, but he also collected the works of classical and European authors. Later, as we shall see, he concerned himself with publicizing the cause of the American colonists in England. His aim was to make his collection 'as useful as possible' over as wide an area as possible.[5]

When Hollis died Horace Walpole described him as 'the most bigoted of all republicans'. 'He was formed to adorn a pure republic,' he said, 'not to shine in a depraved monarchy'.[6] Dr Johnson echoed Walpole's view, adding that Hollis was 'one who mis-spent an ample fortune in paving the way for sedition and revolt in this and neighbouring kingdoms, by dispensing democratical works'.[7] Hollis's biographer, Francis Blackburne, strongly denied Hollis was a republican, but he defined the term so narrowly as 'an enemy to a mixed government, with an executive magistrate at its head', that it would have ruled out many in the eighteenth century who called themselves republicans, including Catharine Macaulay.[8] Blackburne published his biography in 1780 when holding republican ideas was dangerous. Following the Gordon Riots, many of the propertied middle class took fright at what they saw as revolutionary activity appealing to the lower classes. In August 1780 a list of those considered trouble-makers in the London Corporation was sent to Lord Amherst, responsible for suppressing the Gordon Riots. Under 'Republicans

---

[5] Ibid. i. 54, 59–60.

[6] *The Last Journals of Horace Walpole*, ed. John Doran, 2 vols. (1859), i. 287; Walpole, *Memoirs of the Reign of George III*, iii. 220.

[7] John Nichols, *Illustrations of the Literary History of the Eighteenth Century*, 6 vols. (1817–31), vi. 157.

[8] *Memoirs of Thomas Hollis*, ed. Francis Blackburne, 2 vols. (1780), i. 210.

in Principle' it included John Sawbridge, James Townshend, Frederick Bull, and, despite his declared opposition to the rioters, 'John Wilkes (Joiner) "Full of Mischief"'[9] In the volume of her *History* published in 1781, Catharine Macaulay was on the defensive against accusations of republicanism that had been made against her. She was aware that 'republican principles and notions have always been too unpopular in this country to found on them any rational scheme of interest or ambition'. She was writing of the seventeenth century but she could well have been thinking of her own time. It was 'from the conviction only of the integrity of their motives' that, in her *History*, she appeared to be 'partial to the leaders of the republican party'.[10]

'In all changes of the times', wrote Hollis in 1769, 'I remain a true old Whig, almost unic.'[11] He still identified with the seventeenth-century Whig tradition and once described himself as 'a disciple of Milton', who, he added, was 'my hero, and the guide of my paths'.[12] It was Hollis's opinion that 'no man can be a good citizen who is not an honest commonwealth's-man, a character which does not consist in a mere enmity to kingly government as such, but to the encroachments upon the constitutional rights and liberties of the people by the powers in being of any denomination'.[13] Hollis was concerned, Caroline Robbins has argued, 'not with the need to recast the social order nor with the problems of economic inequality but with the need to purify a corrupt constitution and fight off the apparent growth of prerogative power'.[14] With other Real Whigs his objective was to limit executive power rather than oppose the monarchy. They supported a mixed constitution but grew increasingly critical of the growth of ministerial power and its manipulation of members of parliament by bribery.

When the first volume of Mrs Macaulay's *History* appeared, Hollis, as we have seen, greeted it enthusiastically. In January 1765, she sent him the second volume. He wrote to tell her how he 'admired the industry, judgement, energy, elegance, faith-

[9] As quoted J. Paul de Castro, *The Gordon Riots* (1926), 234.
[10] Macaulay, *History of England*, vi, p. viii.
[11] *Memoirs of Thomas Hollis*, i. 428.
[12] Robbins, 'The Strenuous Whig', 444; *Memoirs of Thomas Hollis*, i. 112.
[13] *Memoirs of Thomas Hollis*, i. 118.
[14] Robbins, 'The Strenuous Whig: Thomas Hollis of Lincoln's Inn', 449.

fulness, and magnanimity' of the work. The following March Hollis bought from the library of a Dr Leatherland some 145 volumes, mainly tracts of the civil war period, and 'with the intention of bringing them nobly into use', made an anonymous present of them 'to the ingenuous [*sic*] Mrs. Catharine Sawbridge Macaulay', who, he added, 'is now writing that most important period of our history'. They had cost Hollis £10. 1*s.*[15] In June the following year a further thirty tracts 'published during the civil wars' were sent to her. Again the sender remained anonymous.[16] She must have had some inkling of Hollis's generosity, for he also lent her books and tracts from his own collection. Judging by those included in her *Catalogue of Tracts*, she was the owner of a number of rare and inaccessible sources for the period of the Interregnum. That she was able to use such tracts was, as Caroline Robbins has emphasized, in no small part due to Hollis.[17] When she published her fourth volume which closed 'so important a period', Hollis acknowledged the good use to which she had put his gifts. She was, he wrote, 'a very valuable elegant historian'.[18]

She must also have benefited indirectly from the collecting zeal of Hollis. For apart from gifts to individuals, he gave many gifts of books to the Dissenting academies, to Dr Williams's Library, to the Scottish universities, to the Bodleian, and to the British Museum, to which, it was said, 'he contributed ... many things to its valuable stores from his own collections'.[19] It was to Hollis among others that Joseph Priestley referred when he wrote how 'since the opening of the British Museum many persons are daily contributing to that immense and valuable collection, by sending ancient writings and manuscripts'.[20] Hollis was largely responsible for having the valuable Thomason collection of Civil War tracts presented to the British Museum.[21] Hollis was most responsible for influencing Catharine Macaulay's republican ideas; but he was not alone.

[15] *Memoirs of Thomas Hollis*, i. 264; see also MS of diary of Thomas Hollis, entry for 10 Apr. 1765.

[16] *Memoirs of Thomas Hollis*, i. 269; see also MS of diary of Thomas Hollis, entry for 18 June 1765.

[17] Caroline Robbins, *The Eighteenth-Century Commonwealthman* (1959), 267.

[18] *Memoirs of Thomas Hollis*, i. 410.

[19] Ibid. 82.

[20] Joseph Priestley, *Lectures on History and General Policy*, 2 vols. (1803), i. 376.

[21] Robbins, 'The Strenuous Whig', 424.

Another member of this circle was Richard Baron, the close friend of the Macaulays in the 1760s. In his politics, it was said, he was 'a high-spirited republican, an adorer of Milton . . . Sydney and Locke'. Unlike Hollis, he would have proudly acknowledged the truth of the description. For Baron was a far more outspoken republican than Hollis, who considered him somewhat rash in giving his opinion of books too hastily and not always authenticating the many anecdotes he related about their authors.[22] Sylas Neville revealed that at the height of his popularity, Pitt had 'courted Baron to furnish him with Republican principles'. Pitt's carriage, it was noted 'sometimes stood for four hours at Baron's door'. But when later Baron asked him for financial help, Pitt had called him 'a man unfit to be conversed with'. 'He is such a hot-headed Republican', he was reported as saying, 'that I cannot do anything for him.'[23] On 30 January 1768, the anniversary of the execution of Charles I, when Sylas Neville called on Baron to persuade him 'to dine at the Green Man on calfs head', he found him in bed and too ill to speak. In less than a month he was dead. He died in poverty leaving his family in distressing circumstances. Neville regretted he had not got to know him earlier. When, after his death, he met a friend who had known him well, he was told that although Baron had been 'a very honest man' who 'took great pains in the cause of Liberty', he was 'mad in a certain degree'. 'What seemed madness in him', Neville concluded, 'was only a high degree of enthusiasm'.[24]

There were others of the same circle who, like Baron, expressed more republican sentiments than Hollis. In 1767 when Sylas Neville and Timothy Hollis were discussing the appearance of an enlarged edition of one of Baron's works, they thought it might well run into some difficulties with ministers, as Baron had defended the assassin of the Duke of Buckingham in 1628. But Neville was quite clear 'that if a tyrant or bad magistrate cannot be brought to justice in a solemn & regular manner, every individual has a right to kill him as an enemy of mankind, just as he has a right to kill a mad dog or other fierce beast'. But few would have gone as far as Baron in 1767 when, commenting that the Duke of Cumberland, uncle of George III, 'was even more haughty,

[22] Ibid. i. 61; ii. 578, 581.
[23] *The Diary of Sylas Neville 1767–1788*, ed. Basil Cozens-Hardy (1950), 15, 18, 19, 20.
[24] Ibid. 29, 30, 69.

insolent and wicked than the rest of the Royal Family', he went on to add that the only hope of salvation lay in a 'general rising'. Sylas Neville, it is true, expressed his agreement with him but, more cautious than Baron, thought it a comment that should not be repeated except to 'true friends of liberty'.[25] When with Caleb Fleming, he went to meet Catharine Macaulay, they talked of Neville's desire to go and fight for the Corsicans. Fleming had tried to dissuade Neville, arguing that 'there will be employment for you at home before you can get to Corsica—by a general rising of the people'. It was a subject they later discussed with Mrs Macaulay. Neville recorded that she thought it would be an advantage 'if the people suffer a little more oppression before they rise', adding that 'they may then act with a greater spirit'. She feared that 'if a revolution should happen at present, knowledge is not sufficiently diffused for the settlement of Liberty on a solid basis'.[26] This explains the emphasis she was later to place on the improvement and expansion of education.

What above all Catharine Macaulay shared with Hollis was an admiration for the writings of James Harrington. Harrington's historical approach to politics must have had a particular appeal for her, for she had a passionate belief in history as the key to an understanding of current political problems. She would have welcomed the broad sweep of his analysis, in the context of which he placed the English revolution. Her republicanism, at least in the 1760s and 1770s, owed much to Harrington. She enthusiastically embraced his thesis that property was the basis of political power, and that a change in the balance of property of necessity led to a change in 'the superstructure' or the form of political power. In 1769 she drew heavily on Harrington's imaginary republic of Oceana in framing a republican constitution for Corsica.[27] Earlier Hollis had inserted in the *London Chronicle* an appeal to the people of Corsica to read and learn from Harrington, whose Oceana 'for practicableness, equality, and completeness, is the most perfect model of a common-

[25] Ibid. 23, 26.

[26] An unpublished extract of Sylas Neville's diary quoted in G. M. Ditchfield, 'Some Literary and Political Views of Catherine Macaulay', *American Notes and Queries*, 12 (1974), 70–6, at pp. 72, 74.

[27] Catharine Macaulay, *Loose Remarks on Certain Positions to be found in Mr Hobbes's Philosophical Rudiments . . . with a Short Sketch of a Democratical Form of Government, in a Letter to Signor Paoli* (1767).

wealth that ever was delineated by ancient or modern pen'.[28]

Harrington's *Oceana* was written in the troubled period of 1649–53, when attempts were being made to frame a new constitution. Harrington believed *Oceana* provided a solution, in that while preserving what the Civil War had achieved it effectively created an obstacle to the dangers of 'excessive democracy'. The Civil War confirmed the shift of political power commensurate with the shift that had already taken place in economic. But if ownership of land had now been transferred from the nobility to the gentry, it was important that safeguards should be introduced to prevent any future concentration of property in a few hands, for popular government could only exist where land-ownership was widely diffused through the community. Hence Harrington's insistence on an Agrarian Law, which by limiting the amount of land any one landowner could hold to the value of £2,000 a year, imposing a restriction on dowries of £1,500, and ending primogeniture so that estates should be divided between all the children, effectively, or so he thought, prevented any return of monarchy or aristocracy.[29] In the view of Catharine Macaulay many of the problems Harrington's *Oceana* set out to solve were still present in the 1760s. When framing a Corsican constitution, and later, in her concern for the nature of the American constitution, she too was anxious to avoid 'aristocratical accumulation of property'. In her advice to Paoli she echoes Harrington's Agrarian Law, recommending the equal division of estates between all male heirs on a man's death and, 'in default of such heirs, between his male heirs in the first and second degree of relationships'. But she went further than Harrington in 'debarring females the bringing of dower in marriage', and, as Susan Staves has emphasized, 'far from adding to the rights contemporary women enjoyed, actually would have lessened them'.[30] Catharine Macaulay was not alone in her belief in an Agrarian Law. Earlier Francis Hutcheson had subscribed to it, and later Thomas Spence was to advocate it. Not all her friends, however, thought it feasible. Timothy Hollis discussed it with Sylas Neville and

[28] *London Chronicle*, 19 (1766), 352, as quoted in *Memoirs of Thomas Hollis*, i. 306.

[29] Christopher Hill, *Puritanism and Revolution* (1986), 290, 295.

[30] Macaulay, *Loose Remarks*, 36, 37; Susan Staves, ' "The Liberty of a She-Subject of England": Rights Rhetoric and the Female Thucydides', *Cardozo Studies in Law and Literature*, 1 (ii) (1989), 161–83 at p. 164.

concluded that it 'could not be easily carried into execution' and that abolition of primogeniture alone would be as effective and much easier to achieve.[31]

The source of some of her republican ideas can be traced through Hollis, Baron, and others of the group of Real Whigs, to the writings of Milton and Marvell, Sydney, Ludlow, and Harrington, writings with which they were all familiar. In her own account of the inspiration for her republican ideas, she talked of her early reading of 'the annals of the Roman and the Greek republics'.[32] The importance she placed on rotation as a necessary guard against the dangers of corruption, she wrote, owed something to her reading of the history of the Roman republic, as well as to Harrington. Her recognition of the defects of that republic led to her emphasis on the need for 'fixing the Agrarian on a proper balance'. Had this been done in Rome 'it must have prevented that extreme disproportion in the circumstances of her citizens, which gave such weight of power to the aristocratical party, that it enabled them to subvert the fundamental principles of the government, and introduce those innovations which ended in anarchy'.[33]

She emphasized in a highly traditional manner the need for virtue among citizens of a republic. It was a notion far from confined to her. James Burgh fully endorsed her views. If she felt called on to apologize for 'the seeming preciseness of manners' of the Commonwealth parliament, he wrote, it was in the interests of 'promoting of virtue and religion among the people'.[34] Joseph Priestley was to write of 'virtue and public spirit' as 'the necessary supports of all republican governments'.[35] Richard Price in his *Observations on the Importance of the American Revolution* commented approvingly on how American society consisted of 'an independent and hardy YEOMANRY, all nearly on a level, . . . clothed in home-spun—of simple manners, strangers to luxury'. He called on Americans to maintain at all costs 'those virtuous and simple manners by which alone republics can long subsist'. He confessed to being unable to reconcile himself to 'the idea of

---

[31] *The Diary of Sylas Neville*, 17–18.
[32] Macaulay, *History of England*, i, p. vii.
[33] Ead., *Loose Remarks*, 33–5.
[34] James Burgh, *Political Disquisitions*, 3 vols. (1774–5), iii. 192–3.
[35] Priestley, *Lectures on History and General Policy*, ii. 81.

an immoral patriot; or to that separation of private from public virtue, which some' thought possible.[36] Jacques Brissot, after his visit to America, wrote that 'without morals there can be no liberty' and with Catharine saw 'the morals of the people' as the secret of success of the American revolution. Such virtue he linked with a simple agricultural society of smallholders—'nine tenths of them' living 'dispersed in the country'—thrift, and the avoidance of all ostentation and luxury.[37] It was a sentiment with which John Adams wholeheartedly agreed. In 1776 he told Mercy Warren that he sometimes doubted whether there was 'public virtue enough to support a Republic'.[38] 'Without national Morality' he wrote, 'a Republican Government cannot be maintained'.[39] Among many Americans expressing similar views, Jefferson thought such small farmers 'the most valuable citizens'.[40]

Among contemporaries it was not only Horace Walpole who saw Mrs Macaulay as a 'republican' who wrote 'republican' history. When Edmund Burke published his *Thoughts on the Cause of the Present Discontents*, he wrote that it had been received by the public 'beyond my Expectations'. 'The fiercest Enemies it has yet met with', he later told Richard Shackleton, 'are in the republican faction'. He defined them as 'a rotten subdivision of a Faction amongst ourselves, who have done us infinite mischief ... I mean the Bill of Rights people'. When, a few months later, Catharine Macaulay published her reply, he described her as 'our republican Virago'. Her 'performance' was as he expected, but he admitted that 'none of that set' could do better, adding 'the Amazon is the greatest champion amongst them'.[41] It was high praise from an enemy. But despite the looseness with which the term was often used, nobody ever suggested that republicans were anything but a very small group. As Timothy Hollis remarked to Sylas Neville

[36] Richard Price, *Observations on the Importance of the American Revolution* (1785 edn.), 69, 85. *Observations on the Nature of Civil Liberty* (1776), 43.
[37] J. P. Brissot de Warville, *New Travels in the United States of America, Translated from the French* (London, 1792), pp. xix, x, xi.
[38] *Warren–Adams Letters*, 2 vols. (Massachusetts Historical Society Collections, 72, 73; 1917–25), i. 202.
[39] As quoted Edmund S. Morgan, *The Meaning of Independence* (1976), 25.
[40] Fitzpatrick, 'Rational Dissent in the Late 18th Century', 302.
[41] *The Correspondence of Edmund Burke*, ed. T. W. Copeland, 10 vols. (1958–78), ii. 139–40, 149–50.

when proposing a meeting 'of the mutual friends of Liberty' in 1767, 'there are very few companies of Republicans'.[42]

If originally what attracted Walpole to her *History* was its 'emphatic Whiggism', he became increasingly opposed to her republican views. His political ideas underwent considerable change between the early sixties and the late seventies. In the sixties he had given his full support to the opposition and become progressively more sympathetic to Wilkes. His earlier admiration for George Grenville completely evaporated in the course of the Wilkes affair and he transferred his support to the Rockingham Whigs. But here too he experienced bitter disillusionment. As we have seen, for Burke's *Thoughts on the Cause of the Present Discontents* he had the greatest contempt. He openly expressed his preference for Catharine Macaulay's answer. Yet while more and more disillusioned with his own party he could not wholeheartedly identify with hers. When in 1778 he confessed to the Revd William Cole that 'Mr. Hollis wrote against me for not being Whig enough' and that he was 'offended with Mrs. Macaulay for being too much a Whig', Cole was clearly disconcerted. For both Hollis and Macaulay were 'in their writings determined republicans', and in confirmation of how vaguely the term was used, he went on to add, 'if I greatly do not mistake, this can be no offense at Strawberry Hill'.[43] Yet an offence to Walpole it clearly was. When Catharine Macaulay defended the Parliamentary army in the Civil War, some of the differences between them were revealed. 'I worship liberty as much as she does, detest despotism as much,' Walpole protested, 'but I never yet saw or read of a form of government under which more general freedom is enjoyed than under our own.' The people, he argued, were not capable of government 'and do more harm in an hour, when heated by popular incendiaries, than a king can do in a year'. And what check was there on the people in a republic? 'In what republic', he asked, 'have not the best citizens fallen sacrifice to the ambition and envy of the worst? God grant that, with all its deficiencies, we may preserve our own mixed government.' Two years later he wrote bitterly to Cole that 'no King nor government can long please a people given up to change of all sorts'. With the

---

[42] *The Diary of Sylas Neville*, 18.

[43] *Horace Walpole's Correspondence*, ed. W. S. Lewis, 48 vols. (1937–83), ii. 90–1, 91 n. 3.

description of the two Charleses in her *History* in mind, he added 'a virtuous one shall be abused by Mrs. Macaulay for being uxorious and loving his wife too well: a profligate one shall be abused for the very reverse'.[44]

The influence of Hollis and Baron only became clear when she ventured on her third, and more particularly, her fourth and fifth volumes, covering the years 1640–60. It is surely the explanation of why, as some have argued, her *History* became more republican as it proceeded. Reviewing her second volume the *Monthly Review* thought that while she gave 'a liberal scope to those noble principles [i.e. love of freedom], yet she does not run into the extravagant enthusiasm of republican bigots'.[45] In her third volume she had argued that 'every political distinction and privilege which is partial' impeded 'the entire and equal subjection to the authority of the law'. Such ideas the *Review* found 'much too refined'. 'It is difficult if not impossible for any society', it wrote, 'to subsist long without political distinctions and privileges.' It firmly rejected the notion of a 'community formed on such a levelling plan'.[46] When in the fourth volume, she passionately defended regicide and talked of the fear and horror of the gentry and nobility at the 'growth of opinions which tended to reduce all men to that equitable state of equality', she had gone too far. It was 'not difficult to determine the Writer's bias'. 'Those who contend most zealously for this equality', argued the reviewer, 'only wish to rise to the level of those above them, but would never endure that those beneath them should be advanced to the same station'.[47] In fact sensitive to the accusation of favouring 'a levelling plan', in her fourth volume, she made quite clear why she rejected any attempt at levelling. Although God had given 'equal and impartial privileges to the species in general, yet the difference which exists in the judgment, understanding, sagacity, genius and industry of individuals, creates superiority and inferiority of character, and produces a state of dependence from man to man'. 'The whole art of true and just policy', she thought, lay in preserving natural subordination 'established by God himself' while preventing 'that accumulation of property and influence which the different

---

[44] Walpole, *Memoirs of the Reign of George III*, iii. 122–3.
[45] *Monthly Review*, 32 (1765), 217.
[46] Ibid. 36 (1767), 304–5.
[47] Ibid. 40 (1769), 359, 360.

qualities of men occasion, from producing tyranny, and infringing the general rights of the species'.[48]

In holding such views Catharine Macaulay in no way differed from other contemporary radicals. Earlier Thomas Hollis had argued that 'all commonwealths were founded by gentlemen'.[49] Joseph Priestley reasoned that it was persons of considerable fortune who, because of the education they had enjoyed, were 'best qualified to act for the public good', and who therefore should play the dominant role in government and occupy 'the highest offices'. Those with 'most property at stake' would be 'most interested in the fate of their country'. Three years later he amended the claim to those of 'a *moderate* fortune' who were, he thought, 'more truly independent' than the more opulent.[50] Even Tom Paine, it is suggested, although more democratic in his views than most contemporaries, 'did not entirely reject the contemporary notion that some proof of personal independence should be required of voters'.[51]

Much the same accusation as that of the *Monthly Review* was made against her by Dr Johnson in the anecdote he told to prove 'the absurdity of the levelling doctrine'. One evening at her house he had suggested she should invite her footman to sit down and dine with them.[52] Much later she queried Johnson's version of the occasion and his 'additions, quite foreign to the simplicity of the circumstance as it really existed'. But her own version, while different from Johnson's, is equally revealing. She insisted that in this discussion she had been talking only against *political* distinctions. She was not 'arguing against that inequality of property which must more or less take place in all societies'. Had her servant been paid no wages and worked for her by reason of her station and the privileges it carried with it, she argued, Johnson would have had a point.[53] No more than Harrington could she envisage a society without economic inequality. Social distinctions based on ownership of property were built into her notion of a republic—the only proviso being that no one should be allowed to accumulate so much property as to form an aristocracy.

[48] Macaulay, *History of England*, iv. 355 n. See also the letter written in her defence, signed 'Republican', *London Chronicle*, 25 (1769), 596.
[49] Robbins, 'The Strenuous Whig', 449.
[50] As quoted Fitzpatrick, 'Rational Dissent in the Late 18th Century', 306.
[51] Eric Foner, *Tom Paine and Revolutionary America* (1976), p. xix.
[52] *Boswell's Life of Johnson*, ed. G. B. Hill, rev. L. F. Powell (1934), i. 447–8.
[53] Catharine Macaulay, *Letters on Education* (1790), 167–8.

In her *History*, one critic wrote, 'all the characters and events were viewed through democratic spectacles'.[54] But Catharine Macaulay, it could be argued, was as little a democrat as Harrington. Should they both be seen as aristocratic republicans?[55] When she recommended 'the democratic system' to the Corsicans as 'the only one which could secure the virtue, liberty, and happiness of society', what exactly did she mean by 'democratic'? She made clear she favoured 'a fair and equal representation of the whole people', 'a more extended and equal power of election', shorter parliaments and more frequent elections, the instruction of MPs by those they represented, and a House of Commons more answerable to the people.[56] But as important with her as the form and power of the republic were the measures to be taken to protect it from corruption—namely 'the rotation of all places of trust, and the fixing the Agrarian on a proper balance'. The 'proper balance' was one which 'inclines in favour of the popular side'.[57] Just how much should the balance incline? It is doubtful whether she would have favoured universal male suffrage and the abolition of any property qualification for a vote, but she certainly never entertained the idea of extending the franchise to women. Her vision, like that of the Levellers before her, was of a male republic.

By the time she published the sixth volume of her *History* in 1781 she had no illusions about what was possible of achievement in the existing political climate. Blackburne, writing of Hollis, had said that no radical could 'expect applause in an age when the present doctrines of the majority are so loudly echoed through the land, and when the loyalty of the day is chiefly distinguished by execrations on the principles of Milton, Sidney, Locke, and other patriot writers of past time'.[58] He might equally have been writing of Catharine Macaulay. Her *History*, she protested, was 'without any unconstitutional design, or any wild enthusiastic hope of being

[54] Robert Chambers, *Book of Days*, 2 vols. (1863–4), i. 810.
[55] As was argued by Bridget and Christopher Hill: 'Catherine Macaulay and the Seventeenth Century', *The Welsh History Review*, 3 (1967), 381–402, at p. 398.
[56] Macaulay, *Loose Remarks*, 29; and see her *Observations on a Pamphlet entitled 'Thoughts on the Cause of the Present Discontents'* (1770), 11, 17, 19, 20, 32; *An Address to the People of England, Scotland, and Ireland on the Present Important Crisis of Affairs* (1775), 10, 18; *Observations on the Reflections of the Rt. Hon. Edmund Burke on the Revolution in France* (1790), 48.
[57] Macaulay, *Loose Remarks*, 33, 36.
[58] *Memoirs of Thomas Hollis*, i. iii–iv.

able to influence the minds of a nation in favour of a democratic government, who from the beginning of time have been under the rule of regal sway, and whose laws, manners, customs, and prejudices' were 'ill adapted to a republic'. Was it this seeming impossibility of achieving an English democratic republic which led her, as a fervent anti-monarchist, one who, it was said, 'hates all the royal family and thinks them fools', to omit anti-monarchism from her priorities?[59] What exactly Baron's 'general rising' would have achieved remains unclear but after 1768 there was no more talk of it. Would she have favoured the overthrow of monarchy in her own time by revolutionary means? If she ever entertained the idea in the 1760s she soon abandoned it.

There is no doubt that she and many of her friends were republicans in principle—'speculative republicans' as Lecky called them. Where other countries—Corsica, America, France—were concerned, they were also republicans in practice. But in England, republican ideas played little or no role in the political reform programme put forward by radicals from the 1760s to the 1790s. When Johnson insisted there was a monarchy in heaven, Catharine Macaulay's reply was 'If I thought so, Sir, I should never wish to go there'.[60] But heaven was another country. Where England was concerned it was a different matter. On the same question, Major John Cartwright's attitude was described by his daughter:

> though in forming a new government in another part of the world, Major Cartwright would certainly have preferred a form of government as simply republican as would be consistent with security from anarchy, he never wished in his own country to interfere with its ancient institutions.[61]

'It is doubtful whether any leading radical wished to abolish the mixed constitution in the eighteenth century', writes Colin Bonwick, 'regardless of the theoretical merits of republicanism and their admiration of its effects in America'.[62] James Burgh, for example, while arguing that republicanism had advantages not

---

[59] Catharine Macaulay, *The History of England*, vi (1781), p. vii; Colin C. Bonwick, *English Radicals and the American Revolution* (1977), 22.

[60] Nichols, *Illustrations of Literary History*, vi. 158.

[61] As quoted Dorothy Thompson, *Queen Victoria, Gender and Power* (1990), 91.

[62] Colin C. Bonwick, 'Contemporary Implications of the American Revolution for English Radicalism', *The Maryland Historian* (1976), 33–58, at p. 44.

shared by monarchies, quickly dismissed any idea that he was in favour of 'so great a change in the constitution as would exclude king and lords from parliament', and he saw nothing contradictory in quoting Alfred in favour of shorter parliaments.[63] It is an attitude shared by many radicals in the early nineteenth century, when as Dorothy Thompson has pointed out, the distinctions between monarchy and republic were never clearly defined.[64] When in 1807 Mercy Warren in her *History* accused John Adams of 'a partiality for monarchy' he angrily rejected such an accusation adding 'a mixed government is the only one that can preserve liberty'.[65]

Who were Catharine Macaulay's 'republicans' in the seventeenth century? Surprisingly, she would have included Hampden, of whom she wrote, 'convinced that Charles's affections and understanding were too corrupt to be trusted with power in any degree', he fought for 'the abolition of the monarchy as the only cure to national grievances'. Yet while describing him as 'a great patriot', she thought he carried democracy too far. For if he and Pym had not 'thought too highly of the gross and servile conceptions of the multitude', she wrote, 'much mischief would have been avoided'. It is in Volume IV that she talks of the 'Rise of the Republicans'. The date she gives is 1644, but she quotes Clarendon's observation that they were at that time 'contemptible in their numbers' and 'continually incurring the censure of parliament ... for the republican sentiments which they often let fall'. When Henry Marten expressed the view 'that it was better one family should be destroyed than many', he was asked what he meant by 'one family'. On his answering 'the king and his children', he was confined to the Tower. When Marten had tried to dissuade Clarendon 'from his attachment to the court', he said 'he did not think one man wise enough to govern us all'. It was 'the first word he [Clarendon] ever heard any man speak to such a purpose'. The passage of the Self-Denying Ordinance in 1645 Catharine Macaulay saw as a reflection of how 'great was the increase of influence' of 'the republican faction', for the motion was 'well supported by the whole republican party'. Sir Henry Vane, who

---

[63] Burgh, *Political Disquisitions*, ii. 50, 109.
[64] Thompson, *Queen Victoria, Gender and Power*, 89, 91.
[65] *Warren–Adams Letters* (Massachusetts Historical Society Collections, 5th ser., 4; 1878), 324, 325.

seconded the motion was 'a warm friend to the interests of the public', 'a great man', and the only 'enthusiast in religion ... whom Cromwell could neither flatter nor deceive'.[66]

General Ireton, whom mistakenly she saw as responsible for the Leveller Agreement of the People, was 'a firm republican in principle'. She praised him as a regicide, for 'the justice inflicted on the king, and the abolition of the English monarchy' was chiefly owing 'to his manly and unconquerable resolution'. By his death, she wrote, 'the republic of England ... sustained an irreparable loss'. In answer to those who had accused him of being a 'mere tool of Cromwell's ambitions', she argued that 'if his virtues were not of that sublimer nature to forbear the offered possession of supreme power, he had too much elevation of mind to subject himself to a voluntary servitude'. After the King turned down Parliament's proposals in 1647, Ireton and Cromwell continued to insist on negotiations with him. In consequence 'the republicans who had hitherto regarded them in their interest, began to suspect' them of private bargaining with the King. The so-called sin of Colonel Hacker, accused of guarding the king on the day of his execution, was 'his steadiness to the republican cause'. If it was difficult for a historian to do justice to the memory of 'the few illustrious patriots, who ... acted on the pure principles of public good', Catharine Macaulay had no doubts that the period of the Commonwealth had been 'the brightest age that ever adorned the page of history'.[67]

The Leveller manifesto that she most favoured was *An Agreement of the Free People of England* of 1 May 1649. Significant is the clause with which that Agreement concludes: 'that it shall not be in the power of any Representative, in any wise, ... to level men's Estates, destroy Propriety, or make all things Common'. In her fifth volume Catharine Macaulay explained that the clause was included 'to demonstrate beyond contradiction, that the party were not tainted with any principles of levelling, but those which support the rights of Nature and equal government'.[68] 'That general spirit of levelling which pervades modern society', she

---

[66] Macaulay, *The History of England*, iii. 451, 356 n.; iv. Ch. 3 is entitled 'Rise of the Republicans', ibid. 160, 161 n., 165, 171.

[67] Ibid. iv. 330, 351–2; v. 21, 22, 24, 382; vi. 19, 21, 130.

[68] *Leveller Manifestoes of the Puritan Revolution*, ed. Don M. Wolfe (1944), 409; Macaulay, *The History of England*, v. 9–10 n.

wrote, 'is a new circumstance of corruption among us.'[69] There is an echo here of Harrington's *Oceana* requiring protection from 'Robbers and Levellers'.[70] But the remark was made in 1781 after her fall from fame when her reputation had suffered, and when levelling doctrines were highly suspect. In the volume of her *History* published in that year, she wrote that despite the hostility to republican principles, and 'however erroneous might be the opinion of the few republicans whom opportunity enabled to take an active part in the affairs of England', they were men whose 'conduct was founded on principle because diametrically opposed to their interest, and even their safety'. Nearly all had suffered the fate of 'banishment, an ignominious death, or the entire ruin of their fortunes'. Earlier she wrote of 'those' in 1647 'who were simply honest to the principles of equal and general Freedom, who called themselves Commonwealthsmen, but who were in derision stiled Levellers'. She was anxious not to leave it there. 'Levellers', she wrote, was 'a hackneyed term of reproach, flung out on all occasions by the adversary against the partizans of Liberty'.[71]

There is evidence she had read Winstanley, although she does not refer to him or the Diggers in her *History*.[72] If no True Leveller, the ideas she expressed at different times are sufficiently ambiguous to leave unresolved just how far she was prepared to go towards democracy. Although she frequently expressed her belief in a liberty that involved security of property, 'the *summum bonum* of political happiness', in 1781 she revealed a shrewd scepticism about the way such a principle could be abused. 'If a hoarder, in a time of scarcity, denies to his fellow citizens the most essential necessaries of life under an exhorbitant price, it is his property, and he has a right to act according to his corrupt interest.' There is surely little room for misunderstanding that, but there was more to follow. She commented on the monopolist who 'by his management' could produce 'an artificial famine', but, she asked ironically, should not 'every man' be allowed 'to buy and sell as he pleases'? 'If whole provinces are laid waste to

---

[69] Ibid. vii. 494.

[70] As quoted Hill, *Puritanism and Revolution*, 297.

[71] Macaulay, *The History of England*, vi, pp. viii–ix; iv. 355 and n.

[72] Some of the works of Winstanley were included in her *Catalogue of Tracts*; and see Robbins, *The Eighteenth-Century Commonwealthman*, 19.

accumulate wealth in the hands of individuals, the law ought to secure property, however unjustly obtained. If the public is ever so notoriously defrauded, the same security must guard the property of the individual.' So it was that 'in England, from these false notions of freedom and political good, the basest affections of the human heart are nourished and encouraged'.[73] But her attack is directed more against corruption than against the plight of the propertyless.

Yet by the end of her life her ideas were changing. If there was still no real belief in social equality, she was finding examples of gross economic inequality less acceptable. She had begun to notice and find shocking the contrast between the hovels in which so many lived, and the 'princely palaces' of the rich. She noted 'the respect that riches meet with'. Shrewdly she saw how 'the pleasures of possession are increased by the consciousness that we are enjoying what the bulk of mankind are, from circumstances less fortunate, denied.' She called on the more fortunate to be content 'with plain and simple habitations' and cheerfully to 'sacrifice the use of private advantages to the nobler purpose of a general good'. In France in 1777 the distinction between the squalid conditions of the poor and the noble châteaux of the rich had appalled her. Such 'inequality of property', she came to believe, was 'incompatible with a wise and just government'. Nevertheless when her plan of education was criticized because 'only the rich could carry it into practice' her answer, echoing Priestley, was that it was 'the men of opulence alone who' could 'reap the choicest fruits of the industry and ingenuity of their species'. The 'education of the great, were it properly attended to . . . would be felt in the improved virtue of all the subordinate classes of citizens'.[74]

Events in America and France were to change her ideas. When writing to Thomas Brand Hollis, who as heir to Hollis adopted his name on his death, in 1789 of events in France she revealed how well aware she was of the limited achievement of liberty in England. She thought it would be 'the last of all the nations in possession of complete freedom, for the forms and nature of their government are of a kind to foster, and render inveterate, the

[73] Macaulay, *The History of England*, vi. 211.
[74] Macaulay, *Letters on Education* (1790), pp. v–vi, 305, 307, 330.

worst kind of political prejudices'. History, she argued, revealed that 'the majority of the English nation never engaged in the cause of freedom'.[75]

In the final volume of her *History* Catharine Macaulay appealed to the 'ingenuous and uncorrupted among her countrymen' demanding of them: 'which class of historians have been the real friends of the constitution?' Was it 'those who by humouring the prejudices of all factions, left the judgment of the reader in a state of confusion, or those', like herself, who had 'closely adhered to the purest principle of civil and religious freedom; have marked every deviation from constitutional rectitude, and have not only pointed out the destructive enormities of marked tyrants, but have endeavoured to direct the judgment of the public to the detection of those masked hypocrites, who, under the specious pretence of public good, have advanced their private interest and ambition on the ruin of all that is valuable to man?'[76]

[75] *Memoirs of Thomas Brand Hollis*, ed. John Disney (1808), 42 n. Q.
[76] Macaulay, *The History of England*, viii. 338–9.

9. *Catharine Macaulay, English Radicalism and the American Revolution*

> As the body of the people in America are much more virtuous and understand the nature of liberty better than the body of the people here and have men capable of leading them, he (Caleb Fleming) hopes they will die bravely with their swords in their hands rather than submit.
>
> (*The Diary of Sylas Neville, 1767–1788*, ed. Basil Cozens-Hardy (1950), 31, entry for 2 Apr. 1768)

AMONG the grievances included in their petitions to the king, the Society of the Supporters of the Bill of Rights listed the mismanagement of the American colonies. Parallel to the re-emergence of English radicalism in the 1760s was a developing crisis in relations between the American colonists and the mother-country. Burdened by the costs of an expensive war with France and the need for maintaining American defence, the government embarked on a policy of making the colonists share the expense by the imposition of a series of revenue-raising measures. The Americans reacted with fury. Asserting their financial and administrative independence in internal affairs they raised the cry of 'No taxation without representation'. The colonists' attitude to what they saw as an increasingly tyrannical government was little different from that of many Englishmen. As the Wilkes movement developed so the colonists saw a growing identity of interests between their own grievances and those of English radicals.

It is a curious irony that although Catharine Macaulay's contribution to eighteenth-century radical ideas has yet to be fully recognized by English historians, the influence she had on the ideological origins of the American Revolution is widely acknowledged by its historians. She was, it is claimed, 'among the patriots' best English friends', and 'an important intellectual figure of this generation to the colonists'.[1] American historians, in analysing the

---

[1] Colin C. Bonwick, 'An English Audience for American Revolutionary Pamphlets', *Historical Journal*, 19 (1976), 355–74, at p. 355; Bernard Bailyn, *The Ideological Origins of the American Revolution* (1967), 41.

origins of the revolt of the American colonies, have long stressed the role played by Real Whig ideas, which were 'of central importance in explaining the American Revolution'.[2] Within that body of ideas Catharine Macaulay's *History* played a significant role.

As we saw earlier, Benjamin Franklin knew and admired her *History*. It was one of Jefferson's 'preferred authorities' on a period of history which he regarded as critical.[3] In order to confront 'Hume's "misrepresentations" with "authentic truths"', he suggested Hume should be reprinted, and alongside his account 'in parallel columns' the refutations 'from "honest writers" like Edmund Ludlow, Catharine Macaulay, and Rapin'.[4] He repeatedly recommended her *History* to friends, and listed it twice in the catalogue of his 'Second' library, and again in his 'Fourth'. He was later to purchase her entire eight-volume *History* and to include it in the University of Virginia library. John Adams read the *History* 'with much Admiration'. It was, he wrote to her in August 1770, based 'upon the Plan' he had 'ever wished to see adopted by Historians. It is calculated to strip off the Gilding and false Lustre from worthless Princes and Nobles, and to bestow the Reward of Virtue, Praise upon the generous and worthy only.' He had never seen any history, he wrote, in which 'this exact Historical Morality' had been 'more religiously regarded.' From reading it 'as well as from the concurrent Testimony of all who have come to this Country from England', he 'had formed the highest Opinion of the Author as one of the brightest ornaments not only of her Sex but of her Age and Country'.[5] She was the historian 'whom Washington knew best'.[6] Both Josiah Quincy and Benjamin Rush were familiar with her *History*. In April 1770 Richard Henry Lee of Virginia wrote a letter to Arthur Lee in London lamenting that he had 'not yet read Mrs. McCauley's history', and asking that a copy be sent to him with 'any other of her works that may be published'.[7]

---

[2] Pauline Maier, *From Resistance to Revolution* (1973), p. xii.

[3] H. Trevor Colbourn, 'Thomas Jefferson's Use of the Past', *William and Mary Quarterly*, 3rd ser., 15 (1958), 56–70, at p. 64.

[4] H. Trevor Colbourn, *The Lamp of Experience* (1965), 179.

[5] Letter to Catharine Macaulay dated 9 Aug. 1770, *The Diary and Autobiography of John Adams*, ed. L. H. Butterfield, 4 vols. (1961), i. 360.

[6] Colbourn, *The Lamp of Experience*, 153–4.

[7] *The Letters of Richard Henry Lee*, ed. J. C. Ballagh, 2 vols. (1911, 1914), i. 44.

On at least two occasions documents helpful to her *History* were sent from America. In October 1769 William Palfrey wrote asking Wilkes to pass on to Catharine Macaulay a copy of Hutchinson's *Collections of Original Papers Relative to the History of the Colony of Massachusetts Bay.*[8] The following year Richard Henry Lee sent her Henry Brooke's *Farmer's Letters* (1745).[9] When she had completed four volumes of her *History* the *London Chronicle* printed a letter from a gentleman in Boston to a friend in London. He wrote that despite the prohibition on importing into North America, 'they...have paid Mrs. Macaulay the compliment of allowing the free sale of her *History of England* in all the colonies'.[10] It is on the basis of this apparent familiarity with her *History* that Pauline Maier has claimed that Americans 'shared a characteristic commonwealthman view of English history as expounded in the 1760s by Catharine Macaulay'.[11] It provided, she argues, 'a corpus of ideas about public authority and popular political responsibilities that shaped the American revolutionary movement'.[12]

Catharine Macaulay's *History* was read by many American colonists. In 1774 a writer in the *Monthly Review* felt called on to remind his readers that Americans were 'as well read in the nature and grounds of civil liberty as ourselves'.[13] Recalling the period later, John Adams wrote that '*Cato's Letters* and the *Independent Whig*, and all the writings of Trenchard and Gordon, Mrs. Macaulay's *History*, Burgh's *Political Disquisitions*, Clarendon's *History of the Civil War*, and all the writings relative to the revolution in England became fashionable reading'.[14] How did this situation come about and why?

Many colonists were of dissenting background, their families the victims of religious persecution—that is, much the same background as the majority of Real Whigs. The point was made by Ezra Stiles, the Rhode Island Congregational minister, in a letter to Catharine Macaulay in 1775, when he wrote 'our fathers

---

[8] Colin C. Bonwick, *English Radicals and the American Revolution* (1977), 42 n. 33.
[9] *The Letters of Richard Henry Lee*, i. 42.
[10] *London Chronicle*, 25 (1769), 454.
[11] Pauline Maier, 'John Wilkes and American Disillusionment with Britain', *William and Mary Quarterly*, 3rd ser., 20 (1963), 373–95, at p. 376.
[12] Ead., *From Resistance to Revolution*, 27.
[13] Bonwick, *English Radicals and the American Revolution*, 63.
[14] *The Works of John Adams*, ed. C. F. Adams, 10 vols. (1850–6), x. 202.

fled hither for Religion and Liberty'.[15] Joseph Priestley described the American colonists—more particularly those in New
England—as 'chiefly Dissenters and Whigs'.[16] At the end of the
century the *Anti-Jacobin* wrote that 'the descendents of the
Puritans' were still pursuing 'the same principles which in
England and America have produced so much disturbance'.[17]
Long before the crisis in the American colonies developed, close
ties existed between individuals of similar religious outlook on
both sides of the Atlantic—ties which were often expressed in a
lively exchange of correspondence. In 1760, for example, Ezra
Stiles had contacts with forty-four like-minded individuals in
England.[18]

Between many colonists and Real Whigs there existed a natural
sympathy, particularly when there was any threat from episcopacy
or Catholicism. Often forgotten, as Carl Bridenbaugh reminds
us, is that 'religion was a fundamental cause of the American
Revolution'. If one of the first sources of increased tension between the colonists and Britain in the 1750s was the rumour that
the Anglican church was to found bishoprics in America, the
background to the reaction that rumour provoked lay way back in
the seventeenth century, when many of the first settlers arrived in
New England. As Jonathan Mayhew wrote in 1763, they 'fled
hither as to an asylum from episcopal persecution, seconded by
royal power'.[19] What had been a suspicion became a real threat
between 1763 and 1766, when news of plans for creating an
Anglican episcopate reached the ears of the colonists. The fight
against it was carried on by Dissenters from both England and
America. Thomas Hollis and Jonathan Mayhew, dissenting
minister of Boston, played leading roles in the struggle. With
his eyes firmly directed towards the seventeenth century Mayhew

[15] Letter from Ezra Stiles to Catharine Macaulay, 15 Apr. 1775, Microfilm of Ezra
Stiles's papers, Beinecke Library, Yale University.
[16] As quoted Walter H. Conser, Jr., Ronald M. McCarthy, David T. Tuscano, and
Gene Sharp (eds.), *Resistance, Politics and the American Struggle for Independence, 1765–75*
(1986), 405–6.
[17] As quoted by Anthony Lincoln, *English Dissent 1763–1800* (1938 repr. 1971), 7.
[18] Martin Hugh Fitzpatrick, 'Rational Dissent in the late 18th Century with
Particular Reference to the Growth of Toleration', D.Phil. thesis (University of Wales,
1982), 29.
[19] Carl Bridenbaugh, *Mitre and Sceptre* (New York, 1962), pp. xiv, 225.

wrote to the Archbishop of Canterbury that bishops had 'commonly been instruments in arbitrary reigns of "establishing a tyranny over the bodies and souls of men"'.[20] Similarly in 1774 the Quebec Act was seen as an attempt by government to undermine the liberties of Protestant Englishmen in the North American continent. Much of the correspondence between the American colonists and English Real Whigs was at first concerned more with theological than with political issues. But in the minds of many Dissenters the two were inseparable. 'The stamping and episcopizing our Colonies', wrote the *St. James's Chronicle*, 'were understood to be *only different branches of the same plan of power.*'[21] Slowly as the crisis in relations between England and the American colonies worsened correspondence between English and colonial dissenters turned more overtly political. By the 1760s English and American dissenters shared more than religious sympathies.

The leaders of the Sons of Liberty, like the majority of the Real Whigs, came from the middling and upper ranks of society. The Club of Honest Whigs, in which many of the radicals of dissenting sympathies congregated in London, included Richard Price, Joseph Priestley, and James Burgh among its members. From the beginning they ranged themselves unanimously behind the cause of the American Colonists. When Benjamin Franklin, Josiah Quincy, and other visitors from the American colonies came to London, they were warmly welcomed to the club. Josiah Quincy wrote of it as 'a club of friends of liberty'.[22] A reason given for the failure of his own times to appreciate Thomas Hollis was 'his affectionate attachment to *our late* American colonies' which 'happen at this day, to be deemed *rebellious* to the mother country'. Hollis, it was claimed, would 'undoubtedly class, in the estimation of the vulgar, among the first encouragers and abettors of their disobedience'.[23] According to the Revd B. N. Turner, Samuel Johnson described Hollis as having 'laid the first train of combustibles for the American explosion'.[24] Yet at first Hollis did

---

[20] As quoted Bailyn, *The Ideological Origins of the American Revolution*, 97.

[21] Bridenbaugh, *Mitre and Sceptre*, 259.

[22] Verner W. Crane, 'The Club of Honest Whigs', *William and Mary Quarterly*, 3rd ser., 23 (1966), 210–33 at p. 223.

[23] *Memoirs of Thomas Hollis*, ed. Francis Blackburne, 2 vols. (1780), i, p. iv.

[24] John Nichols, *Illustrations of the Literary History of the Eighteenth Century*, 6 vols. (1817–31), vi. 157.

not see his mission as primarily concerned with the American colonists and it was only as the American crisis emerged and deepened that he started to focus attention more exclusively on them.

From the mid 1750s Hollis sent to America works 'designed by their authors to recommend in some cases the preservation, in others the recovery, of public liberty'.[25] He also encouraged friends to send over copies of their publications. Catharine Macaulay sent Mayhew her *History*. Mayhew was delighted with it. She wrote, he told Hollis, 'with a Spirit of Liberty, which might shame many great Men (so called) in these days of degeneracy, and tyrannysm and oppression'. He was particularly pleased with her treatment of the Stuarts, which gave him 'great pleasure'.[26] Hollis recorded in his diary a note he sent to Mrs Mayhew in 1769 giving notice that he was sending her 'some copies of Blackburne's Considerations on Popery, and Mrs. Macaulay's *History*'.[27]

So even before the Wilkes affair erupted there were close links between individual colonists and Real Whigs in England, but outside them there was little sympathy with the American cause. If there was opposition expressed to the Stamp Act of 1765, a duty imposed on all legal transactions, it was almost entirely confined to Real Whigs, and merchants trading with America. It is true the more moderate Rockingham Whigs supported the repeal of the Stamp Act—mainly for reasons of expediency, to effect a recovery in trade—and called themselves friends of the American colonists, but it was they who drafted the Declaratory Act of 1766 which, by claiming parliamentary supremacy over the colonies 'in all cases whatsoever', effectively extinguished hopes of legislative autonomy. As Benjamin Franklin noted in 1767, the accepted view was that 'the American colonies should exist in a subordinate relationship to the mother country'.[28] But as the London radical opposition developed, sympathy for the colonists grew.

Behind the identity of interests that drew the two together lay a shared view of the English constitution. Pauline Maier has stressed how at first the Sons of Liberty to a man felt genuine

---

[25] *Memoirs of Thomas Hollis*, i, pp. vi–vii.
[26] Colbourn, *The Lamp of Experience*, 63.
[27] *Memoirs of Thomas Hollis*, i. 429–30.
[28] John Sainsbury, *Disaffected Patriots* (1987), 6.

affection for Britain and her constitutional monarchy. What they set out to do was not to replace but 'to defend that constitutional system'.[29] With the majority of English Whigs they celebrated the Glorious Revolution of 1688 as providing unique safeguards of the liberty of the subject. It was seen as 'marking the grand renaissance of Anglo-Saxon principles after the vicissitudes of the intervening centuries and as a triumph for English Liberty'.[30] At first many Americans would have been reluctant to accept Catharine Macaulay's version of 1688 as the source from which present corruption flowed. In this respect, Josiah Quincy was exceptional, for he, like her, argued that thanks to the Restoration 'the science of bribery and corruption hath made amazing progress in England'.[31] What was needed, Catharine Macaulay argued, was not a new constitution but a return to the earlier pure constitution of Anglo-Saxon England before it had been destroyed by the Norman Conquest. It was a view of the past shared by many friends of liberty in America. In *An Appeal to the Justice and Interests of the People of Great Britain in the Present Disputes with America* of 1775 Arthur Lee wrote that 'originally, and before the Conquest, the right of being present in the great council of the nation, in which grants if any were made, belonged to every freeman in the kingdom'.[32] Josiah Quincy admired what he saw as the 'sensible arrangement of "our Saxon ancestors"'.[33] So great was Jefferson's belief in the liberties of Saxon England that in 1798 he began to study Anglo-Saxon.[34] As late as 1824 when the Norman Yoke myth was beginning to fade, Thomas Jefferson continued to subscribe to it. He told Thomas Cartwright that the Tories were descendants of the Normans and the Whigs of the Saxons, and he saw the American constitution as merely a restoration of Anglo-Saxon principles.[35]

Real Whig links with Americans led to a flow of seventeenth- and early eighteenth-century texts to America. Widely dispersed,

[29] Maier, *From Resistance to Revolution*, 271.

[30] Bonwick, *English Radicals and the American Revolution*, 25.

[31] As quoted Colbourn, *The Lamp of Experience*, 80.

[32] Bonwick, *English Radicals and the American Revolution*, 63.

[33] As quoted Colbourn, *The Lamp of Experience*, 80.

[34] Douglas L. Wilson, 'Jefferson vs. Hume', *William and Mary Quarterly*, 3rd ser., 46 (1989), 49–70, at p. 57.

[35] J. R. Pole, *Political Representation in England and the Origins of the American Republic* (1966), 438.

they were read throughout the colonies. Jonathan Mayhew summed
up the reaction to such works when he wrote how having been
'initiated, in youth, in the doctrines of civil liberty, as they
were taught by such men ... as Sidney and Milton, Locke and
Hoadly ... I liked them; they seemed rational.'[36] This familiarity
with such texts led Americans to use much the same language of
protest as Real Whigs and Wilkites. John Adams in 1765 rejoiced
that increasing oppression provided the opportunity for Americans
to become 'Brookes, Hampdens, Vanes, Seldens, Miltons,
Nedhams, Harringtons, Nevilles, Sidneys, Lockes'.[37] When in
1774, Mercy Otis Warren wrote to Catharine Macaulay, she had
little hope that the members of the new parliament would prove
more conciliatory than the old; she warned that if they were not
they would 'soon see the Genius which once animated their
Hamdens, Harringtons and Pym' had 'taken up Residence on
these distant shores'.[38] In 1776 in his search for the principles of
good government Adams found them only in 'Sidney, Harrington,
Locke, Milton, Nedham, Neville, Burnet and Hoadly'.[39]
Seventeenth-century authors seemed increasingly relevant to
Americans as the crisis in relations with the mother country
worsened. As Bailyn has emphasized, 'it was in terms of this
pattern of ideas and attitudes—originating in the English Civil
War and carried forward with additions and modifications ... —
that the American colonists responded to the new regulations
imposed by England on the American colonies after 1763'.[40]
Increasingly colonists looked to history for solutions to their
problems. They saw parallels between their own position and that
of seventeenth-century England, and were dismayed when the
past produced no answers. In 1765, during the Stamp Act crisis,
Jonathan Mayhew lamented that there were 'no similar Examples
from former Times'.[41] In 1768 Andrew Eliot wrote to Hollis 'we
have everything to fear and scarce any room to hope. I am sure
this will put you in mind of 1641.'[42] The Quebec Act, it was

---

[36] Bailyn, *The Ideological Origins of the American Revolution*, 45.
[37] Maier, *From Resistance to Revolution*, 48.
[38] Letter from Mercy Warren to Catharine Macaulay of 29 Dec. 1774, The Adams
Papers, 1639–1889, Microfilm No. 344.
[39] Bailyn, *The Ideological Origins of the American Revolution*, 45.
[40] Ibid. 54.
[41] Maier, *From Resistance to Revolution*, 113.
[42] Bailyn, *The Ideological Origins of the American Revolution*, 120.

said, 'went beyond anything either Charles I or James II had attempted'.[43] The colonists looked to the past for guidance in judging in what circumstances it was legitimate to resist. A study of the Stuart period provided a wealth of indications of the forms taken by repression. Catharine Macaulay's *History* played an important contributory role in accounting for such knowledge of seventeenth-century history.

The flow of ideas between England and America was far from being a one-way process. Those sympathetic to the American cause were equally concerned to publicize the case of the colonists in England; in constructing a body of opinion sympathetic to the American cause, Hollis and others were responsible for bringing over and reprinting many of their writings in England. Often these pamphlets reveal an indebtedness to the work of seventeenth-century writers Hollis had been at such pains to make known across the Atlantic. Bernard Bailyn has vividly described Hollis as 'that one-man propaganda machine in the cause of liberty'.[44] But if Hollis played the prime role he was by no means the only recipient of American pamphlets and tracts. John Wilkes and Richard Price as well as Catharine Macaulay 'regularly received pamphlets from America' sent them by friends and admirers.[45] Americans resident in England were also responsible for the dissemination of revolutionary pamphlets. Both Arthur Lee and Benjamin Franklin were instrumental in getting a number reprinted in England. In publicizing such writings, Edward and Charles Dilly, Catharine Macaulay's publishers, played a crucial role. Catharine Macaulay is said to have regularly supplied them with pamphlets on American affairs, which they reprinted.[46] In the second half of the century the Dillys were 'among the three or four leading publishers of American and American-related material in England'. Of eighty-four pamphlets devoted to the theme of relations between the American colonies and England which were published in America between 1764 and 1770, John Brewer has found thirty-seven that were reprinted in Great Britain.[47] In the twenty years up to 1783 it is estimated that

[43] Maier, *From Resistance to Revolution*, 238.

[44] Bailyn, *Origins of the American Revolution*, 46.

[45] Conser *et al.* (eds.), *Resistance, Politics, and the American Struggle for Independence 1765–75*, 409.

[46] Bonwick, 'An English Audience for American Revolutionary Pamphlets', 358.

[47] John Brewer, *Party Ideology and Popular Politics at the Accession of George III* (1976), 202.

altogether seventy-five revolutionary pamphlets were reprinted in England.[48]

The cause of the colonists was aided by many Americans—merchants, colonial agents, and others—who came to England and were closely associated with the London radical opposition as well as the Club of Honest Whigs. Benjamin Rush of Pennsylvania, for example, frequently visited London. Originally he came to read medicine at Edinburgh. Later he visited Wilkes in prison. John Adams described him as 'a Republican... acquainted with Sawbridge, McCaulay, Burgh, and others of that Stamp. Dilly sends him Books and Pamphletts, and Sawbridge and McCaulay correspond with him.'[49] A friend introduced him to Catharine Macaulay and he was invited to 'her evening Coterie which met once a week'. There in 1769 he met James Burgh and John Sawbridge. The subjects of conversation were 'literary and political'. He noted that Burgh took 'an active and entertaining part in them'. Rush found Catharine Macaulay 'sensible and eloquent'.[50] When Jacob, Benjamin's younger brother, came to England to study law, he was invited to dine at Mrs Macaulay's. Afterwards he wrote a long letter to Benjamin describing the occasion. In the many letters that passed between the Dillys and Rush there are regular references to Catharine Macaulay. In April 1770 she had just been to dine with the Dillys. In January 1771, Edward Dilly told Rush that her fifth volume would be finished shortly. A number of copies of her fourth volume had been sent to America. He hoped Rush would 'recommend the sale of them' to his friends. The following month Mrs Macaulay again dined with them 'together with some friends from America', including Jacob Rush. She had asked to be excused for not replying to a letter from Benjamin Rush but at present all her energies were absorbed in the task of finishing the fifth volume of her *History*. In May 1772 Jacob Rush and the Dillys, 'with a Select Party', dined with her.[51]

The brothers Arthur and William Lee of Virginia by infiltrating

[48] Bonwick, 'An English Audience for American Revolutionary Pamphlets', 356.

[49] Bonwick, *English Radicals and the American Revolution*, 65; *The Diary and Autobiography of John Adams*, ii. 182.

[50] *The Autobiography of Benjamin Rush*, ed. George W. Corner (1948), 61.

[51] L. H. Butterfield, 'The American Interests of the Firm of E. and C. Dilly, with Their Letters to Benjamin Rush', *Papers of the Bibliographical Society of America*, 45 (1951), 303, 304 n. 45, 305, 306, 309.

London radical politics became active Wilkites. They played a substantial role in promoting the cause of their fellow colonists. In 1768 Arthur Lee came back to England, read law, and set up a legal practice. Through Wilkes he knew many of the London radicals including Catharine Macaulay who became a close friend. Like so many other American visitors to London, he often dined with the Dilly brothers. He purchased the freedom of the City and became a member of the Society of the Supporters of the Bill of Rights, where he played a leading role in ensuring that the grievances of the American colonists were included in many of the petitions. Behind a variety of pseudonyms—'Monitor', 'Junius Americanus', 'A Bostonian'—he contributed many articles to the newspapers, more particularly to the *Public Advertiser* and the *Gazetteer*. These newspapers were sent to American editors, 'who were hungry for material'. With his brother he distributed American pamphlets among those they thought influential as well as to friends. It was to them Catharine Macaulay owed her knowledge of John Dickinson's *Letters from a Farmer in Pennsylvania to the Inhabitants of the English Colonies*, a pamphlet for which she had great admiration. In return she sent Dickinson her 'more ardent pamphlets'.[52]

Stephen Sayre of New York was another American who during his residence in London played an active role in Wilkite politics. He was admitted into the Framework Knitters' company and in 1773, with William Lee, was elected Sheriff—for two Americans a remarkable event. On 19 October 1775, Sayre was arrested for being implicated in a plot to kidnap the King. The main evidence against him was provided by another American who had recently become an adjutant in the Guards responsible for defending the Tower of London. But when Sayre was arrested his papers were seized. Among them a letter from Catharine Macaulay was found. Whether it contributed to incriminating Sayre is uncertain but it may well have given her some cause for alarm.[53] As a result of extraordinary government bungling of the case Sayre was freed after five days, but some of his admissions point in the direction of an attempted insurrection. It is an interesting case for it suggests that there was some basis for the American belief that an in-

[52] Staughton Lynd, *Intellectual Origins of American Radicalism* (1969), 26.
[53] Sainsbury, *Disaffected Patriots*, 101.

surrection was planned. Certainly, a year earlier, Josiah Quincy had believed an insurrection was imminent in England.[54]

Henry Marchant of Rhode Island was another who visited London in these years of crisis. Trained as a lawyer, he became Attorney-General of Rhode Island in 1771 and almost immediately was sent to England on legal business, including the job of negotiating the return of money owed to the colony by the British Government since the Seven Years War. An American patriot, he was a friend of both Samuel Adams and James Otis. In England 'he sought out like-minded "Old Whigs" ... political descendants of Milton, Harrington, Sidney and Locke'.[55] He met Richard Price, Wilkes, and Arthur Lee and during his visit became a close friend of Benjamin Franklin. It was Lee who introduced him to Catharine Macaulay. Some time in May 1772, Henry Marchant dined with Lee and Stephen Sayre and 'spent most of the evening with the celebrated Mrs. Macauley ... that matchless spirited Lady'. He recorded that although 'in a very infirm State of Health through long Confinement in her Studies ... *her Spirit rouses and flashes like lightning upon the subject of Liberty, and upon the Reflexion of any Thing noble and generous—she speaks undaunted and freely lets forth her Soul—and disdains a cowardly Tongue or Pen*'.[56] In April 1772 they had 'two Hours Conversation upon Liberty in General'. Marchant noted that she thought the political situation in England was 'fast approaching to Dissolution by the very Means which some there think the greatest Proof of Her Stability'.[57] When he left for home she gave him volumes of her *History* as a gift for the Redwood Library in Newport. They continued to correspond. Five years later he became a member of the Continental Congress.

Through Henry Marchant, Catharine Macaulay came to know the Revd Ezra Stiles, a Congregationalist, and Marchant's minister in Rhode Island. It may well have been Marchant who introduced Stiles to her *History*. In March 1772 Stiles began 'reading the History of England by Mrs. Catherina Macaulay'. In July 1772,

[54] Maier, *From Resistance to Revolution*, 260, 250.

[55] David S. Lovejoy, 'Henry Marchant and the Mistress of the World', *William and Mary Quarterly*, 3rd ser., 12 (1955), 375–98, at p. 390.

[56] *The Literary Diary of Ezra Stiles*, ed. Franklin Bowditch Dexter, 3 vols. (1901), i. 251.

[57] Lovejoy, 'Henry Marchant and the Mistress of the World', 392.

Henry Marchant presented her with a copy of Stiles's *Sermon on the Christian Union* preached in 1760. As an answer to the threat of Episcopacy it proposed a union of dissenting churches. Catharine Macaulay read it with interest and it served to cement a close friendship between them. On 29 April 1772, when Stiles was on a visit to England, he dined with Arthur Lee and Stephen Sayre. As with Marchant, it was Lee who, later the same day, introduced him to Catharine Macaulay. She had apparently 'expressed her Inclination for the Meeting'. Stiles was delighted with her. 'I saluted this amiable Daughter of Liberty with inexpressible pleasure', he wrote, 'heightened with the pleasing manner in which she received me.' They talked together for two hours— during which 'she enquired much of American Affairs'. After this they met frequently, often took tea or dined together. He found her 'good sense and goodness of mind...truely worthy of Admiration' and was impressed by her 'knowledge of Politics, History and Government'. Often they discussed history together. Before Stiles left England she 'expressed a great Desire of seeing America'. As soon as the sixth volume of her *History* was completed she resolved to make the visit. 'I took my Leave of this sensible and most agreeable Lady', Stiles wrote, 'with the greatest Regret.' By September he was back in America but the correspondence between them was to continue for thirteen years, the last letter he wrote to her being in April 1791, just before her death.[58]

Through her reading of John Adams's series of newspaper articles reprinted by Hollis as *Dissertations on the Canon and Feudal Law*, she became interested in knowing the author. In 1770 through his friend Mr Gill she established contact with Adams. He had heard, he wrote, that she was contemplating writing 'an History of the present Reign, or some other History in which the Affairs of America' were 'to have a Share'. 'It would give him infinite Pleasure...if...by any Means in his Power, by Letters or otherways', he could 'contribute any Thing' that would assist her in her work.[59] In the following year Isaac Smith met her. She inquired after John Adams and promised that directly she had finished Volume V of her *History*, she would write to him. On 19

---

[58] *The Literary Diary of Ezra Stiles*, i. 219, 251, 318, 319, 321; iii. 415.
[59] *The Diary and Autobiography of John Adams*, i. 361.

July she did so. They discussed the situation of the colonists, exchanging information. Adams regarded his introduction to her 'as one of the most agreeable and fortunate Occurences[*sic*] of his life'.[60] Through Isaac Smith, Adams had made contact with Edward and Charles Dilly with the object of being sent 'every Book and Pamphlet of Reputation, upon the subject of Law and Government' as soon as it appeared.[61] Among the works the Dillys sent him were James Burgh's *Political Disquisitions*, and in 1775, four copies of 'a small pamphlet published this Day by Mrs Macauly on the present Important Crisis of Affairs'.[62]

From her contact with Adams she was introduced to Mercy Otis Warren, with whom she had a correspondence right up to within a year or so of her death. She had confided in Adams her 'Desire to become acquainted with . . . American Ladies', and Adams's wife Abigail had responded by writing to her.[63] To the women of America Mrs Macaulay was 'sufficiently distinguished by her superior abilities'. She herself while lacking 'eaquil [*sic*] accomplishments' shared their 'esteem for a Lady who so warmly interests herself in the cause of America'.[64] There were many other Americans—some lesser figures like the Baptist minister in Boston, Samuel Stillman, who was a friend of Patience Wright, but also Benjamin Franklin, George Washington, and Elbridge Gerry—who became her friends and correspondents. It is not an unimpressive list of names in the history of the American Revolution. That it was a woman who had such contacts with leaders of the American Revolution is astonishing.

The Wilkite movement was to forge closer ties between the American colonists and Real Whigs. Through the success of the Wilkite opposition Americans saw their own problems being solved. Parliamentary reform by creating a more independent House of Commons would mean instant redress of colonial as well as domestic grievances. How far the grievances of the radical opposition in London coincided with those of the American

---

[60] Ibid. 360.
[61] Letter from John Adams to Isaac Smith, 11 Apr. 1771, *Adams Family Correspondence*, i. 74–5.
[62] Edward Dilly to John Adams in letter dated 13 Jan. 1775, Adams Papers, Microfilm No. 344; see also ibid. for original letter from Catharine Macaulay to John Adams, 11 Sept. 1774.
[63] *Adams Family Correspondence*, i. 177.
[64] Ibid.

colonists was highlighted by the Wilkes affair. Wilkes was seen by the colonists as like them—'a victim of a tyrannical executive'.[65] Seven years before Wilkes's expulsion and re-election for Middlesex a 'Mr. *Adams*, a member of the assembly of Barbadoes' had been 'prosecuted, fined, and imprisoned for resisting the Sheriff in the execution of his duty'. He had been expelled from the assembly, re-elected, and re-expelled. The electors had insisted that it was 'they, and not the assembly' who 'were the judges of the fitness of persons to represent them'. When nevertheless the Governor formally disqualified him, he appealed to the King. The disqualification was reversed for being 'arbitrary, and contrary to the Spirit of the *British* constitution'.[66] No wonder the colonists tended to identify with Wilkes! The strength of the pro-Wilkes movement in America, particularly after 1768, can hardly be exaggerated. On hearing of the expulsion of Wilkes as representative for Middlesex from the House of Commons, Joseph Warren wrote of how it 'filled America with grief'. Towns were named after him. The three children of Nathaniel Barber, a Boston Son of Liberty, were named John Wilkes, Oliver Cromwell, and Catharine Macaulay.[67] As Bernard Bailyn has argued, the conviction 'of the existence of a malign conspiracy against the liberties of Englishmen' that the Wilkes affair so dramatically demonstrated, 'had rapidly taken root in America just as it had in the ranks of the parliamentary opposition in Britain'.[68]

Other parallels between events in England and in the American colonies were not lost on either side: when John Adams in 1776 looked back on events leading up to the Revolution it was 1761 and the argument over writs of assistance (giving customs officers on the mere suspicion of smuggled goods the right to enter premises or homes, if necessary by force) that he saw as marking the 'commencement of this controversy between Great Britain and America.'[69] When two years later, after the publication of No. 45 of *The North Briton*, Wilkes was arrested, his house searched, and many of his papers seized, it was by virtue of a general

---

[65] John Sainsbury, 'The Pro-Americans of London, 1769 to 1782', *William and Mary Quarterly*, 3rd ser., 35 (1978), 423–54, at p. 423.

[66] Ibid.; James Burgh, *Political Disquisitions*, 3 vols. (1774–5), i. 250.

[67] Maier, *From Resistance to Revolution*, 176, 163.

[68] Ian Christie, *Myth and Reality* (1970), 22–3.

[69] *Familiar Letters of John Adams and his wife Abigail, during the Revolution*, ed. Charles Francis Adams (1875), 191.

warrant. Not surprisingly colonists saw little difference between writs of assistance and general warrants. The principle of no taxation without representation found a sympathetic ear among the London radical opposition; when Wilkes's papers were seized in 1763 he had argued that it constituted a threat to the rights of property; the suspension of all legislative functions in New York until such times as it had agreed to permit the quartering of troops in the province had a familiar ring in England, where there was the same resentment of the deployment of troops against the civilian population; in Boston in 1770, when a series of incidents with the military culminated in the massacre of five people, there were echoes of the scene two years earlier in St George's Fields, when crowds gathered outside the prison in the hope of seeing Wilkes emerge on his way to Middlesex. Anticipating trouble the government called in troops. In the fighting that ensued six people were killed and fifteen wounded. The following year the military had been called in to suppress rioting silk-weavers in Spitalfields. When in October 1769 William Beckford, Lord Mayor, was almost deprived of a second term as Lord Mayor by the efforts of the ministry, he compared his experience to that of the 'quasi-legal harassment of the colonists'.[70]

The Society of the Supporters of the Bill of Rights from its inception in 1769 was consistent in its sympathy for, and active support of, the colonial cause. The founder, Horne Tooke, first formulated the close interdependency of the rights of Englishmen and American colonists: 'When the people of America are enslaved, we cannot be free; they can never be enslaved whilst we continue free. We are stones of one arch, and must stand or fall together'.[71] A letter appeared in the *Public Advertiser* which was reprinted in the *Boston Gazette* of 8 May 1769. 'The Cause of Liberty in England and America is ONE COMMON CAUSE' it read, 'the Attacks on both have been made and carried on by the *same Set of Men*, with the same Views, and with the same illegal Violence.'[72]

In June 1768 the Sons of Liberty of Boston, where opposition to the Stamp Act had been centred, sent Wilkes an adulatory letter. Expressed, significantly, in terms of the English revolution

---

[70] Sainsbury, 'The Pro-Americans of London, 1769 to 1782', 429.
[71] John C. Miller, *Origins of the American Revolution* (1943), 322.
[72] As quoted Maier, 'John Wilkes and American Disillusionment with Britain', 388.

of the seventeenth century it referred to Wilkes's 'perseverance in the *good old cause*', which 'may still prevent the great System from dashing to pieces'.[73] It was rapidly followed by similar letters and generous contributions from Virginia, Maryland, and South Carolina. When the South Carolina assembly sent £1,500 to the Bill of Rights Society the governor refused to let it continue in session. The letter of thanks sent by the Bill of Rights Society ended: 'Our cause is one—our enemies are the same'.[74] But it was with the Boston group that Wilkes had closest contacts and it was from them he received up-to-date information on American affairs over the next few years. Through his brother-in-law George Hayley, an agent for Boston merchants, Wilkes became acquainted with William Palfrey and John Hancock. Wilkes was to write to Palfrey that 'the pulse of this nation never beat so high for liberty as at the present moment and all the true friends of it applaud exceedingly the late proceedings of the patriots in America'.[75] When news of the Boston Massacre reached England, Catharine Macaulay sent her condolences to the Bostonians. The only consolation she drew from the tragic event was the opportunity it had given them of exhibiting 'a rare and admirable instance of patriotic resentment tempered with forbearance and the warmth of Courage with the coolness of Discretion'. She put herself at their disposal. If there was any service she could perform for them, they could 'depend upon a faithful and ardent exec[u]tion'.[76]

It was rumoured that if Wilkes's attempt to get into parliament failed, he would retire to Boston. Wilkes and his friends were being pressed to seek shelter in 'the peaceful deserts of America' in the event of arbitrary power driving them from England. As tension increased and war began to be seen as unavoidable, the need was stressed for America to survive in order to provide a haven for refugees from oppression, much as it had done in the seventeenth century. Americans were said to have been

[73] 'John Wilkes and Boston', ed. W. C. Ford, *Proceedings of the Massachusetts Historical Society*, 47 (1913–14), 190–220 at p. 191.

[74] Sainsbury, 'The Pro-Americans of London, 1769–1782', 431.

[75] Sainsbury, *Disaffected Patriots*, 37.

[76] Letter from Catharine Macaulay to the town of Boston dated 9 May 1770 from a transcript of the original (MS 195) provided by the Boston Public Library.

enraptured when it was learnt that Catharine Macaulay talked of 'ending her days on the banks of the Ohio'.[77]

During the Stamp Act crisis Hollis had distributed copies of James Otis's *Considerations on behalf of the Colonists* (1765) among London sympathizers. Later in 1769 John Almon was responsible for publishing a number of American tracts including Otis's *A Vindication of the British Colonists* (1769). In April 1769 Catharine Macaulay wrote to Otis of the admiration felt by 'every Lover of their Country and Mankind' for his 'patriotic conduct and great abilities in defence of your fellow citizens'. To him, as 'one of the most distinguished of the great guardians of American Liberty', she sent her *History*, for she saw 'the principles on which I have written the History of the Stuart Monarchs' as 'in some measure correspondent to those of the great Guardian of American Liberty'. She added that she would welcome an account 'from your own hand of the present state of American affairs'.[78]

In December 1774 Josiah Quincy visited Bath. Like Otis's work, his pamphlet *The Rights of the British Colonies Asserted and Proved* (1764) was well known among the friends of the American colonists. He was described by a hostile press as a most 'pestilent fellow' who 'came over from Boston with the lighted Torch of Rebellion in his Hand, and went Brandishing it up and down the Country, in hopes of kindling the Flame of Civil Discord and Fury'.[79] In his journal he was to record his visit to 'the celebrated Mrs. Macaulay'. Already it seems contact had been made with her by the leaders of the Massachusetts Sons of Liberty, for Quincy recorded how he 'delivered my letters to her' and was then 'favoured with a conversation of about an hour and a half'. He expressed himself 'very much pleased with her good sense and liberal turn of mind'. During the next few days he spent several hours with her. Later he met her brother, Alderman John Sawbridge, who 'spent an hour and a half with me in conversation on American and Parliamentary concerns', as well as 'the Lee brothers, Priestley, Price, Franklin, Brand Hollis'.[80] He attended

[77] Miller, *Origins of the American Revolution*, 323.
[78] *Warren–Adams Letters*, 2 vols. (Massachusetts Historical Society Collections, 72, 73; 1917–25), i. 7–8.
[79] *Memoirs of the Life of Josiah Quincy, Junior of Massachusetts Bay 1744–1775 by his son Jos. Quincy* (1825), 287.
[80] Ibid. 337.

a debate in the House of Commons on American affairs in which Sawbridge spoke in support of the Americans. The unfortunate Quincy died on the voyage home.

When he visited Bath, Catharine Macaulay may have been writing her *Address to the People of England on the Present Important Crisis of Affairs* which was published in 1775. Or it is possible that her meeting with Quincy inspired her to write it. When Edward Dilly sent John Adams four copies, he commented that the author 'though in a very infirm state of Health could not refrain throwing in her Mite into the public Treasury'.[81] It was a passionately pleaded appeal to bring about a change in government policy towards the American colonists before it was too late. From them the ministry had 'attempted to wrest . . . every privilege necessary to freemen;—privileges which they hold from the authority of their charters, and the principles of the constitution'. Americans had been 'stripped of the most valuable of their rights'. The Stamp Act, by which 'they were to be taxed in an arbitrary manner', had met with no opposition in Parliament except, she added, 'from those . . . particularly concerned, that the commercial intercourse between Great Britain and her Colonies should meet with no interruption'. If insistence on 'unlimited obedience' was the price of protection of the American colonists, it represented a threat of unlimited slavery for the subjects of every state. Finally she predicted that 'if a civil war commences between Great Britain and her colonies, either the Mother Country, by one great exertion, may ruin both herself and America, or the Americans, by a lingering contest, will gain an independency'. In the latter event 'all those advantages' enjoyed from their colonies, 'advantages which have hitherto preserved you from a national bankruptcy, must for ever have an end'. She was also to prophesy that if it came to war, England would 'become an easy prey to the courts of France and Spain, who, you may depend on it, will fall upon you as soon as they see you fairly engaged'.[82]

Did she think in the early months of 1775 there was any real chance of a change of heart from the government, or that war could still be averted? Writing to John Adams in September 1774

---

[81] Bonwick, *English Radicals and the American Revolution*, 78; Letter of 13 Jan. 1775, Adams Papers.

[82] Catharine Macaulay, *Address to the People of England, Scotland, and Ireland on the Present Important Crisis of Affairs* (1775), 5–6, 11, 26, 28–9.

she emphasized 'how strenuously and even zealously my Brother Mr. Sawbridge defended the injured rights of America', but she went on to add: 'the hands of the Ministry in both houses are so numerous that opposition serves to no other purpose than to publish the sentiments of individuals not in the smallest respect to obstruct the designs of Government'. Of the Boston Port Bill, the 'Bill for the better regulating the trials of the Soldiery and the Canada Bill' she wrote despairingly that no one had believed the 'government would venture such lengths'.[83] There was increasing scepticism in America of further petitions to the government. As Abigail Adams wrote to Catharine Macaulay, 'having so often experienced their Enefficacy [*sic*] we have little reason to hope'. Faith in the London opposition and its methods had dwindled. America still recoiled 'at the thought of drawing the sword against the state from whence she Derived her origin', but 'like an un-natural parent that state' had 'plunged her Dagger into the Bosom of her affectionate offspring'.[84] In a letter to Henry Marchant dated October 1774 Catharine Macaulay wrote that during the year the situation had 'grown very alarming'.[85] It was a sentiment echoed in a letter written to her by Mercy Otis Warren in December. If she still expressed the hope for better things from the new parliament, she feared there was 'Little Reason to expect it'. She confessed her fear 'lest Britain should be infatuated enough to push the unhappy Americans to the last appeal'. 'Heaven only knows how long we can continue in this state', she went on, 'it is not to be expected that society can subsist long without your government'. It was this, she concluded, that might 'finally drive us to assume such a form as is more consistent with the taste and Genius of a free people'.[86]

By 1775 colonists' attitudes to the constitution had changed. 'My ideas of the English constitution have much diminished', Ezra Stiles had written to Catharine Macaulay in December 1773. So fundamental was the disorder that attempts to 'patch up' this 'broken constitution' were 'almost as discouraging... as to

[83] Letter from Catharine Macaulay to John Adams, 11 Sept. 1774, Adams Papers, Microfilm no. 344.

[84] *Adams Family Correspondence*, i. 178.

[85] Letter from Catharine Macaulay to Henry Marchant dated Oct. 1774, in Marchant papers, Rhode Island Historical Society.

[86] Letter from Mercy Warren to Catharine Macaulay dated 29 Dec. 1774, Adams Papers, Microfilm no. 344.

essay the Recovery of an hydropsical Subject which with many Excellencies in it carries about it the seeds of inevitable death'.[87] An acceptance of Catharine Macaulay's evaluation of the Glorious Revolution had led the colonists from earlier expressions of loyalty and devotion to George III to a total rejection of monarchy.

[87] Microfilm of the Ezra Stiles Papers, Beinecke Library, Yale University.

10. *Catharine Macaulay, the French Revolution, and Burke*

> The French Revolution was attended with something so *new*
> in the history of human affairs; there was something so
> *singular*, so *unique*, in that *perfect* unanimity in the people; in
> that *firm* spirit which baffled *every hope* in the *interested*, that
> they could possibly divide them into parties, and render
> them the instruments of a re-subjection to their old bondage;
> that it naturally excited the *surprise* and the *admiration* of all
> men.
>
> (Catharine Macaulay, *Observations on the Reflections of the
> Rt. Hon. Edmund Burke, on the Revolution in France* (1790),
> 22)

As early as 1768 Catharine Macaulay was watching events in
France with increasing interest. She told Caleb Fleming and Sylas
Neville that she had heard there was 'a great spirit of Liberty
beginning' there.[1] Nine years later she went to see for herself.
The Franco-American alliance she had prophesied in 1777
in the event of the American crisis leading to war had yet to
be concluded, although there were rumours of its impending
announcement.[2] The full impact on France of the American
Revolution had still to be felt. Yet already something of the
enthusiasm expressed in the 1760s by English radicals for the
resistance of the American colonists was manifest in France.
When that resistance developed into war, and more particularly
when, during that war, the American colonists met with any
success, there was no small pleasure taken in seeing the old
enemy treated in this way. French sympathies were all on the side
of the rebellious colonists. Among liberals in France, as Catharine
Macaulay discovered, the Declaration of Independence stirred
already latent ideas into life, ideas that rejected the Ancien
Régime and the whole established order on which it rested. They

---

[1] G. M. Ditchfield, 'Some Literary and Political Views of Catherine Macaulay',
American Notes and Queries, 12 (1974), 70–6, at p. 74.

[2] Catharine Macaulay, *An Address to the People of England, Scotland, and Ireland, on
the Present Important Crisis of Affairs* (1775), 28–9.

led straight towards 1789 and the Declaration of the Rights of Man.

France's intervention on the side of the colonists had cost her dear. It was a major factor contributing to the financial crisis which by 1786 made French financial reform an urgent necessity. Defeating all attempts at reform was the resistance of the privileged classes. Faced by widespread revolt and economic breakdown, in August 1788 the king agreed to call the Estates-General—the first time since 1614—in a desperate attempt to resolve the nation's financial problems. The attempt failed, and a revolution resulted.

From early in the war with the American colonists, France supplied arms to the rebels. Some French officers like La Fayette volunteered to fight for them. He returned to France to be welcomed as a national hero, played a directing role in drafting the Declaration of the Rights of Man, and for a period played a leading part as commander of the newly organized National Guard. To George Washington in October 1789, Catharine Macaulay referred to him as 'your friend and élève' who 'has acted a part in this revolution, which has raised him above his former exploits because his conduct has been directed to the good of his distressed countrymen'.[3] Benjamin Franklin, the American envoy in Paris, was fêted wherever he went. Brissot wrote of him as 'the genius who has liberated America, and shed over Europe the torrents of his light'.[4] On his death in 1790 the National Assembly went into mourning for three days. In January 1778, Catharine Macaulay reported that the French were 'all American mad', and went on to caution Lord Harcourt that 'even your Lordship would not be well received in France if you were not an American'. According to her 'all the enlightened French' passionately wanted 'a large empire established on a republican basis to keep the monarchies of the world in order'.[5] Soon after she returned, the treaty of alliance was signed between France and the American colonies. It was the beginning of the end of the struggle. Three years later the war was over and American independence a fact.

[3] *Correspondence of the American Revolution*, ed. Jared Sparks, 4 vols. (1853), iv. 283.
[4] J. P. Brissot de Warville, *New Travels in the United States of America*, Translated from the French (1792), 230.
[5] *The Harcourt Papers*, ed. E. W. Harcourt, 14 vols. (1876–1905), viii. 109.

1. *Catharine Macaulay's Visit to France, 1777–8*

As it gave an opportunity of meeting so distinguished an English republican, the visit was enthusiastically welcomed. It is possible she had visited France earlier. Thomas Wilson in a letter to Polwhele dated January 1776 referred to her as 'just returned from Paris'. He expressed his pride in the honour shown her by many 'persons of the first rank, and the literati' who had entertained her in Paris.[6] The 'strong and powerful recommendations' of Lord Harcourt were responsible for her meeting with many of her French contacts.[7] It is unclear how far ahead her journey to France had been planned, although the many recommendations she took with her suggest the visit was not taken on the spur of the moment.

The ostensible reason for her visit was ill-health. She was certainly ill, but she may also have felt it necessary to be 'peculiarly cautious' in order 'to give no offence to the administration of her country . . . by appearing to have any other views in her excursion to France . . . than for the benefit of and restoration of her health'.[8] To Lord Harcourt, she stressed her ill health when she left England. As a consequence of getting into a 'tepid bath rather too cool and after a hot day' she had been attacked by a high fever. Bath doctors, but whether exclusive of James Graham she does not say, 'despairing of her life' sent her to Nice for a change of air.[9] Persistent illness and the slow and painful progress she made towards Paris did not augur well for the visit. On reaching Paris the doctor recommended by Horace Walpole advised against her going further. 'Commodious and elegant apartments' were found for her near the Palais Luxembourg.[10] Slowly she began to recover, and finally felt able 'to partake of that agreeable society' to which her friend Lord Harcourt had provided an introduction.[11] During the rest of her stay in Paris 'her apartments were crowded with visitors, and her invitations to dinner daily multiplied'.[12]

[6] Richard Polwhele, *Reminiscences in Prose and Verse*, 3 vols. (1836), i. 22. Wilson's letter almost certainly should have been dated 1777.
[7] *The Harcourt Papers*, viii. 105.
[8] Mary Hays, *Female Biography*, 6 vols. (1803), v. 301.
[9] *Harcourt Papers*, viii. 105–6.
[10] Hays, *Female Biography*, v. 297.
[11] *Harcourt Papers*, viii. 106.
[12] Hays, *Female Biography*, v. 301.

Among those she met were the chevalier de Rigemont, the abbé de Colbert, and the duc de Harcourt (no relation of her correspondent), who called on her several times and offered her 'all the civilities which are usually offered by that polite people to women of consequence, and', she added, 'would have made a dinner for me if I could have stayed to have accepted it'.[13] She also met the ducs de La Rochefoucauld-Liancourt—François-Alexandre and his cousin Louis Armand, both liberal in their outlook. Their estate at Rochefoucauld, it was said, became 'le principal foyer de l'opposition libérale'. François-Alexandre was one of the nobility who enthusiastically embraced the new ideas. A man of some culture, his home attracted scientists and men of letters, statesmen ('les plus indepéndans') and distinguished foreigners. He became a member of the 'patriot' party, and, almost certainly, one of the Committee of Thirty that played a directing role within that party. When the Estates-General assembled in 1789 he shared the opinions of the minority of the nobility and signed the protest against the decisions of the majority. Yet he was never anything but a devoted supporter of the monarchy. After the massacre of the Champ de Mars in August 1792, he continued to preach loyalty to the Crown. Getting wind of his imminent arrest and execution he fled to England, and later, in 1793, went to the United States. He saw France as having tried a new kind of government analogous to the new republic in the United States—'la plus sage assurément de toutes celles qui ont existé'—and was convinced that had the experiment lasted, the United States could have given France some useful lessons.[14] His visit to England in 1768 was the first of many. On it he may well have met Catharine Macaulay. At the time of her stay in Paris Catharine described him as 'very friendly and polite'.[15] One of the few 'patriots' who survived the Revolution, he returned to France in 1799.

She was particularly moved by the kindness shown to her by the Count of Sarsfield, who called on her every day during her stay in Paris 'to offer his services'. Directly she could venture out he arranged a dinner for her and invited 'the ladies of the highest

[13] *Harcourt Papers*, viii. 107.

[14] Frédéric Gaëtan, comte de La Rochefoucauld, *Vie du duc de La Rochefoucauld-Liancourt*, 2 vols. (Paris, 1827), i, 17, 20, 37.

[15] *Harcourt Papers*, viii. 107.

rank in his family to the entertainment'.[16] Was it indicative of how
undermined her confidence was that she felt it necessary to
emphasize their rank? Mme du Bocage and Mme Geoffrin (one of
the most prominent of the *salonnières*), Mme Grigson, and Turgot,
Controller-General at the time of her visit, were also among those
who came to meet her. She spent a day with Turgot, among a
large party meeting Marmontel and the widow of Helvétius.[17]
According to an anecdote Brissot recounted to illustrate her
hatred of monarchs, when dining with Turgot in Paris in 1774 (an
indication that she had been to France before 1777), he had asked
her whether she had visited Versailles. She replied 'I have no
desire to see the residence of the tyrants, I haven't yet seen that of
the Georges'.[18]

Before her departure, Horace Walpole had told his friend Mme
Du Deffand of Mrs Macaulay's visit and asked her to see that
Catharine was well looked after and entertained. Mme du Deffand
in her younger days had formed her own salon and been a brilliant hostess. She readily agreed to do all that Walpole requested
of her, and expressed impatience for Catharine Macaulay's arrival,
asking only that when she came she should bring her some tea.
The impending visit rather frightened her. Mme du Deffand
thought 'Mme. Macaulay a bien l'air de ne pas souper', and,
she explained to Walpole, as she herself never dined, proposed
to introduce Catharine Macaulay to Mme Necker, wife of the
minister of finance, to ensure she met many celebrated people and
received several invitations to dine. The illness of both Mme du
Deffand—she was to die three years later—and Catharine
Macaulay postponed their meeting until early December. When
finally it happened it was not entirely successful. Mrs Macaulay
had 'l'air d'un spectre', and talked only in a very low voice. They
apparently discussed her *History* but the conversation did not flow.
Mme du Deffand was disappointed.[19]

Benjamin Franklin, the American envoy in Paris, was among
those she saw during her stay there. According to Wilkes, she

---

[16] Ibid.

[17] Hays, *Female Biography*, v. 297–8.

[18] *Mémoires de Brissot*, ed. M. F. de Montrol, 4 vols. (1830), ii. 237.

[19] *Lettres de Mme du Deffand à Horace Walpole*, ed. Mrs Paget Toynbee (1912), 378,
367, 388; and see Dena Goodman, 'Enlightenment Salons: The Convergence of
Female and Philosophic Ambitions', *Eighteenth-Century Studies*, 22/3 (1989), 329–50,
at pp. 333–4.

was fearful of the consequences of revealing too close a friendship with Americans, and refused an invitation to dine with him.[20] Her later letter to Franklin confirms Wilkes's story. There were a great many Americans in Paris. She did not seek them out, but 'those who were eminent for their learning or talents seized every opportunity of observing the fair historian and mingling in the societies she was accustomed to frequent'.[21] Just before she left Paris, she wrote an apologetic letter to Franklin explaining that since Habeas Corpus had been suspended in England, 'any suspicion of my having held a correspondence with your countrymen on this side of the water' would have had dire consequences for her. This was why she had not entertained him at her hotel and had not seen more of all her American friends in Paris.[22]

During the visit she was constantly made aware of the excitement generated by the American rebellion. The 'same earnest wish' that American independence should be achieved and an American republic set up, she had found, was shared by 'the vulgar . . . through hatred and jealousy of the English'. Such hatred came as something of a shock to her. She had been told, she recorded, that this spirit was 'universal through all the continent of Europe'. Had she any faith in Lord North's ministry, she wrote on her return, she would have thought it her duty 'to have acquainted him with the dreadful storm which hangs over this devoted country'.[23] She was surprised at how little the existence of a monarchy seemed to impinge on French society. 'If it was not for the necessity of a passport to go out of France, and being asked at the gates of the several French towns whether you have anything in your coach contrary to the orders of the King,' she explained, 'you would not know by any thing you heard spoken by the people of any rank,—especially the better sort, that you lived under the power of a Monarch.' How different this was from England, where, as she told Lord Harcourt, 'we are fond of rattling our chains in our ears which is the most provoking part of the servile disposition' which prevailed among the English. What

[20] *Letters from the Year 1774 to the Year 1796 of John Wilkes, Esq. Addressed to his Daughter, the Late Miss Wilkes*, 4 vols. (1804), ii. 61–2.
[21] Hays, *Female Biography*, v. 301.
[22] The Benjamin Franklin Papers, MS of letter dated 8 Dec. 1774, Ref. 7: 138, The American Philosophical Society, Philadelphia.
[23] *Harcourt Papers*, viii. 109–10.

was more, she confessed, she never heard any member of the royal family mentioned. Nevertheless she discovered that her French friends were all too aware of living under a monarchy. After complimenting her on her 'genius' and 'literary power', the quality in her which the French regarded as the next highest compliment was her 'hatred of kings'.[24]

The poverty and wretchedness of the lives of the French peasantry—'an indigent and miserable people' who 'appeared thinly scattered over wild and dreary plains'—made a deep impression on her. She contrasted their way of life with that of the French monarchy and aristocracy. When offered a description of the palace of the prince of Condé at Chantilly by a Dr Nash, after thanking him, she replied that 'she would spare him the repetition, since she could receive no pleasure in hearing of the splendour of one mortal, while the misery of thousands pressed upon her recollection'. The following day on the way to Paris she stopped to change horses, when her carriage was immediately surrounded by a crowd wretched in their appearance and begging for alms. She burst into tears, crying 'My God! my God! have mercy on the works of thine own hand!', and distributed money and all the provisions she had with her. Much later in the day after a long silence she turned to her companion and said 'you saw yesterday the habitation of the prince of Condé, and his family at dinner!' She had no need to say more.[25] Despite persistent fever cutting short her visit, she left expressing the hope of returning when she was better and able to enjoy 'the pleasure of French society'. She had found agreeable 'the manners and present opinions of the Parisians' and been 'quite charmed with the decent rational system of social life'. The 'apprehension of a war with France' was not merely a matter of public concern but a bitter disappointment of 'a private gratification'.[26]

Her brief visit may seem inadequate grounds for suggesting that at this time Catharine Macaulay had more than a passing interest in French affairs. She was clearly gratified at the notice taken of her and flattered by the attentions of the great. But in 1777 her mind was more on happenings in America than France.

[24] Ibid. 108–9.
[25] Hays, *Female Biography*, v. 295–7.
[26] *Harcourt Papers*, viii. 108, 114.

2. *The Role of Catharine Macaulay's* History *in French Revolutionary Politics*

Following her visit at least two sets of her *History* were sent to France.[27] The warm welcome she received during her visit from those aware of her reputation as a republican historian suggests her *History* was not without relevance to the French. As was noted in Ch. 2, the reception in France of David Hume's *History of England* was very different from that in England. It 'enjoyed a spectacular success' and even before its translation and publication, there is evidence it was widely read. Among others Voltaire, Rousseau, and Helvétius praised it in extravagant terms above all for its impartiality, precisely the quality the English denied it. Extracts from the volume on the Stuarts were published in French journals. The main reason for the popularity of Hume's *History* in France lay in the powerful case he made out for the retention of monarchy in preference to a republic. Conservative opinion found in it a reassuring defence of the Ancien Régime. If before the revolution it was regarded as of particular relevance for the situation in France, when the revolution came, events gave it a new immediacy. Laurence Bongie sees Hume's *History* as representing 'a contribution to French counter-revolutionary thought... almost totally ignored by historians to this day'.[28]

Hume had anticipated its popularity in France when negotiating for its translation. Thinking of the decline in respect for both the Catholic church and the monarchy to which the recurrent persecutions of Protestants and the struggles with the Jansenists had contributed, he wrote that, 'considering some late transactions in France, your Ministry may think themselves obliged to a man, who, by the example of English history, discovers the consequences of puritanical and republican pretensions'. He pointed out that his principles were 'tolerably monarchical' and that, unlike most Englishmen, he abhorred 'the low practice... of speaking with malignity of France'. When his *History* was reviewed in 1760 by the *Journal étranger*, they remarked that Hume 'quoique Anglais, républicain et protestant, a toujours parlé des Français avec estime, des rois et des catholiques avec modération'.[29] Between 1760 and the French Revolution, atti-

---

[27] Ibid. 113.
[28] Laurence Bongie, *David Hume* (1965), pp. vii–viii.
[29] Ibid. 14, 16.

tudes in France were to change, most rapidly of all after the
revolution in America. Just as in the 1760s English Whigs had
needed a different version of seventeeth-century history from that
of Hume, so in France those destined to become future revolutionaries sought to combat the conservative use to which Hume's
History was put. This change in the French political climate
can be traced in the changing response to Catharine Macaulay's
History—long before any translation was mooted. When in 1764
the *Journal encyclopédique* reviewed the first volume, no doubt with
an eye on the censors, it warned its readership of the wicked and
seditious purposes of the author. The attention of readers was
drawn to 'des efforts criminels qu'elle fait pour inspirer à ses
concitoyens la haine de la royauté, et du mépris pour la mémoire
des princes les plus respectables de la Grande-Bretagne'. The
reviewer was outraged by her republicanism. '*Quiconque entreprend
de concilier la monarchie avec la liberté est un rebelle dans le sens le plus
noir et le plus étendu*'.[30] By 1778, soon after Catharine Macaulay's
visit, and only a few months after France had allied herself with
America against Britain, the atmosphere was very different. The
same journal now talked of the 'justesse des idées, la solidité du
jugement... et les profondes connaissances qu'elle a de la nature
humaine'.[31] Later they were again to attack her—if more gently
than earlier—for her anti-monarchist prejudices.

There had been talk of translating her *History* into French in
1778. The offer came from the duc de Harcourt. She greeted it
'with great satisfaction' and immediately ordered from her publishers, Messrs Dilly, an octavo edition to be sent him. But the
proposed translation negotiated through the good offices of Lord
Harcourt, never appeared. Possibly his Lordship changed his mind
after reading her recently published *History of England from the
Revolution to the Present Time*. When unacknowledged she wrote
telling him how hurt she was by his 'silence' as she prized his
'approbation so much'. She hoped her treatment of William—'our
great deliverer as he is called'—had not 'disgusted' him. But even
at the risk of sacrificing a French translation, she refused to
retract. If his Lordship examined her principles more closely, he
would find that this latest of her publications in no way departed
from those of previous volumes. He must see, she wrote appeal-
ingly, how impossible it was for her 'to treat with approbation

---

[30] *Journal Encyclopédique* (1764) as quoted Bongie, *David Hume*, 58–9.
[31] Ibid. 60.

characters who have laid the foundation of our ruin by a funded debt, and by reducing the art of corruption into a system'. If he could give his 'free sentiments on the volume' it would give her 'great pleasure'. Whether or not he ever complied, no more was heard of a translation. Her suspicion that she had offended him was almost certainly right. Elizabeth Montagu's letter to Viscount Nuneham in which she expressed her delight that Mrs Macaulay 'will no longer love the House of Harcourt, and the House of Harcourt will not love her', certainly suggests as much.[32]

Among many French anglophiles who spent a period in England in the 1780s were two men who saw her *History* as of direct and compelling application to France. They were political journalists in a period when official censorship rendered it difficult to make a living. Both the Comte de Mirabeau and Jacques Brissot de Warville were widely travelled. Brissot visited the United States in the late eighties and Mirabeau travelled extensively throughout Europe.

Mirabeau was one of the Committee of Thirty which assumed leadership of the 'patriot' party. In the first year of the Revolution he played a leading role in the Constituent Assembly. A moderate, he believed in constitutional monarchy and saw sovereign power as shared between king and people—a view held by many English radicals. Somewhat surprisingly we find him using Milton to convince the opposition of the need for freedom of the press and the ending of censorship. In 1788 he published *Sur la Liberté de la presse*, a rough translation of Milton's *Areopagitica*. In the introduction, perhaps anticipating some criticism of his source, he wrote that 'si dans quelques-uns de ses écrits Milton s'est montré républicain violent, il n'est dans celui-ci, où il s'adresse à la législature de la Grande-Bretagne, qu'un paisible argumentateur'.[33] While convinced of the efficiency of the monarchical form of government Mirabeau nevertheless felt it could be more effective as well as more popular if limited in its powers. Yet in 1789, at the time when King and Constituent Assembly left Versailles for Paris, he translated and published with a preface by himself *Théorie de la Royauté d'aprés la Doctrine de Milton*. His biographer described it as extracts from all Milton's republican

[32] *Harcourt Papers*, viii. 113–14.
[33] Mirabeau, *Sur la liberté de la Presse* (1788), 7, 8.

writings, and commented that 'aprés les événemens des 5 et 6 octobre, la publication d'un tel livre était non-seulement un libelle, mais un crime de haute trahison dans un membre de l'assemblée nationale'.[34] It was a remarkable piece of daring. The stories illustrate how much the writings of Milton and others in the seventeenth century were seen as of relevance to the eighteenth. It was not only English Real Whigs who were familiar with the seventeenth-century Whig tradition.

At other times Mirabeau was cautious. On the proposed abolition of feudal rights and privileges he was less than enthusiastic, even if driven by events to side with those in favour of abolition of tithes. It was over some of his colleagues' opposition to the king's right of executive veto, an issue that was to divide the patriot party, that Mirabeau finally drew back. Mme Roland had never trusted him. She thought him too anxious to defend the king, and his determination to give the king an absolute veto confirmed her opinion that he placed more importance on monarchical power than on that of the people. As Étienne Dumont commented, Mme Roland 'ne crut jamais à la possibilité d'allier la liberté avec la monarchie, et voyait un roi avec la même horreur que madame Macaulai'.[35] Mirabeau had hoped for a reform involving nothing more than the creation of a constitution modelled on that of England. Catharine Macaulay's writings contributed to his knowledge of the English constitution. Profoundly attached to the English-style monarchy, he saw its role in France as that of checking the growing threat of political radicalism from the Constituent Assembly.

An ambitious man, Mirabeau would have liked nothing better than to have become a minister. The decree of 9 November, which laid it down that no member of the Assembly could also be a minister of the Crown, put paid to that. Catharine Macaulay would certainly have approved the decree. It was ironic, given his preoccupation with Mrs Macaulay's account of Cromwell and his warning against a republican form of government, which served only 'l'ambition d'un seul', that his own colleagues saw him as a potential Cromwell.[36] After the November decree he resorted to

---

[34] Étienne Dumont, *Souvenirs sur Mirabeau* (1832), 172.
[35] Ibid. 397.
[36] In Macaulay, *Histoire d'Angleterre depuis l'avènement de Jacques Ier jusqu'à la Révolution*, 3 vols. (1791–2), ii, p. xx.

political intrigue in a hopeless attempt to gain the co-operation of
a king who refused to play the role of constitutional monarch. But
the king never trusted him and his advice was totally disregarded.
While plotting for the restoration of monarchical authority, he
continued to take an active part in the Constituent Assembly, and
in January 1791 became its President. His death three months
later ended this ambiguous career. Mary Wollstonecraft was one
of his admirers; despite the reputation he had for a total lack of
scruples, she did not think him 'utterly devoid of principle—far
from it'.[37]

In 1784–5 Mirabeau visited London. If he met Catharine
Macaulay as he claimed, neither she nor anyone else made mention of it. Yet later he described her face 'dont la mâle austerité
rappelle les traits de Porcia'. Thomas Wilson he thought responsible for encouraging her 'talent naissant' so that 'l'élève surpassa
l'attente du maître'.[38] But Mirabeau certainly knew her *History*
and during his visit to London he conceived the idea of a French
translation. His dissatisfaction with Hume's history and concern
to answer it made him anxious to translate Mrs Macaulay's work.
He expressed impatience with Hume's belief in 'established
order', demanding 'si l'ordre établi est mauvais, doit-on regarder
comme constitutionnel l'usage qui l'empêche d'être bon? Cet
ordre fût-il même excellent, quelle autorité humaine peut
empêcher une nation de le changer?' Later when the translation
was announced it was described as a 'correctif' to Hume.[39]
Mirabeau never claimed to be competent to translate the *History*
and writing home from England he instructed a friend to contact a
Monsieur Durival to find out whether he had 'leisure to translate'
it. The *History*, he added, had 'made much noise in this country,
and the lady who wrote it, being a republican in principles, it will
probably meet with a more extensive sale than Watson's *Philip*'.
He expressed his astonishment that the work 'ne fut pas déjà
traduit en France' and went on to suggest that a Monsieur
Guiraudet might be prepared 'to go shares in the undertaking'.
To convince his friend of the worth of the enterprise he included
in his letter an extract from her *History*. 'Judge from the following

[37] *Collected Letters of Mary Wollstonecraft*, ed. Ralph M. Wardle (1979), 235, in a
letter to Gilbert Imlay dated Aug. 1793.
[38] In Macaulay, *Histoire d'Angleterre etc.* (1791), i, v n. i, vi.
[39] As quoted Bongie, *David Hume*, 114–15.

character of James the Second', he wrote, 'whether this manner will do.'[40] Difficulties in finding a translator in part account for the long delay before the translation appeared.

In October 1786 Mirabeau wrote to Jacques Brissot to congratulate him on his reply to a certain M. Chatellux, a member of the Académie Française who had fought in the war in America as a major-general, and who had just produced a history in which he casually dismissed the struggles of the American colonists. It was the Americans alone in the eighteenth century, Mirabeau wrote, who had taken up the torch of reason kindled by their seventeenth-century predecessors. If anyone needed convincing they had only to read 'l'excellente histoire de mademoiselle Macaulay' and compare what she wrote about the principles of the Levellers with all that had been written by Americans during the recent war.[41] Mirabeau asked Brissot to take on the translation of her *History*. Brissot, although an admirer of her *History*, was not enthusiastic. Making a literal translation he felt would be tedious, and would not meet the needs of French readers. He recommended a work based on Mrs Macaulay's *History* but specially edited for the French.[42] Mirabeau, unconvinced, continued his search for a translator. Finally a M. Debourge was chosen and with Brissot discussed the difficulties involved. According to Brissot, Debourge later abandoned the translation, a task taken on by a M. Guinguène, who in turn passed it on to some hack translator at so much a page. The final translation Brissot condemned as 'détestable'. He rejected any idea that Mirabeau was responsible for it. His knowledge of English would not have been up to it.[43]

The first five volumes of Catharine Macaulay's *History* were translated in two volumes in 1791 and 1792. The *Moniteur* called the work 'l'un des plus importants que l'on ait entrepris depuis la révolution'.[44] By the time any of it appeared, both Catharine

---

[40] A French translation of Robert Watson's *History of Philip II of Spain* (1777) enjoyed great popularity. Mirabeau, *Letters during his Residence in England*, 2 vols. (1832), ii. 230, 234; id., in Macaulay, *Histoire d'Angleterre depuis l'avènement de Jacques Ier jusqu'à la Révolution*, i, p. viii.

[41] Brissot, *Correspondance et Papiers*, ed. C. Perround (1911), 102.

[42] *Mémoires de Brissot*, ii. 232.

[43] Ibid.

[44] *Gazette nationale, ou le Moniteur universel*, 9 Oct. 1791.

Macaulay and Mirabeau were dead, but it was under Mirabeau's name that the translation together with an introduction and 'un précis de toute l'histoire d'Angleterre, jusqu'à l'avènement de Jacques II' appeared. As he had worked on it 'il en sentait croître l'importance'. When the French Revolution intervened to delay the translation, Mirabeau handed the work over to a friend to finish explaining to him that 'cette traduction n'est pas dans nos circonstances, un ouvrage ordinaire . . . Il existe tant de points de contact et de rapport entre ces événements, ces personnages et nous, qu'on se trouvera faire l'histoire des deux révolutions'. So great was the importance Mirabeau attached to getting the translation published that he himself corrected the proofs.[45]

Jacques Brissot, although trained as a lawyer, rarely practised his trade and became increasingly involved in radical pamphleteering. Accused of libelling Marie-Antoinette, he was imprisoned for two months in the Bastille, and according to his enemies was only freed after agreeing to some kind of deal with the French police. In the 1780s, when a number of political clubs blossomed in Paris, it was Brissot who founded the Société des Amis des Noirs, a political club with anti-slavery objectives. Among the mass of new journals that began to appear once censorship ended, his *Patriote Français* became a regular publication. During his visit to London in the early 1780s he met Richard Price, Joseph Priestley, and Jeremy Bentham, but it was to his friendship with 'l'illustre historienne Macaulay' that he attached greatest importance. Already familiar with Stuart history and profoundly influenced by it, he too welcomed Catharine Macaulay's *History* as an answer to 'les principes serviles de Hume'. 'Madame Macaulay a eu le courage', he wrote, 'de s'écarter de la route des autres historiens, de s'en frayer une nouvelle.' If people still needed convincing that the *History* was her work and hers alone, he explained later, they had only to talk with her, for her conversation had 'tous les caractères de cette dignité, de cette énergie républicaine que respire son histoire'. It was during his visit to London he became convinced of the importance of a translation of her *History*. 'Je n'ai plus qu'un souhait à former', he wrote, 'c'est que son Histoire soit traduite en français'. At the same time he expressed the hope she would write a history of the American

---

[45] In Macaulay, *Histoire d'Angleterre*, i, pp. viii–ix.

Revolution so that Americans would know how to avoid the mistakes the English had made in the seventeenth century.[46]

Brissot visited the United States in 1788. During his visit he met John Adams and Washington. It was Catharine Macaulay who introduced him to Washington as 'a warm friend to liberty, and a man of the [*sic*] first rate abilities'. Brissot was her 'great friend'.[47] By the time Washington received Catharine Macaulay's letter Brissot was back in France, having hurried home when news of the impending meeting of the Estates-General reached him. On reaching France he was amazed at the progress of events since he had left.

Unlike Mirabeau, Brissot was at heart a republican with ideas close to those of Catharine Macaulay. In his *Mémoires* he recorded how when she was accused of too marked a partiality for republicanism, he defended her partiality: 'Mais pouvait-elle s'en défendre, quand elle avait à peindre les excès tyranniques qui signalèrent les ministères des Buckingham, des Laud, des Strafford?' It was only 'la partialité pour les personnages' which discredited historians, and she was not guilty of that charge.[48] Like her he approved of laws against 'excessive *material inequality*'. But like Harrington, he favoured controlling the amount of property the rich possessed, not taking it away from them; perhaps his reading of Catharine Macaulay had made him familiar with Harrington's *Oceana*: Brissot too was a firm advocate of limiting the period of office of all functionaries and not allowing their re-election without an interval. With her he was critical of the English constitution, seeing the House of Commons as manipulated by the executive. He argued that the English parliament represented property not the people. In many ways, however, Brissot was more of a democratic republican than Catharine. There were times, as in September 1792, when he saw as she did not that it was 'within the class of citizens called *people* that one finds the most sincere republicans. Why? Because the people have more good faith, more good sense, fewer prejudices, less self-seeking calculation than the other classes'.[49] Yet for all his criticism he believed the English constitution could still 'servir de

---

[46] *Mémoires de Brissot*, ii. 229, 231–2, 237; *Journal du Licée de Londres*, 1 (1784), 34.
[47] Sparks, *Correspondence of the American Revolution*, iv. 283.
[48] *Mémoires de Brissot*, ii. 230.
[49] Norman Hampson, *Will and Circumstance* (1983), 184–6.

modèle aux sociétés qui voudraient changer leur régime'. He added that unfortunately the nature of the English constitution 'était peu connu en France'.[50]

For Brissot legislative power resided with the people, but like Catharine Macaulay he had doubts whether without more education they could exercise that power responsibly. France, he argued in December 1790, was not ready to become a republic. Provisionally power must be shared with the King. For all the reservation he had expressed earlier, events of June 1791 were temporarily to change Brissot's mind. Whether ready for a republic or not, there could no longer be any question of restoring the king to the throne. Together with Condorcet he pressed for the proclamation of a Republic directly after the flight of the king, but the Constituent Assembly dithered.[51] The moment for declaring a Republic passed. Brissot became leader of the group of deputies known as Brissotins, or later as Girondins. In March 1792 they formed the Ministry. But it was in the earlier period 1791–2 that Brissot became prominent. Finally in power and with the Paris Commune pressing for more radical policies, he was less happy about the idea of popular sovereignty. His earlier lack of confidence in the people resurfaced. Brissot's popularity with the Commune declined, and he was finally denounced by it on 2 September 1792. Together with most of the English expatriates, Brissot had argued for mercy to be shown to Louis XVI. They were not alone in seeing the parallels between the trial of Charles I and that of Louis XVI and questioning the legality of both. What worried many was that if the king was executed a French Cromwell would emerge. During the debate in the Convention over the fate of the King, the analogies between the situation in 1648/9 and 1792 were recognized and led to renewed importance being attached to a study of Stuart history. The view that 'la mort violente ou juridique d'un tyran n'a jamais servi véritablement la cause de la liberté, et n'a fait que placer la tyrannie dans d'autres mains' was expressed by many moderates.[52] Yet despite their opposition, in January 1793 the king was executed. On 30 October 1793, together with twenty other Girondins, Brissot was executed in his turn.

---

[50] *Mémoires de Brissot*, ii. 206–7.
[51] Hampson, *Will and Circumstance*, 172.
[52] As quoted Bongie, *David Hume*, 135.

When Brissot condemned the translation of Mrs Macaulay's *History* that bore Mirabeau's name, it was after the event and Mirabeau was dead. There were political reasons for Brissot to distance himself from Mirabeau. But if their political objectives were different, both had supported constitutional monarchy, although in Brissot's case it was from fear of the alternative rather than any conviction of its inherent merit. Both had read Mrs Macaulay's *History* and were convinced of its relevance for revolutionary France. Both were fascinated by the character of Cromwell as she depicted him. 'Ce Cromwell, tout-à-la-fois démagogue astucieux, intrigant fanatique, artificieux augure, ambitieux tribun', Mirabeau wrote, 'qui parvient à la dicta-ture, protecteur et souverain d'un pays où il prêcha l'égalité'. Attempting a comparison between the English and French revolu-tions Mirabeau's argument gives way to an impassioned plea to the people of France: 'Il nous faut un roi'. A republic, he argued 'n'a jamais été que la chimère des peuples libres, qui n'a duré qu'un jour'. It was inevitably a transitional form of government 'propre à servir par ses vices même . . . l'ambition d'un seul qui n'ose d'abord se montrer'. Brissot confessed that 'l'histoire de Charles Ier et de Cromwell m'avait singulièrement frappé'. But it was 'ce dernier' that fascinated him, 'déchirant dans son enfance le portrait de son roi, terminant sa carrière par le faire décapiter, et ne devant qu'à son genie le grand rôle qu'il avait joué dans la révolution anglaise'. Significantly he thought it not impossible 'de renouveler cette révolution'.[53]

In 1790 the debate between Brissot and Clermont-Tonnerre, a constitutional monarchist much influenced by Hume's *History*, over the *Comités de recherches* centred on their very different views of the Long Parliament. That such a debate could happen reveals 'how Stuart history influenced in an immediate sense the for-mulation by both sides of many political problems of the day'. It shows the importance of Hume's history, but it also makes clear that Mrs Macaulay's *History* 'had begun to play an equally important role in countering its conservative effect'.[54]

Other French liberals knew Catharine Macaulay's work and reputation. Some like Henri Bancal des Issarts had met her. A

[53] Mirabeau, i.e. Macaulay, *Histoire d'Angleterre*, ii, pp. xii, xx; *Mémoires de Brissot*, ii. 54–5.
[54] As quoted Bongie, *David Hume*, 105–7, 113.

lawyer from Clermont-Ferrand, he moved in the same circle as Brissot, Condorcet, and the Rolands, and was a close friend of Tom Paine, whose works he translated, and of Thomas Christie and Helena-Maria Williams, both of whom were living in Paris during the Revolution. He regularly contributed to Brissot's *Patriote Français* and was a member of his Société des Amis des Noirs, and of the Société des Amis de la Constitution, later to become the Jacobin Club. In England from November 1790 to June 1791, he made contact with as many radicals as he could including Catharine Macaulay and Mary Wollstonecraft. Described as 'a brave and thoughtful man but an ineffectual politician', he did not return to France until after the Terror.[55] Mme Roland much admired Catharine Macaulay and saw her as 'un être au-dessus de son sexe'.[56] She too had spent time in England and may have met Catharine Macaulay. In November 1790 she wrote to Bancal that if she could devote some time that coming winter to improving her English 'ce sera pour lire l'histoire de Mme Macaulay'. In March 1791 she wrote again to Bancal in London asking if he had yet met Mrs Macaulay. 'Son esprit, ses talents, sa trempe républicaine', she wrote, 'me paraissent la rendre bien intéressante'. She had asked Brissot to lend to her and had started to read the first volumes. Later she referred to it as 'une inspiration toute républicaine'.[57] A few days before her execution she expressed the wish, had she survived, of becoming the Catharine Macaulay of France.

Such figures as Mirabeau, Brissot, Bancal d'Issart, Condorcet, Mme Roland and others 'did indeed actively publicize Catharine Macaulay's history of the English revolution as most suitable to replace the hated royalist account by Hume'.[58] When François Guizot (1787–1874) was preparing his *Histoire de la Révolution d'Angleterre* (1826), acclaimed at the time both for its scholarship and impartiality, he remarked that his study of both English and French pamphlets of the period had taught him that 'le public français fut plus occupé qu'on ne pense de la révolution anglaise'.[59] If this was true of the seventeenth century, it was also

---

[55] Claire Tomalin, *The Life and Death of Mary Wollstonecraft* (1974), 135.
[56] Dumont, *Souvenirs sur Mirabeau*, 397.
[57] *Lettres de Mme Roland*, ed. Claude Perraud, 2 vols. (1900), ii. 191, 246.
[58] Bongie, *David Hume*, 86.
[59] François Guizot, *Histoire de la Révolution d'Angleterre, depuis l'avènement de Charles Ier jusqu'à la restauration de Charles II*, 2 vols. (1826), i, p. xxvi.

true of the revolutionary period in France. Guizot thought that despite the efforts of Mirabeau 'les déclamations de Mistress Macaulay' had not succeeded in upsetting the authority Hume's *History* carried in Europe.[60] Nevertheless when in February 1792, the *Moniteur* reviewed the translation of her *History*, which dealt with 'la querelle du peuple avec ses rois', a period 'la plus intéressante de l'histoire d'Angleterre', it talked of Hume as 'partial à force d'impartialité'. It was a reproach, it added, that could not be made against Mrs Macaulay, and it rejoiced that the period had found 'une digne historienne dans cette courageuse amie de la liberté britannique'.[61] Whether or not in consequence of this review, Madame Roland, in 1793, suggested that copies of the *History* were difficult to obtain. But five years later, after the Terror, the Ministry of the Interior recommended that Catharine Macaulay's *History* be included among those suitable for distribution as school prizes 'à la clôture des Écoles et dans les fêtes nationales'.[62]

3. English Radicalism and the French Revolution

In 1790 Catharine Macaulay published her answer to Burke's *Reflections on the Revolution in France*. It was the last thing she wrote. This substantial pamphlet—like Burke's—is as much, if not more, about English radicalism as it is about the French revolution. What is fascinating is that after a gap of twenty years the debate with Burke over interpretations of the 'Glorious Revolution' was reopened, but now in a very different situation. The American revolution had forced English radicals to rethink some of their ideas. Among the mass of pamphlets written during the 1770s and 1780s two had been profoundly influential. Thomas Paine's *Common Sense* (1776) attacked 'the much boasted Constitution of England' which he described as 'the base remains of two ancient tyrannies . . . the remains of monarchical tyranny in the person of the king . . . the remains of aristocratical tyranny in the persons of the peers'. He confessed to a 'strong aversion to monarchy, as being too debasing to the dignity of man'.[63] The pamphlet undermined the notion that a balanced constitution

---

[60] Ibid., p. xvii.
[61] *Moniteur*, 14 Feb. 1792, 184.
[62] Bongie, *David Hume*, 119.
[63] Eric Foner, *Tom Paine and Revolutionary America* (1976), 11, 76.

guaranteed freedom, but it also rejected the idea of an original pure and uncorrupted constitution of the Anglo-Saxons towards the reattainment of which all reforms were directed. Above all what was new in Paine's writing was an appeal to an audience quite outside the 'political nation'. It marked the gradual emergence of a popular radicalism. The other pamphlet that greatly influenced the radicals was Richard Price's *Observations on the Nature of Civil Liberty* (1776) in which he appealed to them to widen their vision. With Paine he called for an abandonment of appeal to historical precedent in favour of natural rights. Radicals must look beyond narrow national interest to the rights of all men. Both pamphlets were in Catharine Macaulay's library.

After the American revolution English radicals looked with a more critical eye at the English constitution. In the final volume of her *History* in 1783 Catharine Macaulay repeated her earlier analysis of the shortcomings of 1688/9, but now relating it to contemporary radical demands for parliamentary reform. It was important, she stressed, that, at a moment when the calamities of the nation had been brought home to 'every disinterested citizen', instead of 'throwing a veil over the defects of the revolution' its weaknesses should be understood. 'Under the specious appearance of democratical privilege, the people' were 'really and truly enslaved to a small part of the community'. In order to destroy corruption, she demanded the abolition of rotten boroughs, the extension of the franchise, the expansion of the number of county members, but also, if these proved insufficient, vote by ballot, 'a mode used in every wise government in all cases of election'.[64] The American revolution raised the whole question of where sovereign power was located. Was the authority of the people ultimately superior to that of parliament, and at what point was armed resistance to a corrupt administration justified?

If little came of attempts at reform by English radicals between the outbreak of the war with America and the French revolution, they served to keep the issue of parliamentary reform alive. John Sawbridge was one who, with great persistence, carried on the fight by introducing a series of motions for shorter parliaments between 1771 and 1786. They never met with anything but indifference or hostility, and there were massive votes against them.

[64] Catharine Macaulay, *History of England*, viii. 330, 337, 339.

Catharine, we have seen, admired his dedication but was clearly sceptical about what if anything it achieved.[65] (If we have little direct evidence of her attitude to the politics of the 1780s, the two cartoons in Pls. 12 and 13 suggest her *History* remained essential reading for those concerned with a radical reform of parliament.) By the end of the 1770s little progress had been made in winning support for a programme of parliamentary reform. The gulf between those wanting only a modicum of reform that would reduce the worst corruption, and those demanding fundamental reforms, remained as wide as ever. But in the years preceding the outbreak of the French Revolution there was a revival of radical politics, particularly as the centenary of 1688 approached. Informal Revolution societies had existed in many towns from the beginning of the century and organized the celebrations for the anniversary of the 'Glorious Revolution'. Few had survived, but now they re-emerged and grew in strength. The almost quiescent Society for Constitutional Information also revived. To their programmes there was now added not only parliamentary reform but the repeal of the Test and Corporation Acts.

Long before the storming of the Bastille, Catharine Macaulay and other English radicals had been following events in France with considerable interest. When they finally erupted there was tremendous excitement. When Catharine Macaulay wrote to congratulate Washington on becoming President, her delight at news of the French Revolution is barely contained. 'All the friends of liberty on this side of the Atlantic', she wrote, were 'now rejoicing for an event which in all probability, had been accelerated by the American Revolution'.[66] To Thomas Brand Hollis, Catharine Macaulay confessed to feeling flattered that the French had adopted 'a limited monarchy' as their chosen form of government. It was, she believed, 'the best form of government for a great and luxurious nation'. She saw events in France as the prelude to 'the full emancipation of all Europe from the shackles which . . . violence, ignorance and superstition had effected'.[67] Events in France had made her more critical of the American

---

[65] Letter from Catharine Macaulay to John Adams, 11 Sept. 1774, in *The Adams Papers*, Microfilm No. 344.
[66] *Correspondence of the American Revolution*, iv. 283.
[67] *Memoirs of Thomas Brand Hollis*, ed. John Disney (1808), 42.

constitution. Although she once thought 'such a system of government would be invulnerable', the growth of corruption in the English legislature since 1688, and the recent creation of the Constituent Assembly in France, had changed her mind. She told Washington she feared 'ill consequences' could result from giving members of the legislature the power not only of 'establishing offices, of regulating the quantum of their salaries', but also of 'enjoying themselves the emoluments arising from such establishments'. The French had 'effectively secured themselves from the return of aristocracy in their government, by confining the legislature to one equal assembly'. It had made her doubt the adequacy of a two-chamber legislature. 'May not your upper House in length of time acquire some distinction', she demanded of Washington, 'which may lay the grounds for political inequality among you?' She thought the Americans by being 'exempt from the evils of aristocracy', had not the same aversion to them 'as now happily exist among the French'.[68] 'We are full of wonder, in this part of the world,' she had written to Washington earlier, 'and cannot conceive how such things should be'.[69] She thought the French had set an example ... unique in all the histories of human society' by overthrowing a despotic regime through the combination of 'the firmness of their union, the universality of their sentiments and the energy of their actions'.[70]

The sermon preached by Richard Price when the London Revolution Society met in 1789 was far from commemorating the virtues of the 'Glorious Revolution'. If 1688 had provided an opportunity of securing men's natural rights, it had failed to use it. The Crown retained far too much power. Liberty of conscience was still denied to many by the failure to repeal the Test and Corporation Acts. So unequal was the state of representation that many were denied the 'right to choose our own governors; to cashier them for misconduct; and to frame a government for ourselves'. The sermon echoed Catharine Macaulay's views expressed in her answer to Burke eighteen years earlier.[71] What now inspired this emphasis on the inadequacies of 1688, and the

---

[68] *The Writings of George Washington*, ed. Jared Sparks, 12 vols. (1834–7), 68–72.
[69] *Correspondence of the American Revolution*, iv. 283.
[70] Ibid.
[71] Richard Price, *Discourse on the Love of our Country*, 3rd edn. (1789), 34; Catharine Macaulay, *Observations on a Pamphlet entitled Thoughts on the Cause of the Present Discontents* (1770).

demand for increased representation and the repeal of the Test and Corporation Acts, was the example France provided. Set beside the principles established by the American Declaration of Independence and the French Declaration of the Rights of Man, the Bill of Rights had achieved little. Price ended his sermon by moving a resolution congratulating the National Assembly on the Revolution. 'Disdaining national partialities and rejoicing in every triumph of Liberty and Justice over Arbitrary Power', the French Revolution encouraged 'other nations to assert the unalienable rights of Mankind'.[72]

It was Price's sermon that provoked Burke into writing his *Reflections on the Revolution in France*. Burke defended the aristocratic Whig tradition which he saw as originating in 1688. He accused English radicals of using the example of France to provoke a revolution at home, or at least a measure of parliamentary reform. Neither, Burke argued, was needed. Apart from 'a few idle, insignificant, speculative individuals', the 'excellencies of the English constitution' were '*obvious* to every observer' and '*unanimously*' bound 'their affections to its principles, its rules, and its dictates'.[73] His anger was directed at the London Revolution Society and the Society for Constitutional Information but its particular focus was Richard Price.[74] It was Price's assertion of popular sovereignty to which Burke took exception. Price had claimed that 'the King of Great Britain owes his right to the Crown by the choice of the people'. It was this that made him 'the *only* lawful king in the world'.[75]

Once again the argument was about what exactly 1688 had and had not achieved. The facts of 1688, Catharine Macaulay argued, '*might warrant a plain thinking man* in the opinion that the present reigning family owe their succession to the choice or assent of the people'.[76] In 1783 she had written of William's crown as one 'bestowed by the free voice of the people'.[77] Burke countered that far from being chosen William had been a necessity. He denied

[72] G. S. Veitch, *The Genesis of Parliamentary Reform* (1965), 122.

[73] Catharine Macaulay, *Observations on the Reflections of the Rt. Hon. Edmund Burke, on the Revolution in France* (1790), 43–4.

[74] Edmund Burke, *Reflections on the Revolution in France*, ed. Conor Cruise O'Brien (1988), 93–4.

[75] Ibid. 96.

[76] Macaulay, *Observations on the Reflections of the Rt. Hon. Edmund Burke*, 10.

[77] Macaulay, *History of England*, viii. 331.

the right of the people 'of chusing their own magistrates, and of deposing them for ill-conduct', arguing that such a right had 'only existed in that Convention of the two Houses in 1688'.[78] Catharine Macaulay made it clear that while she thought the people undoubtedly had such a right, it should '*never* . . . be exercised by a people . . . satisfied with their form of government', who had 'spirit enough to correct its abuses'.[79] No more than Price did she want a revolution.

Burke contrasted the French revolution with that of 1688, and the new French constitution with that which emerged from the 'Glorious Revolution'. He defended the Ancien Régime and argued that no revolution had been necessary. In framing a new constitution the Constituent Assembly had acted illegally. Catharine Macaulay suggested that before censuring the new French constitution and setting up that of England as a model for all nations, it might be wise for would-be critics to ask whether that constitution they recommended bestowed 'the *greatest* possible happiness on the people'. If it did not and there were defects in it, then the remedy lay in reform. But such a remedy had not been open to France. The Third Estate had decided 'to redress their own grievances without waiting the effect of *humble* petitions and *discordant* councils'.[80] The only remedy was to start afresh and create a totally new constitution.

Catharine Macaulay's sympathies were with the Constituent Assembly. She thought it right not to replace Louis XVI although there were 'the *strongest presumptions* of the most *attrocious* [*sic*] guilt' against him, for to have replaced him would have created difficulties 'in the way of their liberty, instead of improving it'. If the King had suffered it was his own fault, the result of 'a conduct which, to say the best of it, was altogether imprudent'. If Price had not been moved by 'the mortifications and sufferings of a *very few persons*', it was because such sufferings 'led the way, or secured the *present and future happiness of twenty-four millions of people, with their posterity*'. Given the animosity that had existed between the 'aristocratists and Democratists on the eve of the Revolution', she had been surprised at the moderation shown in the treatment of their enemies. Compared to wretches forced by '*destitute poverty*'

---

[78] Macaulay, *Observations on the Reflections of the Rt. Hon. Edmund Burke*, 12.
[79] Ibid. 18.
[80] Ibid. 33, 36.

to robbery, who had been broken on the wheel, she thought hanging might be regarded as 'a *mild* punishment'. She appealed to her readers to remember all those sufferers who 'have fallen in *one hour* to the *rage* and *outrageous pride* of kingly despots'.[81] Burke expressed his concern with the 'mortifications of the Queen of France' and lamented that the age of chivalry was dead.[82] Society, she replied, must be freed from such '*false* notions of honour'. The 'honour' of the age of chivalry had been nothing but 'methodized sentimental barbarism'. When Burke condemned the congratulatory address of the Constituent Assembly to the King at the beginning of 1790, Catharine Macaulay argued that it was couched in 'a language the *best* adapted to sooth [*sic*] the personal afflictions of the King'. It was an address promising him 'as loyal an attachment to his person . . . as could have been exacted by the authority of which he was dispossessed'.[83]

Burke resorted to the notion of an ancient law from which the rights of Englishmen were inherited 'as a patrimony derived from their forefathers'. Catharine Macaulay saw that by this device Burke sought to evade the issue of natural rights—'a *novel* or a *mischievous* doctrine' as he saw it, which 'if brought before the eyes of the people' would lead to 'the *utter downfall* of every order in the church and state . . . and with the *general* pillage of the rich'.[84] What Burke had omitted from the theory of ancient rights, she retorted, was the Norman Conquest, which had destroyed such rights. Those subsequently won back had been granted to the people with the agreement of monarchs who as easily as they had given them could take them away. So the only firm basis on which the constitution could stand was the natural rights of man. The 'boasted birthright of an Englishman' she had always regarded as 'an arrogant pretension' for it suggested 'a kind of exclusion to the rest of mankind from the same privileges'. It was 'built on a beggarly foundation' for men's right to freedom was made to depend on 'the *alms* of our princes'.[85]

Arguing for the greater rights of large property-owners to polit-

---

[81] Macaulay, *Observations on the Reflections of the Rt. Hon. Edmund Burke*, 18–20, 23, 25–7.

[82] Ibid. 53; Edmund Burke, *Reflections on the Revolution in France*, 170.

[83] Macaulay, *Observations on the Reflections of the Rt. Hon. Edmund Burke*, 54, 56–7.

[84] Ibid. 44–5.

[85] Ibid. 30–2.

ical power—a point not so very different from that made by
Catharine Macaulay and other radicals earlier—Burke claimed
it was 'the great masses' of property which formed 'a natural
rampart about the lesser properties'.[86] This justified the claim of
'the rich and opulent' to the 'right to the predominant sway in
society'. But Catharine had changed her mind. She now argued
that any property-owner, however small, was equally anxious
to protect his property, and that it was 'this sense of personal
interest' in 'every rank of society' which provided security of
wealth. Were 'men in an inferior state of fortune' to place themselves under the protection of the 'rich and opulent', abuse of
power was inevitable. Those with power 'would be sure to take
the *first* care of themselves'. The only way to avoid such abuse
was by 'a *fair* and *equal* representation of the *whole* people'—
particularly necessary in 'a mixed form of government'. If the idea
of rights confined to the privileged was no longer acceptable,
there was only one rational alternative—the notion of 'the *native*
and *unalienable* rights of man'.[87]

The *philosophe* Condorcet, a close friend of Brissot, Mme
Roland, and Thomas Paine, was familiar with Mrs Macaulay's
History. Aware of her political sympathies he anticipated her
answer to Burke when in July 1790 in his 'Sur l'Admission des
Femmes au droit de Cité', he asked:

croit-on que mistriss [*sic*] Macaulay n'êut pas mieux opiné dans la
chambre des communes que beaucoup de représentants de la nation
britannique? N'aurait-elle pas, en traitant la question de la liberté de
conscience, montré des principes plus élevés que ceux de Pitt, et une
raison plus forte? Quoique aussi enthousiaste de la liberté que M.
Burke peut l'être de la tyrannie, aurait-elle, en défendant la constitution
française, approché de l'absurde et dégoutant galimatias par lequel ce
célèbre rhétoricien vient de la combattre?[88]

The French Revolution was described by Mrs Macaulay as 'an
event, the most *important* to the dearest interests of mankind, the
most *singular* in its nature, the most *astonishing* in its means'. But
in 1790 she believed it was too early to judge it as Burke had done

---

[86] Burke, *Reflections on the Revolution in France*, 140.
[87] Macaulay, *Observations on the Reflections of the Rt. Hon. Edmund Burke*, 40–1,
47–8, 94.
[88] *Œuvres de Condorcet*, ed. A. Condorcet O'Connor et M. F. A. Arago, 12 vols.
(1847–9), x. 119.

and to reach the conclusion that 'truly popular government' was incompatible with 'the human constitution'. After such 'convulsive struggles' as inevitably accompanied revolutions, there must be a period of recovery. It was no good looking to history for guidance as it 'furnished *no example* of any government in a large empire, which in the strictest sense of the word' had 'secured to the citizen the *full* enjoyment of his rights'. 'Ancient authors, or . . . comparisons from ancient times' were therefore irrelevant. What was happening in France was unique. She had no doubts of the dangerous repercussions of Burke's reasoning on attitudes towards the revolution in France. The effect of his pamphlet was 'to rouse all nations and all descriptions of men against them [the French], and thus to *crush in their ruin all the rights of man*'.[89] She did not live to see the results of the hostility it generated not merely towards that revolution but towards radicals at home. Nor did she live to see the second stage of the revolution. In the year of her death Thomas Paine published his answer to Burke, *The Rights of Man* (1791), in which he too compared the situation in France with that in England. He contrasted the new broad suffrage of the French with 'the narrow and "capricious" British franchise, the frequent assemblies based on electoral districts with the seven-year parliaments and the system of rotten boroughs, the French guarantee of freedom of conscience with the disabilities faced by religious Dissenters in England'. He too rejected Burke's recourse to historical precedent—although with him this rejection was not new. 'Every age and generation must be as free to act for itself, *in all cases*, as the ages and generations which preceded it.'[90] If Catharine Macaulay had lived to read Paine, she would almost certainly have agreed. But how would she have responded to the next phase of the revolution in France? Would she have defended the execution of Louis XVI as she had of Charles I? How would she have reacted to the execution of Brissot and of so many of those who had fêted her in 1777? Would she, with her American friend Ezra Stiles, have remained loyal to the revolutionaries and confident that liberty would triumph? Stiles, appalled at the decline in American sympathy for the revolution when news of

[89] Macaulay, *Observations on the Reflections of the Rt. Hon. Edmund Burke*, 6, 81, 86–8.
[90] Foner, *Tom Paine and Revolutionary America*, 216; Thomas Paine, *The Rights of Man*, ed. H. Collins (1969), 63.

the king's execution reached America, felt called on, despite his earlier decision to keep out of politics, to defend regicide publicly. He was writing a history of the judges responsible for executing Charles I who had fled to New England at the Restoration. He now wanted to vindicate not only those responsible for the execution of Charles I but those who had executed Louis XVI. The people, he argued 'not merely . . . have a right to judge their rulers but . . . civil rights and liberty cannot permanently endure in conjunction with hereditary sovereignty or aristocracy'. The people alone were capable of achieving emancipation and creating such 'a rational government policy . . . as would be intelligible to the plainest rustic'. Such emancipation must start, he wrote 'in popular societies, connected, spreading and growing up into general popular exertion'.[91] From being a sincere admirer of the British constitution Stiles, who had learnt from Catharine Macaulay, had become a republican and a democrat.

[91] Edmund S. Morgan, *The Gentle Puritan: A Life of Ezra Stiles 1727–1795* (1962), 458–9, 461.

11. *Conclusion*

There was a certain detachment and independence in her commentary that entitles Mrs. Macaulay to more serious study than she normally provokes.

(Caroline Robbins, *The Eighteenth-Century Commonwealth-man* (Cambridge, Mass., 1959), 361.)

TWO years before Catharine Macaulay's death William Graham matriculated at St Edmund Hall, Oxford. Three years later he graduated BA and in 1795 took his MA.[1] It is a measure of his admiration for Catharine, and her influence on him, that at the late age of 30, he decided to go to university to study divinity. As the Revd William Graham, he occupied a living at Misterton in Leicestershire—perhaps deliberately choosing to be near his sister Elizabeth Arnold.[2] In 1797 he remarried. His wife was a Miss Cave of Walcote.[3] Just over a century later a Revd James Graham, great-grandson of the doctor, of Much Cowarne Vicarage, Bromyard, wrote to *Notes and Queries*, asking for information about Mrs Macaulay and the whereabouts of her statue and portraits.[4]

Her brother John Sawbridge died in February 1795 at 'his town-residence in Gloucester Place, Portman Square'. He was buried at Olantigh; 'a numerous and respectable tenantry, together with very many faithful and affectionate domestics, weepingly followed the hearse'.[5] His epitaph, written by a friend, opened:

> Here *Sawbridge* lies:—a man of worth approv'd,
> In virtue stern,—yet mild, rever'd, belov'd.[6]

Of Catharine Macaulay's friends, Richard Baron, Thomas Hollis, and James Burgh were long since dead. In 1775, suffering

---

[1] *Horace Walpole's Correspondence*, ed. W. S. Lewis, 48 vols. (1937–83), xxxiii. 84–5 n. 8.

[2] Ibid.

[3] John Nichols, *History and Antiquities of the County of Leicester*, 4 vols. in 8 pts. (1795–1815), pt. 1, 312.

[4] *Notes and Queries*, 9th ser., 4 (1899), 238.

[5] *Gentleman's Magazine*, 65 (1795), 217.

[6] *The Kentish Gazette*, 22 May 1795, in a poem by J. Burnby.

from consumption, Augustus Toplady moved to London, where he died three years later. Dr James Graham turned from medicine to religion and founded the 'New and True Christian Church'. He died insane and in penury at Edinburgh in 1794. Three years later, John Wilkes died at his home in Grosvenor Square. The ranks of the Real Whigs were depleted. Caleb Fleming had died in 1779, Timothy Hollis in 1790, Richard Price a year later. Priestley lived until 1804. Of the group closest to Catharine Macaulay in the 1760s and 1770s only Sylas Neville survived well into the nineteenth century. One of the most active radicals in the 1780s and 1790s was Thomas Brand Hollis, heir to Thomas Hollis, and a close friend of Thomas Paine. In the last ten years of Catharine Macaulay's life, when there is little information about her, there is evidence of her friendship and correspondence with Brand Hollis. It was with him she discussed the events of 1789.

Was it coincidence that both husbands, and so many of her friends—Richard Baron, James Burgh, James Graham—were Scots? The link between the Scottish Enlightenment and English Dissenters was close. Many Dissenters after an Academy education went on to Scottish universities. Both Richard Baron and Thomas Hollis owed their initial interest in seventeenth-century texts and their recovery to Francis Hutcheson. Among his other pupils was Thomas Brand Hollis. But Wilkes's campaign against Bute was more than an attack on an individual. Behind it there lurked a profound distrust of all Scots, an attitude shared by many of his supporters. It went with their hatred of the Stuarts. John Sawbridge, for example, saw all Scots as 'tinctured with notions of despotism'.[7] It raises the question of what he really thought of his two brothers-in-law. His sister, in this instance, seems not to have shared his prejudices.

In 1792 Mary Wollstonecraft regretted that Catharine Macaulay had died 'without sufficient respect being paid to her memory', but she was confident that 'posterity' would 'be more just'.[8] Was she right? Women have always been more generous in their acknowledgement of Catharine Macaulay's remarkable gifts, recognizing perhaps how great were the obstacles facing their sex

---

[7] *Gentleman's Magazine*, 65 (1795), 216–17, 253.

[8] Mary Wollstonecraft, *Vindication of the Rights of Woman*, ed. Miriam Kramnick (1978), 206.

and what determination and courage it took to overcome them. Mary Wollstonecraft was one of the few women in Mrs Macaulay's time who recognized her worth. When in 1790 she reviewed her *Letters on Education*, she commented on her 'sound reason and profound thought which either through defective organs, or a mistaken education seldom appears in female productions'.[9] 'The very word respect', she wrote in the *Vindication*, reminded her of Catharine Macaulay. She was 'the woman of the greatest abilities, undoubtedly, that this country' had produced. Mary Wollstonecraft saw her as 'an example of intellectual acquirements supposed to be incompatible with the weakness of her sex'. But 'in her style of writing . . . no sex' appeared, for 'like the sense' it conveyed, it was 'strong and clear'. Her sound understanding and 'her judgment, the matured fruit of profound thinking, was a proof that a woman' could 'acquire judgment to the full extent of the word'.[10] In the early nineteenth century Mary Hays also wrote glowingly of the 'lady who, by her writings, and powers of her mind, has reflected so much credit on her sex and country'.[11] A comparison of Macaulay and Wollstonecraft early this century talked of 'the little taper which Mrs. Macaulay had set burning', which was 'caught up into abler hands'.[12] As far as active campaigning on behalf of women's rights goes, Catharine Macaulay cannot be compared with Mary Wollstonecraft. As we have seen, she was not primarily concerned with women's rights. But she was more actively involved in politics and the writing of political polemic than Mary Wollstonecraft. If one compares their writings it is arguable that Mrs Macaulay's work had far more influence on eighteenth-century politics than anything written by the younger woman. But such comparisons are beside the point. They were both quite remarkable women. Mary Wollstonecraft recognized the exceptional qualities in Catharine Macaulay and selected her work for particular praise.

In the nineteenth century Alicia Lefanu could laugh at Mrs Macaulay's idiosyncrasies, but they did not blind her to the unique qualities she possessed. 'Let us be just to the memory of a very uncommon female', she wrote, 'who rose above the dis-

---

[9] *Analytical Review*, 8 (Sept.–Dec. 1790), 241–54, at p. 254.
[10] Wollstonecraft, *Vindication of the Rights of Woman*, 206.
[11] Mary Hays, *Female Biography*, 6 vols. (1803), v. 287.
[12] Dorothy Gardiner, *English Girlhood at School* (1929), 456.

advantages and deficiencies of education, at a time that literature was not cultivated among women as it is at present. Small could not be the industry and perseverance of a woman, who, under the circumstances, was able to rank with the historians of her country; nor was the merit inconsiderable of that person, who was admired by Cowper, and quoted with approbation by Mr. Fox.'[13] In the present century women have continued to praise her. In 1929 Dorothy Gardiner saw her as 'the pioneer' among the 'very few and isolated' women in the eighteenth century who 'with much mental conflict' were beginning 'to visualize the place of women not merely in the home, but in human society', and who 'pondered over the causes of feminine inadequacy, and . . . drew conclusions from experience within their own knowledge'.[14] Nor was this a lone view. It was echoed in the 1950s when she was described as 'the woman born before 1750 who challenged most directly the prevalent conceptions of her time'.[15] But if occasionally she was mentioned in passing, nobody since the early nineteenth century had concentrated attention on her until, in 1949, Lucy Donnelly's article in the *William and Mary Quarterly* appeared. It is significant, and indicative of the relative importance assigned to her by historians on both sides of the Atlantic, that the article came from America. It was intended to rescue a remarkable woman from obscurity. In this it certainly succeeded. There was no absence of praise: 'an amazing figure', 'a *femme forte*', 'a woman of power and resource' whose achievement 'was truly astonishing'.[16] Yet the tone is often condescending if not denigratory. It has been aptly described as that of 'jocose depreciation'.[17] Mrs Macaulay, it is claimed, had only 'a background of superficial reading'. As evidence, John Adams is cited as saying he always 'knew her learning to be superficial'. Of the history she planned to write 'only the volumes of Stuart history were accomplished' and that 'only after an interval of years'. It 'deserved only its ephemeral

---

[13] Alicia Lefanu, *Memoirs of the Life and Writings of Mrs. Frances Sheridan* (1824), 234.

[14] Gardiner, *English Girlhood at School*, 454.

[15] Doris Mary Stenton, *The English Woman in History* (1957), 306.

[16] Lucy Donnelly, 'The Celebrated Mrs. Macaulay', *William and Mary Quarterly*, 3rd ser., 6 (1949), 173–207, at pp. 174, 179, 189, 203.

[17] Susan Staves, ' "The Liberty of a She-Subject of England": Rights Rhetoric and the Female Thucydides', *Cardozo Studies in Law and Literature*, 1 (1989), 161–83, at p. 181 n. 6.

success' for 'Republican zeal, energy and industry, however useful in controversy, are insufficient qualifications for an historian; and only on the grounds of sex can the plea of being a pioneer in the field be urged for' her.[18] Three years later Daisy Hobman was to deny some of these criticisms: 'A woman whose friends included George Washington, and whose writings, however much they have been discredited subsequently, were based upon research in an age when feminine scholarship was altogether exceptional, must have been remarkable, and, in fact, there does emerge from the scanty data of her life, the outline of a forceful and original personality'.[19] This view was echoed four years later when she was described as 'the first woman to attempt the writing of history on a large scale, based on materials in manuscript as well as in print'.[20] A more recent estimation of her *History* has recognized not only that 'she could be acute and sensible in her use of evidence and . . . read widely in the pamphlet literature of the period', but that she was familiar with manuscripts.[21]

Male critics have been less admiring of her qualities. In 1883 one wrote of her as 'a weak and foolish woman'.[22] Two years later when Gainsborough's portrait of her was exhibited at the Grosvenor Gallery, the Catalogue referred to her *History* as 'this elaborate crudity and pretentious book' which would 'soon pass into the oblivion of waste paper'. Could the author have ever seen her *History* let alone read it? He felt called on to add that 'nevertheless so great was the admiration for the author . . . that she received extraordinary marks of public esteem'.[23] There was no accounting for public taste. Among nineteenth-century historians William Lecky (1838–1903) was almost alone in recognizing her importance. She was, he wrote, 'the ablest writer of the New Radical School'.[24] Early in this century Elie Halevy devoted one sentence to 'the republican and feminist, Mrs. Macaulay'

---

[18] Donnelly, 'The Celebrated Mrs. Macaulay', 183, 190, 194, 201.
[19] Daisy L. Hobman, 'Mrs. Macaulay', *The Fortnightly*, 171 (1952), 116–21, at p. 116.
[20] Stenton, *The English Woman in History*, 306.
[21] *History and Hope: The Collected Essays of C. V. Wedgwood* (1987), 481.
[22] R. E. Peach, *Historic Houses in Bath* (1883), 117.
[23] Catalogue of the Grosvenor Gallery 'Exhibition of the Works of Thomas Gainsborough, R.A.' (1885), 94.
[24] W. E. H. Lecky, *A History of England in the Eighteenth Century*, 8 vols. (1878–9), iii. 206–7.

who 'found "poison" in Burke's writings'.[25] A literary critic described her as 'the celebrated female historian' who 'was a red republican'.[26] 'The poor lady', wrote a historian, 'is now remembered solely as the object of some of Dr. Johnson's coarsest, but certainly not his least amusing jokes.'[27] There has been little recognition of her by historians of English radicalism. Maccoby makes no mention of her.[28] More recently some social historians have acknowledged her existence and expressed their admiration that such a woman could survive in eighteenth-century society. 'A woman hoping to be accepted intellectually', writes Roy Porter, 'had to run an obstacle race. Catharine Macaulay... one of the few women to do so, was jeered off the track.'[29] Historians of the American Revolution have been almost alone in acknowledging her importance and the wide influence of her ideas. She was 'one of the most brilliant women of her generation'.[30]

Little appreciated is that for most of her life Catharine Macaulay was a sick woman. She had been 'unfortunately born with a very delicate constitution'. From her 'earliest infancy to the age of maturity' she was constantly ill.[31] When Sylas Neville and Caleb Fleming visited her in 1768 they commented on her diet of milk and vegetables on account of a bilious complaint.[32] Her medical problem was never satisfactorily diagnosed. Partly it was a nervous condition which emerged whenever she was under strain; overwork on her *History*, the effort of producing a volume a year, the increased criticism and hostility she encountered as she embarked on the period of the 1640s—all coincided with periods of ill health. For Catharine Macaulay, coping first with fame and then its decline, anxious over the increasingly unwelcome and

---

[25] Elie Halevy, *The Growth of Philosophic Radicalism* (1928, repr. 1972), 146.

[26] *Mrs. Montagu—Queen of the Blues: Her Letters and Friendships from 1762 to 1800*, ed. Reginald Blunt, 2 vols. (1923), 1. 234.

[27] Sir George Otto Trevelyan, *The Early History of Charles James Fox* (1901), 129 n. 1.

[28] Simon Maccoby, *English Radicalism 1762–1914*, 6 vols. (1935–61).

[29] Roy Porter, *English Society in the Eighteenth Century* (1982), 36.

[30] C. C. Bonwick, 'The English Audience for American Revolutionary Pamphlets', *Historical Journal* 19 (1976), 355–74, at p. 355.

[31] James Graham, *A Short Inquiry into the Present State of Medical Practice*, 2nd edn. (1777), 18.

[32] G. M. Ditchfield, 'Some Literary and Political Views of Catherine Macaulay', *American Notes and Queries*, 12 (1974), 70–6, at p. 74.

possessive attentions of Wilson, hounded by gossip and defamatory reports, the strain of being continuously in the public eye must have been severe. Little wonder if sometimes she was preoccupied by ill health, became a near hypochondriac, and desperately tried out new remedies and cures. She was far from alone among eighteenth-century women who were frequently unwell with illnesses rarely diagnosed. It is indicative of how frustrating and unfulfilled the lives of the great majority of women were; a reflection of the boredom, confinement, and repression they suffered. For those few who ventured into the public domain, who entered fields hitherto monopolized by men, and attempted to lead independent lives, the pressures were as great if not greater. Men's resentment of women who rejected their allotted role, and invaded their spheres of influence and power, was focused on them. There was no limit to the weapons that were used against them to attack, hurt, undermine, and, if possible, destroy. What is surprising is that any women survived. Many became bedridden, some were psychiatric cases, but Catharine Macaulay not only survived but, refusing to admit defeat, continued to behave in exactly the same way as before.

For a woman who by all accounts had been of striking appearance if not beautiful, it must have been difficult to accept the loss of her youth and looks. Her solution was 'to paint'. After her return from France in January 1778, Wilkes commented how she was 'very ill indeed. . . . she was painted up to the eyes, and looks quite ghastly and ghostly'. In April 1778 he found her looking 'as rotten as an old catharine pear'.[33] When Catharine visited Philadelphia in 1785 Sarah Vaughan recorded that she 'had heard in company that her teeth are false, has plumpers in her cheeks to hide the hollowness toothlessness gives, and that she paints'.[34] We have seen how she stayed only briefly in New York 'being desirous of returning from the South, before the sickly season comes on in that climate'.[35] After leaving Mount Vernon, she wrote to George Washington of 'the great fatigue' she had felt on her return to New York. The Washingtons had been concerned at 'the

[33] *Letters from the Year 1774 to the Year 1796 of John Wilkes Esq. addressed to his daughter, the Late Miss Wilkes*, 4 vols. (1804), ii. 61–2, 193.
[34] As quoted Linda K. Kerber, *Women of the Republic* (1980), 227 n. 68.
[35] *Letters of Richard Henry Lee*, ed. J. C. Ballagh, 2 vols. (1911–14), 359.

distresses' she must have suffered 'on acct. of the intemperature (*sic*) of the air'.[36] Washington's biographer writes that 'about 44 . . . she suddenly displayed a fondness for gaudy dress and began to apply rouge with a purposeful hand'.[37] Yet when she visited America one newspaper described how 'not caring to embellish her person by any vain pomp in dress or equipage' she appeared 'in quite a plain, yet elegant stile'. In July of the same year when she visited Washington at Mount Vernon, she told Mercy Warren that it was the state of her health which had persuaded her to reside in the south of France.[38] This background of nearly continuous ill health almost certainly explains far more than her 'painting'.

Now, two centuries after her death, how are we to assess her character? What kind of a woman was she? It was a question to which an unknown contributor in the *Town and Country Magazine* of 1769 addressed himself. The 'mother, aunts, sisters, and the circle of good women who form the assembly' in his correspondent's neighbourhood, ever since they had read her *History* were 'upon the tenter-hooks of impatience to know what kind of woman' she was. His correspondent—clearly male—admitted he too was 'not void of the same curiosity'. The unknown contributor revealed he was 'acquainted with the lady'. He found her a woman 'of uncommon ease and affability of behaviour'. 'You cannot talk with her ten minutes', he wrote, 'without perceiving that she is a woman of sense; but you may be ten years in her company, without suspecting her to be an author.' As an observer of her first marriage, he confirms all that Richard Baron had been told by George Macaulay. Dr Macaulay was 'in a married state an object of envy'. He confessed he did not know 'any man more happy . . . in a wife, not only as to her person, sense and prudence, but her family economy'. He was informed, moreover, that she was 'as remarkable for her discharge of the parental . . . as of the conjugal duties'. What makes his verdict interesting is that he admitted he was 'no admirer of her political system', so cannot be accused of being prejudiced in her favour. But, it could be

---

[36] *Notes and Queries*, 5th ser., 9 (1878), 421.
[37] Douglas Southall Freeman, *George Washington*, 7 vols. (1948–57), vi. 39.
[38] *Warren–Adams Letters*, 2 vols. (Massachusetts Historical Society Collections 72, 73; 1917–25), ii. 257.

argued, this was an early verdict before fame had gone to her head.[39]

The language reserved for distinction in women was always overdone, the praise deliberately exaggerated. It meant the frontier between admiration and scorn was blurred. A writer could move easily from such praise to the sharpest of satire. Satire is an insidious form of comment, for provided the wit is sharp enough, it has a durability that can resist the most committed of scholarly questioning. Long after Catharine Macaulay was forgotten, her works no longer read, and her kind of radicalism overtaken by events, the satire remained. Often it is all that is remembered about her. In 1930 one of her descendants in a letter to *Notes and Queries* complained how unfair it was with 'so much to her credit with posterity' that 'her immortality' seemed almost certain to rest on Johnson's version of the footman anecdote. Sadly he offered his tribute 'to the cause of truth and justice she upheld so stoutly'.[40] It is all too easy today to accept uncritically the judgements of her most vocal contemporary opponents. Very few historians who have referred to her since her death have failed to take over much of the ultimate rejection of her in her own times—and assumed that reports of her arrogance, lack of human warmth, cold calculation, and immorality were true, quite apart from accepting contemporary evaluations of her *History*. Part of the trouble is that she is no longer read. As one biographer wrote of her *History* early in the nineteenth century, while at the time of its publication 'it was read with some avidity', it had since 'fallen into so much disrepute, as scarcely ever to be inquired after'.[41] 'This *History* was at one time held in high esteem by some,' commented one account early this century, 'but has been for many years practically forgotten'.[42] Yet lack of familiarity with her work cannot justify acceptance of her character as painted by her most hostile critics. Somewhere something is out of joint. The portrait of her painted by such critics is curiously at odds with that of those closest to her. First there is Elizabeth Arnold, sister

---

[39] *Town and Country Magazine*, 1 (1769), 91.

[40] *Notes and Queries*, 159 (1930), 111–12.

[41] Alexander Chalmers, *The Genal Biographical Dictionary*, 32 vols. (1812–17), xxi. (1813), 45.

[42] Robert Pierpoint, *Catharine Macaulay 'History': The Marble Statue in the Entrance Hall of Warrington Town Hall*, 2 parts (1908–10), i. 2.

to William Graham, and as Mary Hays was later to recall, 'an excellent and amiable woman'.[43] Sisters-in-law have no reason to love the wives their brothers choose, but despite all she had heard against her, Mrs Arnold met and immediately liked Mrs Macaulay.

After Catharine Macaulay was dead, Mrs Arnold told Mary Hays that 'as a wife, a mother, a friend, a neighbour, and the mistress of a family', Catharine 'was irreproachable and exemplary'. What makes the account convincing is that this was not what Mrs Arnold had expected. She was surprised by the woman she met and came to know. The reputation Catharine enjoyed was clearly very different from the reality—so efficient had been her character-assassination. 'I have seen her marked out by party prejudice as an object of dislike and ridicule', Mrs Arnold told Mary Hays, 'I have seen her bowed down by bodily pain and weakness: but never did I see her forget the urbanity of a gentlewoman, her conscious dignity as a rational creature, or a fervent aspiration after the highest of attainable perfection. I have seen her humble herself in the presence of her Almighty father; and with a contrite heart, acknowledging her weakness, and imploring his protection; I have seen her languishing on a bed of sickness, enduring pain with the patience of a christian, and with the firm belief, that the light afflictions of this life are but for a moment, and that the fashion of this world will pass away, and give place to a system of durable happiness.'[44]

Much earlier Richard Baron was surprised by the warmth with which George Macaulay praised Catharine Macaulay's character and protested her admirable abilities as both wife and mother.[45] Not only was George Macaulay devoted to her but, unusual in a husband at the time, he seems fully to have appreciated her talents. What of her second husband, William Graham? Two years after Catharine Macaulay's death, Isaac D'Israeli (1766–1848) published his *A Dissertation on Anecdotes*, in which one anecdote amounted to a 'heavy charge' against Catharine Macaulay. According to D'Israeli she was responsible for deliberately destroying parts of manuscripts in the British Museum 'when she came to any passage unfavourable to her party, or in

[43] Hays, *Female Biography*, v. 292 n.   [44] Ibid. 305–6.
[45] See Ch. 1; *The Diary of Sylas Neville, 1767–88*, ed. Basil Cozens-Hardy (1950), 20.

favour of the Stuarts'. Eventually her behaviour was noticed, D'Israeli held, 'and she was watched'. The accusation turned out to be based on one case—that of Harleian manuscript 7379, a collection of state letters—which he held would 'go down to posterity as an eternal testimony of her historical partiality', for it had 'four pages entirely torn out'. Proof that such destruction was at her hand, D'Israeli argued, was that on the day that the alleged vandalism occurred, 12 November 1764, Catharine Macaulay had been working on the manuscript.[46] At the time of the alleged dilapidation D'Israeli was yet to be born!

The correspondent in the *Gentleman's Magazine* for 13 August 1794 who protested against this slander of Catharine Macaulay was clearly on her side. He had gone to the British Museum to investigate and applied to the librarian concerned at the time, Dr Morton, for further information. The answer he received was that there was no evidence that Mrs Macaulay was responsible for tearing out the pages, but 'on the contrary' it appeared 'that the said three leaves [there is some confusion on both sides as to whether it was three or four pages that were missing] were *already wanting* when the Manuscript was sent down to the reading-room' for her use. On the basis of this testimony he appealed to the public 'to judge of the candour and impartiality' of D'Israeli. Although the letter to the *Gentleman's Magazine* was signed 'An Old and Constant Reader of the Gentlemans Magazine' his true identity was not concealed. The letter from Dr Morton was addressed to the Revd William Graham.[47]

D'Israeli persisted in his accusation. He claimed he had 'received information from a quarter of undoubted authority' that 'the Female Historian and dilapidator had acted thus more than once, and when accused, insolently *confessed* it'. The library, it was claimed, had refused her further access. (The library later officially denied the vandalism charge.) That such acts of vandalism occurred so long before made authentication difficult, but there were 'several gentlemen', regular readers in the British Museum, to whom these facts were '*well known*'. Unfortunately his residing at such a distance from the capital prevented his supplying names without the owners' permission. Dr Morton's

---

[46] *Gentleman's Magazine*, 64 (1794), 685.
[47] Ibid., 685.

evidence was dismissed. He was after all 'in a very advanced period of life', and 'not unfriendly to Mrs. Macaulay's political party'.[48]

Why, thirty years after the event, and only after Catharine Macaulay's death, did D'Israeli choose to make the allegation? As a royalist, the author of *Commentaries on the Life and Reign of Charles I* (1828–30), he cannot have been sympathetic to Catharine Macaulay's *History* or her republicanism. He was ambitious, extremely anxious to win approval, and in the 1790s his prejudices against Catharine Macaulay would have found a sympathetic ear. While acknowledging the popularity of his literary anecdotes, his biographer concedes 'he was not very accurate'.[49] Nevertheless we have reason to be grateful to him for his attack, for it provoked William Graham into a passionate, but tempered defence of 'a most worthy and amiable woman...who, from party-spirit, had been much abused and misrepresented'. Unlike her critics, he had lived with her 'near twelve years' and in the intimacy of domestic life had 'had an opportunity of knowing her better than any other person'. He 'never knew or ever heard of a more perfect character'. She possessed 'a sacred love of truth, a detestation of every base and unworthy action, a heart filled with the purest benevolence and kindness to the whole human and brute creation'. He confessed that until he came to know her he had never met 'such an equanimity and placidness of temper' and would have thought it 'incompatible with human nature'. Finally, he wrote movingly, that if he possessed any virtue or good quality, it was 'to her' he was 'indebted for it'.[50]

But it is not only the opinions of those closest to Catharine Macaulay which are at odds with her public image, but her own writings. It is true that at times she can be long-winded and pedantic, but so can most writers. At other times she writes 'with strength and spirit'.[51] Often there is humour, and an ironic wit. In her judgements of people, even those she most regarded as enemies of her cause, she is consciously striving to be fair. In

[48] Ibid. 817, 996; Isaac D'Israeli, *Curiosities of Literature*, ed. The Earl of Beaconsfield, 3 vols. (1881), ii. 446 n.
[49] S. L. Lee in *Dictionary of National Biography*.
[50] *Gentleman's Magazine*, 65 (1795), 6.
[51] *A Series of Letters between Mrs. Elizabeth Carter and Miss Catherine Talbot*, ed. Montagu Pennington, 4 vols. (1809), iii. 84.

considering her fourth volume, the *Critical Review* commented that 'she cuts off Laud's head with very little ceremony', but, it went on, 'she gives him fair play, as she everywhere does to the characters of the princes Rupert and Maurice'. Far from sharing all her conclusions, the reviewer praised her as 'open and candid' for making clear at the outset her own political position.[52] If she passionately defended the execution of Charles I she also strove 'to do justice to that part of his conduct which [she] thought truly great'.[53] Hence the very different opinions of her characterization of Charles I. Some thought her far too tolerant. Moved by suffering, acknowledging courage in the face of adversity, often she gives people the benefit of the doubt. The exception of course is Cromwell. Examples of her fairness in historical judgements have been dismissed as her 'outward attempt of impartiality'.[54] Can we expect more of any historian?

A learned woman with claims to scholarship, she struck many as austere. Her passion for politics and her dedication to the radical cause inspired all her conversation. One suspects she had little time for small talk. She worked extremely hard, was fascinated by her subject, and saw her *History* as an important part of the political education of contemporaries. But her outward confidence and self-assurance are belied by her sensitivity to criticism, and the bitterness of her response. The happiness of her two marriages suggests a very different woman lurked behind the public figure. The nervous ailments that beset her are additional evidence of vulnerability, as perhaps is the importance that religious certainty came to have for her.

'This lady', wrote the *European Magazine* in 1783, 'who has experienced more of the extremes of adulation and obloquy than any one of her own sex in the literary world'.[55] It was a rash claim but not an unfair assessment. What makes her life so intriguing is precisely this wide swing of the pendulum of fortune, and the reasons that lie behind it. She was deliberately victimized—above all for her dangerous politics and republicanism—and the method used to discredit her *History* and vilify her as a person was to

[52] *Critical Review*, 27 (1769), 9–10, 1.
[53] Catharine Macaulay, *History of England*, vi, p. xii.
[54] Lynne E. Withey, 'Catharine Macaulay and the Uses of History: Ancient Rights, Perfectionism, and Propaganda', *Journal of British Studies*, 16 (1976), 59–83, 71.
[55] *The European Magazine and London Review*, 4 (1783), 330.

exploit the weakness of her position as a woman. As a correspondent to the *St. James's Chronicle* wrote in 1778 of the accusations against her of plagiarism, 'many parties have been raised against Mrs. Macaulay as an Historian, for some malignant Purpose or other, endeavouring to undermine her Reputation'. He concluded that such attacks had 'the Appearance of wanton Insult, and bare-faced falsehood'.[56] By the time she wrote her sixth volume she was shrewd enough to recognize that 'the reputation of authors are attacked in order to decry their works'.[57] She was attacked, it was said, 'by petty and personal scurrilities, to which it was believed her sex would render her vulnerable'.[58] So did, but she never hesitated in her response. A historian 'must look down with contempt on the angry crowd, nor suffer their fierce and loud clamours in any respect to divert him from pursuing the grand object of his honest ambition'.[59]

For six years or more after the publication of her first volume of *History*, Catharine Macaulay enjoyed general acclaim. With it came fame, something for which women were ill prepared. Authorship, Mary Wollstonecraft commented, was 'a heavy weight for female shoulders, especially in the sunshine of prosperity'.[60] Catharine Macaulay was suddenly 'exalted on the dangerous pinnacle of worldly prosperity, surrounded by flattering friends and an admiring world'.[61] Fame assumed a public presence and no woman was expected to have one. After years of being addressed as 'a person of your eminence', 'the celebrated Mrs. Macaulay', 'our incomparable female historian', it is not surprising that she began to need such praise and came to rely on it.[62] It made it all the harder to accept criticism. When former friends became enemies and admirers turned against her, it was a bitter blow to her pride and morale. Many women would have admitted defeat and given up the struggle. Not so Catharine Macaulay. But is it any wonder that under the pressure of society's censorious

---

[56] *St. James's Chronicle*, No. 2733 (19 Sept. 1778).

[57] Macaulay, *History of England*, vi, p. xiv.

[58] Hays, *Female Biography*, v. 292.

[59] Macaulay, *History of England*, vi, p. xiv.

[60] Mary Hays, *Emma Courtney* (1796) as quoted Claire Tomalin, *The Life and Death of Mary Wollstonecraft* (1974), 128.

[61] Hays, *Female Biography*, v. 305.

[62] As she was called by Augustus Toplady, *Jackson's Oxford Journal*, Josiah Quincy, Mercy Warren, and George Washington respectively.

eye some women reacted eccentrically? How was an intelligent woman aware of the assumptions made about 'learned' women to behave? Mary Hays, seeking to account for 'the eccentricities of conduct' of which learned women were accused, wrote of the frustrations of 'those of superior minds' destined to remain obscure onlookers.[63] But for those like Catharine Macaulay who were so much in the public eye, the divide between fame and infamy was razor-thin.

Criticism was to be expected from those who opposed her political ideas, but it is sometimes forgotten how many sharing those ideas and identifying with her radicalism were deeply prejudiced against her sex. Often behind the words of fulsome praise and acclaim there lurk profound reservations about women if not deep hostility. By any standards John Wilkes, distributor of the notoriously bawdy *Essay on Woman*, was lascivious and profligate. He appeared, says his biographer, 'to revel in libertinism', he 'adopted a new mistress almost as often as he bought a new suit of clothes'.[64] His mercenary marriage ended in separation. The substance of the court case was 'that her husband having used her ill, did in consideration of a great sum which she gave him out of her separate estate, consent to her living alone . . . and covenanted under a large penalty never to disturb her'.[65] Yet despite the agreement, after the separation Wilkes continued to attempt to extort money from her.[66] If not as undisguisedly profligate as Wilkes, many of those men who were most vociferous in their praise of her were reluctant to grant women any recognition or role in public life. Even the doting Wilson, it will be remembered, wanted 'no more than one Mrs. Macaulay'.[67]

In America Independence brought no change in attitudes to women. Although nothing in the American constitution prevented women from occupying federal office, there was no attempt to test such an unwritten right until long after the Revolution. Indeed, Thomas Jefferson, who expressed such warm approval of Catharine Macaulay's *History*, saw no changed role for women as a consequence of the Revolution. He hoped 'our good ladies . . . are

---

[63] As quoted Tomalin, *The Life and Death of Mary Wollstonecraft*, 197.

[64] Horace Bleackley, *Life of John Wilkes* (1917), 358, 359.

[65] Anon., *The Laws Respecting Women* (1777), 57.

[66] William Purdie Treloar, *Wilkes and the City* (1917), 3.

[67] *The Gazetteer and New Daily Advertiser*, 10 Sept. 1777.

contented to soothe and calm the minds of their husbands returning ruffled from political debate'. After he became President,
when his Secretary of the Treasury tentatively suggested he
appoint women to office, Jefferson bluntly rejected the idea. 'The
appointment of a woman to office', he wrote, 'is an innovation for
which the public is not prepared, nor am I.' Much later he
explained that even the purest democracy must exclude women
from the franchise in order 'to prevent deprivation of morals and
ambiguity of issue'.[68] John Adams, one of the great leaders of the
Revolution, was not without his prejudices where women were
concerned, even though he was married to Abigail Adams, a truly
remarkable one. It was Abigail who in 1776, when considering
'the new Code of Laws' which she supposed it would be necessary
for him to make, wrote begging him to 'remember the ladies' and
to 'be more generous and favourable to them than your ancestors.
Do not put such unlimited power into the hands of the husbands'.
She pointed out the irony that men should be so concerned with
freeing nations while 'retaining absolute power over Wives'. Even
if she meant only to address the legal subordination of married
women, they were brave words. She went on gently but firmly to
warn her husband that if women were not considered, they would
'foment a rebellion' and would not hold themselves 'bound by any
Laws in which' they had 'no voice, or representative'. Jokingly
John Adams dismissed her plea. Men knew 'better than to
repeal' their 'Masculine systems'.[69] Later, angered by the treatment he received in Mercy Otis Warren's history of the American
Revolution, there was an acrimonious exchange of letters in which
he finally claimed that 'History' was 'not the Province of the
Ladies'.[70]

In France, Jean-Pierre Brissot defended Catharine Macaulay
against those who claimed the *History* was not her own work. He
believed she had 'justified women against any reproach ... that
they are not suited to a scientific career and are incapable of
producing anything great or useful'.[71] But in 1787, when writing
of what he saw as the changed and more rational attitudes to

---

[68] As quoted Richard B. Morris, *The Forging of the Union, 1781–9* (1987), 190.
[69] *Familiar Letters of John Adams and His Wife Abigail, during the Revolution*, ed.
Charles Francis Adams (1875), 149–50.
[70] *Warren–Adams Letters* (1917–25), i. 361.
[71] *Mémoires de Brissot*, ed. M. F. de Montrol, 4 vols. (1830), ii. 231.

political crises, he excluded women from playing any role. 'In times of trouble', he held, 'women should only be the secret consolation of their husbands.'[72]

The revolutionary times in which Catharine Macaulay lived involved momentous changes but where the position of women was concerned the situation remained the same. If, as the author of *The Female Advocate* wrote in 1774, 'the sentiments of all men of sense' were 'more enlarged than they formerly were', throughout the life of Catharine Macaulay they were to remain 'very contracted'.[73]

Today it is difficult to appreciate just how extraordinary a figure Catharine Macaulay was in the eighteenth century. Relatively few women wrote at all, no other woman wrote scholarly history, and no other woman—and very few men—embarked on such an ambitious project as was involved in her eight-volume *History*. It was, *The Critical Review* acknowledged in 1783, 'one of the most signal instances ever known to the literary world, of the extraordinary abilities and persevering exertions of a female writer'. There were other distinguished women in literature, but she alone had 'had the boldness to contend for the palm in the field of history'.[74] As has been emphasized, the description of her in the *Dictionary of National Biography* as 'historian and controversialist' is one that 'could have been given to no Englishwoman before her'.[75] Politics was not a sphere in which women played any role, yet Catharine Macaulay actively participated in London radical politics of the 1760s and 1770s. No other woman had such familiarity with both the Wilkites and the London Commonwealthmen. No other woman was regarded with such respect and admiration by both American and French patriots. But we must get it right; it is true that part of her uniqueness is that she did things no other woman had done. Yet there is a danger that by emphasizing 'the remarkable woman' we lose sight of the important historical character, and that importance has nothing to do with her sex. The view that 'only on the grounds of sex can the plea of being a pioneer in the field be urged for' her must be rejected. As the first historian of the eighteenth century to attempt

[72] As quoted Norman Hampson, *Will and Circumstance* (1983), 99.
[73] Mary Scott, *The Female Advocate* (1774), p. vi.
[74] *Critical Review*, 55 (1783), 216.
[75] Stenton, *The English Woman in History*, 306.

a republican history of the seventeenth century, she deserves more study than she has so far received. Her *History*—and its popularity—illustrates how vital the seventeenth century still was to both Commonwealthmen and Wilkites. It makes the point that any understanding of eighteenth-century radicalism must start from the seventeenth century. Her influence on radical ideas in England, and the contribution she made to the changing nature of radicalism in the last three decades of the eighteenth century, make her *History* and political polemic of no small importance. Her role in familiarizing Americans with the history of the seventeenth century and reinforcing their conviction that events of that earlier century were being replayed in their time, the contribution her interpretation of the 'Glorious Revolution' had in finally severing relations with the mother country, her being the first English radical to visit the United States after Independence, and on terms of familiarity with many of the leading figures in the American Revolution both before and after the Revolution—all this has not been lost on American historians who have recognized her importance. That her writings also had relevance for many French patriots in the early years of the Revolution is less well known.

Now, two hundred years after her death, Mary Wollstonecraft's hope that 'posterity' would 'be more just' to her memory may be in process of becoming fact. The *Rivista storica italiana* in 1986 carried a 67-page article on the importance of Catharine Macaulay in English radical historiography. In the course of her presidential address to the American Historical Association in 1987, Natalie Zemon Davis, in considering the relationship between individual historians poised in their brief moment of time and the whole field of historical study, compared Catharine Macaulay with David Hume. The fact that among five chosen historians she should have been one, and her work treated on an equality with that of Hume, would have delighted her. In her relationship to other historians with whom she disagreed she is seen as putting 'history's higher goals' before 'private rivalry'. In her refusal to be deterred by loss of reputation she put those same goals before self. She would not have found the verdict displeasing. More recently her analysis of the 'Glorious Revolution' has been seen as anticipating 'in a number of ways some of our current historiography, for instance, John Brewer's *Sinews of Power: War, Money and the English State, 1688–1783*' (1989). An eminent Russian historian gave a paper at the historical conference held in Paris to commemorate the French Revolution. His subject was the contribution made by Catharine Macaulay's *History* to revolutionary thought.[76] Perhaps, before long, we may even have some acknowledgement from English historians of her importance in the development of English radicalism.

[76] Rolando Minuti, 'Il problema storico della libertà inglese nella cultura radicale dell' età di Giorgio III. Catharine Macaulay e la Rivoluzione puritana', *Rivista storica italiana*, 98 (1986), 793–860; Natalie Zemon Davis, 'History's Two Bodies', *American Historical Review*, 93 (1988), 1–30, esp. 12–18; Staves, ' "The Liberty of a She-Subject of England" '; Professor M. A. Barg in a paper delivered in Paris in 1989 at the bicentenary celebrations of the French Revolution.

CATHARINE MACAULAY'S WORKS

The History of England from the Accession of James I to that of the Brunswick Line, 8 vols. (London, 1763–83): i (1763), ii (1765), iii (1767), iv (1768), v (1771), vi (1781), vii (1781), viii (1783).

Loose Remarks on Certain Positions to be found in Mr. Hobbes's 'Philosophical Rudiments of Government and Society', with a Short Sketch of a Democratical Form of Government, In a Letter to Signor Paoli (London, 1767).

Observations on a Pamphlet entitled 'Thoughts on the Cause of the Present Discontents' (London, 1770).

A Modest Plea for the Property of Copyright (Bath, 1774).

An Address to the People of England, Scotland and Ireland on the Present Important Crisis of Affairs (Bath, 1775).

The History of England from the Revolution to the Present Time in a Series of Letters to a Friend [the Revd Dr Wilson], i (Bath, 1778).

Treatise on the Immutability of Moral Truth (London, 1783).

Letters on Education with Observations on Religious and Metaphysical Subjects (London, 1790).

Observations on the Reflections of the Rt. Hon. Edmund Burke, on the Revolution in France (London, 1790).

WRITINGS ON
CATHARINE MACAULAY

'Account of the Life and Writings of Mrs. Catherine Macaulay Graham', *The European Magazine*, 4 (1783), 330–4.

BECKWITH, MILDRED CHAFFEE, 'Catharine Macaulay: Eighteenth-Century Rebel', Ph.D. thesis (Ohio State University, 1953).

—— 'Catharine Macaulay: Eighteenth-Century Rebel', *Proceedings of the South Carolina Historical Association*, 1958, 12–29.

DITCHFIELD, G. M., 'Some Literary and Political Views of Catherine Macaulay', *American Notes and Queries*, 12 (1974), 70–6.

DONNELLY, LUCY MARTIN, 'The Celebrated Mrs. Macaulay', *William and Mary Quarterly*, 3rd ser., 6 (1949), 172–207.

FOX, CLAIRE GILBRIDE, 'Catherine Macaulay, an Eighteenth Century Clio', *Winterthur Portfolio*, 4 (1968), 129–42.

HILL, BRIDGET and CHRISTOPHER, 'Catharine Macaulay and the Seventeenth Century', *The Welsh History Review*, 3 (1967), 381–402.

HOBMAN, DAISY L., 'Mrs Macaulay', *The Fortnightly*, 171 (1952), 116–21.

SCHNORRENBERG, BARBARA B., 'The Brood-Hen of Faction: Mrs. Macaulay and Radical Politics, 1765–75', *Albion*, 11 (1979), 33–45.

—— 'An Opportunity Missed: Catherine Macaulay on the Revolution of 1688', *Studies in Eighteenth-Century Culture*, 20 (1990), 231–40.

STAVES, SUSAN, '"The Liberty of a She-Subject of England": Rights Rhetoric and the Female Thucydides', *Cardozo Studies in Law and Literature*, 1 (1989), 161–83.

WITHEY, LYNNE E., 'Catharine Macaulay and the Uses of History: Ancient Rights, Perfectionism, and Propaganda', *Journal of British Studies*, 16 (1976), 59–83.

INDEX